THE OTHER SIDE OF THE DESK

A 20/20 Look at the Principalship

Janet Tareilo

ROWMAN & LITTLEFIELD EDUCATION
A division of
ROWMAN & LITTLEFIELD PUBLISHERS, INC.
Lanham • New York • Toronto • Plymouth, UK

Published by Rowman & Littlefield Education
A division of Rowman & Littlefield Publishers, Inc.
A wholly owned subsidary of The Rowman & Littlefield Publishing Group, Inc.
4501 Forbes Boulevard, Suite 200, Lanham, Maryland 20706
http://www.rowmaneducation.com

Estover Road, Plymouth PL6 7PY, United Kingdom

British Library Cataloguing in Publication Information Available

Library of Congress Cataloging-in-Publication Data

Tareilo, Janet.
  The other side of the desk : a 20/20 look at the principalship / Janet Tareilo.
     p. cm.
  Includes bibliographical references.
  ISBN 978-1-60709-664-1 (cloth : alk. paper) — ISBN 978-1-60709-665-8
(pbk. : alk. paper) — ISBN 978-1-60709-666-5 (electronic)
  1. School principals—United States. 2. Educational leadership—United
States. 3. School personnel management—United States. I. Title.
  LB2831.92.T37 2009
  371.2'012--dc22

                                                         2009044886

Printed in the United States of America

This book is dedicated to all those school leaders

who already make a difference in the lives of children

and to the ones who someday will.

You know the real reasons we do the job.

CONTENTS

ACKNOWLEDGMENTS

I have always wanted to play the piano well enough that I could make the great Liberace jealous. When I am in the shower and I pretend the nozzle is a waterproof microphone, I could challenge Barbara Streisand to a karaoke sing-off match and win. Monet and van Gogh, if they were alive today, would probably ask me for painting lessons when they saw my sketches of stick figures and bowls of fruit.

In my mind, I can play the piano, sing, and paint as well as or better than the masters in those fields. Unfortunately, as I said, this is only in my mind. What I know how to do, what I know I can do, and what I know I do well, is to take care of children as a campus principal. But I didn't learn how to be a school leader without having the help and love of others along the way.

I would first like to acknowledge my mother, Esther, who taught me survival of the fittest. She overcame many obstacles, disappointments, and challenges and unknowingly passed on her spirit of determination and independence to me. Without my grandfather, Bruce, I would have missed the opportunity to have someone in my life who gave me unconditional love. I can still hear him call me "Jinnet," and when I hold close to my chest his worn and tattered coat that I have kept all these years since his death, I realize my love for him has never died and never will.

I cannot even imagine the path my life would have taken if it had not been for 207 Mt. Nebo and the family who lived there. They are my Reeders, and each and every one of them holds pieces of my heart and soul that make me who I am. No words have been written that I could ever borrow that would truly reflect what the family means to me.

I am grateful to friends, colleagues, and mentors who have held my hand, supported my efforts, and believed in me when my tired and discouraged soul could find no rest. Ted, Pat, Sandy, Trampas, Suzanne, Markye, and Donna—each one of you gave me gifts that I treasure and hold dear. You gave me your time, your kindness, and your words of encouragement. I will be forever grateful.

Years ago when I was in high school, I met a boy in study hall. He sat there day in and day out cracking jokes and making the people around him laugh. I just wanted to sit in study hall and read my books without any interruptions. I guess after thirty-three years of marriage to that young boy, you could say he interrupted my life.

I loved him then and I love him even more today. Kirk, you still make me laugh. To my daughters Amanda and Jenny, there is no possible way for me to explain how much love I have for you both. It is an endless waterfall that will never stop. You both amaze me when I think of what strong and independent women you have become. I am so proud to be your mother.

The events and stories in this book took place over a time span of twenty-four years in public education. Some of the faces of the people and the things I encountered along the way are just as clear as if it all happened yesterday. I genuinely hope I gave to the children and the people in my care as much as they gave to me.

PREFACE

There is no question that being the principal of a school requires a person to be not only knowledgeable but prepared and ready to accept the ever-changing responsibilities facing the principalship. Whether one assumes the position on an elementary or secondary campus, the deciding factor regarding the success of the school and its students is most assuredly the leadership ability the principal possesses. By examining leadership theories in college preparation classes, candidates for the position of school leader begin to understand the importance of developing their own leadership capacity. In addition, these candidates also need to learn about the real-world leadership skills required on a campus to sustain continued learning and make their lives easier.

Many graduates of principal preparation programs profess that they did in fact receive excellent training and preparation during their university coursework. However, leaders for today's schools face so much more than gum chewing or skipping classes. Future principals also need to learn about the real world of an administrator from the stories and voices of those who have lived through the experience. Being a principal is not an easy job. The shortage of candidates for the principalship is steadily growing, and the issue of applicable and real-world preparation must be addressed.

This book offers stories and collected memories from my journey through sixteen years as an elementary principal. I grab the reader's attention and involve you in some of the most unforgettable conversations and events that took place during those sixteen years. I continuously paint pictures of the teachers, parents, and children who made my principalship exciting and unique. Words of wisdom, checklists, and suggestions for developing the leadership abilities needed to survive the daily expectations for a principal are found in each chapter.

School leadership is hard work and requires those who choose the profession to do so with a strong and willing sense of commitment. The results of that commitment are not dependent on how much money the principal has or where he or she lives, but by what the principal does for the many children who pass in and out of his or her life. Those children need someone who cares about them in an individual and meaningful way. That is the primary reason why the stories in this book were selected. I have changed names, genders, and taken some liberties with time frames but never the events.

Nothing can really prepare a future principal for the challenges to be faced when taking on the role of a campus leader, but the heartfelt stories that emerge from each chapter offer a small glimpse of the passion and determination that should be inside every person who becomes a principal.

FOREWORD

Who am I as a principal? This question perhaps more than any other confronts each individual who enters the principalship, whether it is his or her first position, second, or beyond. There is not a clear answer to this question, nor should there be, particularly given the evolving nature of the principalship in today's schools. Rather, as the German poet Rilke explained, "We must live in the question, so that we come to understand our 'self' and eventually live into the answer." The question of who one is as a principal is a question made increasingly difficult in a rapidly changing world and the demands that such a world places on education and its workers. There are tensions fostered by these demands, pressing on the daily lives of principals and teachers working to prepare students for their roles and responsibilities as members of society.

As I read each chapter in *The Other Side of the Desk*, I found myself reflecting on the world of the principalship, intrigued by the disclosure of the author's own "self" and her beliefs, values, and assumptions about the day-to-day work of the building principal. In particular, I realized that Tareilo has set an important example for the student of the principalship—the reader—by sharing her insight and understanding of the complex and challenging world of the principalship. The power of Tareilo's work, in part, is that not only does she present her "principal self" through rich narrative expression, but more importantly she has given the reader an invaluable gift of insight based on real-world experience, grounded equally in her own lessons learned as a principal and in the work and experiences of others with whom she interacted.

In today's world of principal preparation, programs are defined, in large part, by the demands of state and federal standards and accountability and the licensure and certification requirements of state and professional accrediting entities, and by the ideological and political positionings found within schools and colleges of education. And in today's world of principal practice, these demands are paralleled in the schools and classrooms. Public school administrators face challenges today that have made the path of the principalship more and more difficult. As a superintendent and building principal in school districts in Oklahoma, my days were dominated with what I called "mystifications and false consciousness." Most problems seemed to emerge from a cloud of mystification that veiled the reality of teaching and learning, and the work of educators in schools. The problems we face as building and district administrators present us with the challenge of answering the question "Who am I?" and the responsibility of examining this question through the lens of each decision and each action we undertake. There is a constant in this question, which demands that each decision and action is made with a critical concern for the "reality" of the situation we are addressing, the consequence for all involved in the situation, and the "reality" we are constructing by our decision and action.

The number of books on the market today addressing the principalship is vast, yet few move beyond the theoretical and present a more pragmatic and "lived-experience" approach. We live in a world made increasingly complex and problematic by conflicting political and ideological agendas, changing demographics, and economic tensions. And in this world, education is the common ground for all children and parents. At the school level, holding this common ground is the work of the principal, work that is at once both challenging and crucial to the well-being of all. Preparing principals to enter the leadership role of building administrator and accept all the responsibilities therein requires insight and understanding of the nature of the principal's work.

The need for a book that brings to the foreground a level of practical insight grounded in experience and tempered by understanding is without question, and *The Other Side of the Desk* meets this need, providing the reader with a window into the reality of the principal's work. Tareilo demystifies the "reality" of the principalship, bringing clarity of vision and understanding through her examination of the different dimensions of the principal's work. In a time when "reality" for the American public has been popularized in contemporary and pop culture through television and screenwriters' versions of "reality shows," drawing society into a media-controlled and dramatized world, Tareilo takes the reader inside the "real" work of the principal, examining the reality of the principal's life and work through sixteen years of professional experience.

The Other Side of the Desk offers professors and students of principal preparation programs a well-written and critically insightful work on the "real" work of the principalship. Each chapter brings to life the world of the building administrator, providing a pragmatic and honest look at what it means to be a principal in today's schools. In this book, tempered by an understanding of and a value for theory made accessible and practice seen through the lens of experience, the reader will find a meaningful, and at times humorous, beginning to the journey of answering the question "Who am I as a principal?"

Dr. Patrick M. Jenlink
Professor of Doctoral Studies
Department of Secondary Education and Educational Leadership
Stephen F. Austin State University

1

KNOW THYSELF

William Shakespeare said it best when he wrote, "To thine own self be true." How appropriate are his words for school leaders. Before a principal can begin to lead a staff toward sustained school achievement or can even expect to gain the trust and respect of a staff, the principal must know what personal beliefs he or she holds dear. Today's schools and the children and community they serve need a self-assured and capable administrator.

If you are looking for a chapter that will ask you to pick out your favorite color or geometric shape to determine your leadership capacity and tell you what that color or shape says about your "true" personality, this is not the chapter for you. In fact, you might want to skip this chapter, because the stories and examples that are given may strike too close to home for some of you.

. What I propose to do is to relate real-life experiences that have caused me to understand how my personal style of leadership came into being. It is my hope that through these stories, you will see yourself in some of the circumstances and begin to realize your own true potential as a leader. In order to lead people and establish ideals for an organization, you, as a leader, must know what you believe in.

If you are reading this book, you are probably one of three people: First, you are in the process of preparing for the principalship; second, you are beginning your first principalship; or third, you have been a principal for some time and need to be reminded of why you do the job. Whoever you are and wherever you are in your leadership walk, being a school principal is a wonderful position in which to exemplify your personal leadership skills.

TO THE WANNABES

Let me first applaud you. I know you can't see me, but at the present time I am patting you on the back and shaking your hand. If you have recently read a newspaper or watched a newscast, you are very aware of the problems and concerns facing the educational system. You know about the importance of school safety and the accountability issues that are nationwide. You are aware of the needs of children and the duties that a principal faces on a daily basis. And yet, you are studying and preparing to fill the shoes of a school leader. I feel certain each one of you believes in your heart that you will make a difference—and you will.

FOR THE NEWBIES

So, this is your first year in the principalship. The board has voted on you, the superintendent has introduced you to the staff and faculty of your school, and you are sitting in your new office waiting to prove yourself as a campus leader. So, what do you believe in? Yeah, I'm talking to you. You have the job, you are the boss. Now what? The people of that school—from the custodian to the counselor—are looking at you to help them with instruction, discipline, and the management of that school. If you do not have a belief system in place, get one quickly!

Matthews and Crow (2003) noted that whenever anyone starts a new endeavor, acquiring skills and knowledge is necessary. The principalship is no different. You have to look at things and situations from different angles and perspectives. You have to have a deeper understanding about the decisions and choices you will make. The preparation program you

completed led you to this place in your life. The courses and requirements of the classes gave you a safety net for trying out your personal
leadership style, and with that certificate in hand you are ready for the
best and the worst. Yet, I ask you again: What do you believe in?

NEVER FORGET THE VETERAN

At this very moment, you are wearing your favorite T-shirt. You know,
the one that says, "Been there, done that." You may even work with some
newly assigned principals who still have that unwavering spirit of enthusi-
asm and joy for the principalship. What do they know, right? Don't forget
that this was how you felt a few years ago, before the duties and the responsibilities of the principalship were placed on your shoulders.

Or, you are one of those fortunate people who still loves coming to the
school every day and being involved in the lives of children. You are the
heart and soul of the campus, and that fact is very evident when the children and the parents are glad to see you. You still love your job. I would
venture to say this is because you have a tried-and-true belief system in
place that has guided you from your first moments in the principalship.

Regardless of where you are in your career, the job of the principal is
worth doing. While some days will leave you haggard and worn, other
days will fill you with such joy and amazement that *Ripley's Believe It or
Not* will be knocking on your door for the story. But before we go any
farther, I still must ask you to continue considering this question: What
do you believe in?

DEFINING SCHOOL LEADERSHIP

Examining the essence of school leadership does not always focus on the
ability to manage people or situations. Do not always assume that because you see people in positions of leadership they are capable, caring,
or trustworthy. (Does the word *ENRON* come to mind?) Researchers
and writers are forever describing the traits and characteristics of strong
and effective leaders.

John Maxwell's numerous books provide countless aspects of leadership to read and reflect upon. Pedler, Burgoyne, and Boydell (2004, 6)

define leadership as "principally being concerned with recognizing, mo-
bilizing, and taking action in the face of critical problem issues." Bennis
and Nanus (2003, 19) tell us that leadership is "what gives an organization its vision and its ability to translate that vision into reality." And the
list goes on and on. No matter what author or what source you use, the
most important things to consider are what a leader says, how he or she
says it—and then, how the leader walks that talk.

The evolution of the principalship has moved from completing mun-
dane managerial duties such as opening the doors or being the forceful
hand of discipline to that of instructional and contingency leadership (Matthews and Crow 2003). Because the hours are long, the compensation is
low, and the stress is increasing, the principalship does not look too ap-
pealing to some (Tirozzi and Ferrandino 2000). Yet every year, university
classrooms are filled with bright-eyed optimists who are actively seeking
a leadership position on a school campus. Lists of the responsibilities of
the principal could fill the next few pages. Duties that you never thought
would be associated with school leadership happen on a daily basis. But
you'll find that out for yourself when you take on the role.

With the many duties and overwhelming responsibilities, the person
who takes it on must be truly called to do the job. And yes, if you are
listening to a little voice inside your head calling you to be a principal,
you are perfect for the job!

Many days, I would leave my campus thinking about the preparation I
had received and realizing it had been limited in cultivating the leadership
skills I needed to make a difference. Did anyone notice that I cleaned up
a bathroom situation that not even the custodian would touch? Was there
anyone watching as I stood between a parent and a teacher who were
verbally ripping each other apart? Did anyone overhear my conversation
with the superintendent as I was pleading for no more budget cuts? And
who was with me in the parking lot at 6:00 a.m. as my car drove in and
6:00 p.m. as my car drove off? Probably, no one.

My leadership walk did not come from the pages of a textbook but
from living the job day in, day out. I cannot begin to tell you what you
will face during a week or even a day. I can only guarantee you that no
two days will ever be the same. The one thing that must reverberate inside your head (you and the little voice can always talk about it together)
is that the campus and the people who live and work inside the school's
walls trust you to handle and deal with any and all circumstances that

arise. It is you they will look to for answers and direction, and it is you who must have some. As Bennis and Nanus (2003, 126) said, "Leadership in the 21st century is not a job for wimps, but then it never was."

Educational leadership at the campus level focuses on the effectiveness of the campus principal. There is no guessing or wondering if this is true. It simply is. The success of the children, the culture of the campus, and even the cleanliness of the school are a direct result of the leadership influence of the principal. I have always been a rather assertive, nay, I say, aggressive person and have never really had a problem telling people what to do. So when it came to taking care of the children on my campus or the schools I was in charge of, I usually was compared to a small, angry Chihuahua dog snapping at someone's ankles. I have since learned that calm and persistent people get just as much accomplished as angry, snapping Chihuahuas. It's just not as much fun.

One of the first concepts you must accept about school leadership is the fact that it takes a combination of abilities to lead and manage. Many books and authors describe leadership and management as two separate, yet necessary, qualities needed by principals. Bennis and Nanus (2003) describe the difference between them: A manager is prone to do things right, while a leader is constantly seeking to do the right thing.

Do you see the connection between the two? Do you understand that your particular leadership style cannot be separated from your managerial style, and that in certain situations you must call on your ability to do both? No matter what style of leadership you follow, whether you have a Type A personality or live for procrastination, you have accepted a position that calls on you to be effective and productive.

You have probably heard and studied several of these definitions regarding effective school leadership. But what do they mean to you? That is the purpose of this first chapter, to ignite in you the reasons you will make a successful leader and to make you aware of the gifts that you already possess.

IDENTIFYING PERSONAL STRENGTHS

When you start this journey of campus leadership, consider exactly what brought you to this place. The role and responsibilities of the principalship are limitless. In any given instance, you are called upon to be a nurse, a counselor, or a babysitter. On good days, you actually get to touch instruction by being in the classrooms and watching student learning take place. This is by no means a job for the weak of heart or a spineless coward. Some life situation or circumstance gave you the strength and ability to face the daily responsibilities of the principalship.

Layder (2004) suggested that the unique events that happen in our lives make us into unique people. He also noted, "What we have done or have not done in our past will have influenced who we have become" (2004, 135). The people in your life or the manner in which you overcame adversity created in you a determination and a commitment to do your best. Here is your chance to let your life lessons serve you well.

MOTHER

For me, being the oldest child and only daughter of a single mother gave me several opportunities to be proficient at decision making, creative budgeting techniques, and accepting responsibilities that came my way. Because of our financial situation, my mother had to work two jobs to support the family. She would leave her day job, come home for something to eat, then leave for her night job. In order to make this process run smoothly, I was responsible for having the house clean, cooking some kind of dinner, and watching my two younger brothers. As a child, I will admit, I resented this. But as an adult, I see the gifts she really gave me.

Because of our circumstances, I had to share some of her responsibilities as a mother and a parent. Little did I know that those formative years would instill in me the character and strength I would need to serve as a campus leader. I am a firm believer that our childhood experiences create road maps for us to use as we face challenges, deal with difficulties, and learn what it takes to laugh. While my childhood may not have been the likes of the Brady Bunch, what I learned developed in me a belief system that I carried into the principalship for sixteen years. I'd like to think I became a unique leader because of the uniqueness of my childhood and the lessons I learned from my mother about strength and survival.

With my first trip down memory lane completed, take a moment and think about your own experiences that made you the person you are and readied you to take on the principalship. Hopefully, you had role models who exemplified integrity, honesty, and kindness. A grand-mother, a father, someone who was so involved in your life that what he or she taught you still influences the decisions you make and your interpersonal skills.

Whether that person is living or not, the question is, would he or she be proud of you right now? When you were accepted into graduate school, completed the coursework, graduated, and were named princi-pal of a school, who was the first person you wanted to call and tell the good news? For me, it would have been my Big John.

BIG JOHN

When I was nine years old, we moved into a rental house owned by John Lester Reeder, whom I called affectionately "Big John." He lived two houses down with his wife, Dorothy, their seven children, and their dog Prissy. For the next forty-one years, this close-knit family allowed me to be a part of them. Big John instilled in me the belief that if you are going to do a job, do it right or don't do it at all.

I had begun my college career wanting to pursue a medical degree and eventually become a pediatrician. But even though I possessed great zeal for the medical profession, the chemistry department did not believe my passion for medicine was enough to pass the course. I can remember sitting with Big John talking this over with him. He asked me if becoming a doctor was what I really wanted to do. Before leaving for college I had made him a promise that I would become a doctor. And now, as I sat with this man who had taught me to do my best at every-thing, that promise was quickly fading.

After several attempts at finding myself, I decided to enter the field of education. For years, Big John had been suggesting that I consider becoming a teacher. After several years of schooling, a husband, and one daughter, I graduated with an elementary teaching degree and became a sixth-grade teacher. After six years in the classroom, I was ready for a change and headed back to Big John for advice. I asked what he thought about my leaving the classroom and taking on a program director's posi-tion. He calmly put his book down, pushed his glasses up on his fore-head and started this conversation:

"How many children do you affect right now?"

"About 75."

"How many children will you affect if you take this job?"

"About 300."

"Then, you have no choice."

After our conversation, I accepted the position and returned to graduate school to begin work on my master's degree in education. During the course of this time, I also decided to become a principal. The principals I served with were such inspirations, and I felt certain I had what it took to be a campus leader.

So off I went to seek Big John's advice and had the same conversation as before.

"How many children do you affect right now in your director's position?"

"About 300."

"If you become a principal, how many children will you affect?"

"Between 350 and 450."

"Then, you have no choice."

Big John passed away six months before I became a principal. As I was driving home from accepting my first principalship, I was in tears because I couldn't call him and tell him what we had achieved—to let him know I was on my way to making a difference in children's lives.

However, Big John's legacy to me was not the simple gift of good advice. He taught me to persevere, work hard, and accomplish much. In December of 2004, I received my doctorate in education. The promise I had made to Big John was fulfilled. I had become a doctor, a Doctor of Education, and I knew just what he would say:

"How many children do you affect right now as a principal?"

"About 500 to 600."

"If you get your doctorate, how many children will you affect?"

"When I get my doctorate, I hope to influence principals who will touch thousands of lives in their careers."

"Then, you have no choice."

When Big John passed away, the family started a belief system that involved pennies. A member of the family read or heard an old saying that when you find a penny on the ground, it means that someone up in heaven is thinking about you. On the day of my graduation from the doctoral program, I wanted so badly to find a penny on the ground. I was sure that Big John was watching and would send me a penny.

I parked my car in the parking lot, grabbed my gown and hood, and started walking toward a reception the college had planned for the master's and doctoral graduates. From the parking lot to the second floor of the education building, my head was down and my eagle eyes were looking for a penny. Of all days to find one, this day counted the most.

Not finding a penny anywhere on the ground, I went to the reception, mingled, introduced my family to professors and fellow graduates, took pictures, and still hoped for a little disk of copper to magically appear. That didn't happen. As the time for graduation approached, I headed up to the third floor, where we had left our gowns while we were attending the reception. I so wanted Big John to see what I had accomplished. If I found a penny, somehow, maybe, I would know he approved. Now, I am not a spiritualist by any means, I just wanted one blasted little penny to show up. That's not too much to ask.

When I reached the third floor, I found I was the first one there. I began putting on the heavy black robe and placing the light blue hood over my arm just as we had been shown. As I turned around in all my regalia, I looked down—and there on the edge of a desk, I saw two pennies. Big John was there. He had given his nod of approval. My day was complete.

His influence sustained me for many years, through several colleges and degree plans, until finally I achieved the goal I had established for myself that allowed me to keep the promise I had made him almost thirty years before. But he was not the only person in my life who helped me.

GRANDPA

The one person in my life whom I always wanted to please was my grandfather, Bruce Scrimshire. As a child, I thought he was a giant of a man, and I loved him more than anyone or anything else in my world. He was the youngest of three children, born in the Indian territory of Oklahoma in 1896. His family was very poor and he learned at an early age to never waste anything and to be grateful for everything. Whenever I was near him, I knew I was loved. At his side, I learned to watch the clouds for impending bad weather, turn off the lights when I left a room, and when onions were ready to be pulled from the ground. But one of the most important lessons he taught me was the value of my name.

In one of our many conversations, he once told me that we come into the world with only one sure thing, our names. We may come from different backgrounds, different situations, but the choices we make affect not only our life but the name we hold. The memory of that conversation and the impact it had on me saw me through six years as a classroom teacher, a directorship, sixteen years as a principal, and three years as a college professor.

Because he lived in a small rural community, everyone knew who he was. At the mention of his name, people would always speak so highly of "Mr. Bruce." He had achieved the life lesson he wanted me to learn. His name constantly spoke for him and his actions. Grandpa passed away before I achieved my first principalship. But his voice and his words still influence me, especially when I see my name on my office door at school, when I see it in a program at a conference, and especially when I hear one of my students call me "Dr. T."

These two men played such important roles in my childhood, making me who I am and helping me establish my belief system at an early age. Along with the strength I learned from my mother, they were instrumental in helping me develop my character and my determination. Not to mention the fact that if the educator thing didn't work out, I could work as a weather girl, an energy conservationist, or an onion farmer.

So who are you and what led you to seek the principalship? What person or persons caused you to realize your strengths, your gifts? Whom did you want to call when you decided to become a school leader or when you became a principal? These visitors in our lives gave us a glimpse into theirs so we would be able to touch others. I truly believe that as you are sitting there reading these words, you are hearing their voices either inspiring you or challenging you to do your best, become something, and give back. Whatever the words were, however they were said, you became something very important. You became or are on your way to becoming a school principal, a job some would never even attempt. I am proud of you.

If you are a newly appointed principal, you may be wondering what kind of school leader you want to be. Will you use the theories you learned in college or your life lessons to lead you? Will you use the books you read, such as Wess Roberts' *Leadership Secrets of Attila the Hun* or *The Caring Administrator*? How will you know what to do when an angry parent storms the school, the buses are late, or the cafeteria runs out of corn dogs before all the classes have had their lunch? It all circles back around to what you believe in, what your priorities are, and your personal leadership style.

As you know, every coin has two sides. The same thing goes for developing a belief system. I have been continually asking you what you believe in because I am certain that you cannot even lead a group of chickens across the road if you don't have a strong belief that you will get to the other side. Once you have established these beliefs in your leadership thinking, I want to you to think about what you will not believe in or accept.

As a principal, I learned to accept some situations. I learned to turn my head one time if a teacher was late. I learned to accept lesson plans that were not turned in on time. It was even alright if a teacher forgot a meeting. In saying what I learned to accept, I need to also share with you what I would not accept. These are just a few on my list of What I Don't Believe In:

I do not believe in humiliating a child.

I do not believe harsh words can heal wounds.

I do not believe in wasting time.

I do not believe in hurting another individual with rumors or gossip.

I do not believe that worksheets take the place of teaching.

I encourage you to stand before your staff in the very first faculty meeting and tell them your beliefs about the children, their teaching, and the expectations you have. And with your very next breath, tell them what you do not believe in.

You could even turn this into a staff development exercise by asking them to write their own belief creeds for their classrooms. These non-negotiables are so ingrained in me and my thinking that I am not willing to compromise nor allow any staff member to move me from these beliefs. What are yours? What are you willing to sit down right now and declare as your personal leadership non-negotiables?

Before you set foot on a campus as an administrator, remember what you used to do. You were a teacher. You were chosen for this position

of leadership because you were able (or will be able) to convince an interview committee that you possessed the necessary qualifications and
beliefs to achieve great things. The responsibilities of school leadership
are endless and varied. Your abilities to solve problems, address issues,
and ensure success for the children will surely require you to reflect on
those events and the people in your life that made you strong, taught
you to endure, and placed you firmly in the belief system you still carry
today.

RECOGNIZING PERSONAL NEEDS

The job you have chosen to undertake will require personal stamina,
strength, endurance, and a great sense of humor. There will be some
days when all you have time to do is put your purse or briefcase under
the desk before the school day comes at you full force. When you experience a few of these days, you may find yourself completely exhausted
and dreading the next day before you even leave that evening. Your
physical and mental health are two personal aspects I don't want you to
simply disregard. The school, the teachers, and the children depend on
your constant presence to lead, guide, and nurture them.

During my years as a principal, I always wanted the staff to know
they could come and talk to me about anything anytime I was available.
While this open-door policy developed a sense of trust and understanding between the staff and me, it also caused me to come to the school
on the weekends, use vacation time to catch up on paperwork, and let
caffeine take the place of blood running through my veins.

Learn this tidbit early: It is OK to close your door. Yes, I have said
it. It is OK to close your door. It is even alright to let your secretary tell
people you are busy and will have to get back to them (except for the
superintendent, of course). You can even tell the receptionist to hold
all your calls. Otherwise, you will become a pack mule as you carry bag
after bag of work home, leave it in the back seat of the car, and then
feel guilty because your tired, worn body could not move another inch
once you reached your house. You have to learn to take care of yourself,
let time management skills become your new friend, and rely on other
people to help you.

I was very fortunate in my career as a principal to have a curriculum person who watched over me. When my days were filled with daunting tasks, certain meetings had caused stroke-level blood pressure readings, and some teachers had forgotten my non-negotiables, Suzanne would simply come and take me away from the campus. We would head to Sonic Drive-In for a large Ocean Water or go sit at the ball field and watch baseball practice. For a few minutes, I was able to regain my composure (and usually get my temper in check) and refocus.

Suzanne saw the need for a mental-health moment and acted upon it. I advise you to find a person who will do that for you. I have also had two secretaries who would simply come and close my door, knew when to bring me a lunch, and would literally stand guard at my office door. You have to consider these people as guardian angels who have been placed in your school world to watch over you and, quite possibly, save the life of the next person who wanted to ask you a question.

Regarding your office, make this a place of solitude. Surround yourself with pictures of your family, vacation sites you've visited, or your favorite artwork. I once knew a principal who kept nothing personal on his desk or in his office. He only kept the phone and a yellow notepad on his desk. It was not his home, just the place he worked.

Well, consider this: If you arrive at school by 7:00 a.m. (depending on the time school starts) and you leave at 7:00 p.m. that night, disregarding the hours you sleep, haven't you really spent more time at school than at home? When parents, visitors, teachers, and children enter your office, is it a welcoming place? For your mental health, make yourself comfortable.

Your regard for your physical health is just as important as knowing when to have a Sonic break. Recognize the need to eat or get out of your office sometimes. Usually on Fridays, I would wear my tennis shoes, tell the secretary "I'll be on campus," and take off for the classrooms. I would visit teachers, talk to the children, or drop in on second-graders in the gym and dance the chicken dance with them.

Let me caution you about that. While dancing the chicken dance with a paraprofessional, we fell; I broke my kneecap and was in a knee brace for six weeks. There is a reason second-graders and not the principal learn the chicken dance. Earnestly look for those times to simply enjoy the campus and the children. Take a few moments to find pleasure in the art of teaching and recognize the artists on your campus. Your health and well-being are just as important as the health and well-being of the campus.

SITTING IN THE CHAIR

When I became a principal the first time, I was given permission to buy some new furniture. Knowing the amount of money that had been designated and my frugal nature (some would call me cheap), I found the perfect chair. However, there was one drawback. The upholstery material was pink. For years after that, when I was waving my banner of "I'm the principal and you're not," I would make reference to sitting in the pink chair as if it were the throne of a kingdom. Phrases such as, "When you sit in the pink chair . . ." or "As long as I sit in the chair . . ." would fly from my mouth in times of stress or need.

Well, I do not sit in the chair anymore, but you do or will. When you accepted your kingdom, you also accepted the throne and all that comes with it. And with any monarchy comes absolute power and decisions that only you can make. Then there are those college preparation courses that told you to create a school community, involve all the stakeholders, and give everyone an opportunity to buy in to the success of the school. I am here to tell you, that is exactly what you need to do—most of the time. However, for some situations, the responsibility of decision making is in your hands and your hands alone.

Remember when I told you about how my grandfather taught me to watch the clouds for the different cloud formations? He also told me to watch the sky and if it ever "split" with the top half turning dark and the lower half of the split remaining light, with a touch of a green tint, bad weather was coming. Well, it came.

On one occasion, I noticed that the temperature took a sudden drop and the winds increased. Looking up to the sky, I saw the split happening. We turned on the weather radio, called the central office, and waited. Around 1:00 p.m., the storm that my grandfather had warned me about years before hit a nearby city, with several small tornadoes touching down and causing drenching rains, and this line of thunderstorms was headed our way.

I pulled on my yellow raincoat and red rain boots (no joke, I still have them) and started walking the campus. As I walked through the halls a barrage of questions came from the teachers.

"What do you want us to do?"

"What should we tell the kids?"

"If the parents come in, do we let them take their children?"

"Do you want us to pull out our emergency kits?"

Within seconds, I answered the questions, sent the assistant principal in one direction, the instructional specialist in another direction, told the secretary that if the parents called to inform them we had the situation under control and to assure them their children were safe, and started moving students from the metal, stand-alone gym facility to the safety of the main school building.

The metal-framed gym was connected to the school by heavy metal poles and an overhang made of siding. In a matter of minutes, we were moving children in bucket-brigade style from the gym to the main building. The wind was so high that many of them would have fallen if we had not hung on to them. Back inside the building, the lights had gone out and the teachers had already moved their classes into the hallways. For the most part, everyone remained calm, and the storm passed right over us. Without the help of the support staff, the teachers taking care of their children, and administrative personnel taking on additional responsibilities, we would not have gotten through that day.

Because you sit in the chair, people will be looking at you to provide the answers and the actions associated with the security, safety, and well-being of everyone inside the school. Keep your bag of tricks filled! Whatever you decide to do in any situation, remember this guideline, "What is the best way I can solve this problem that will benefit my school and my children in the timeliest manner?"

Whenever you begin your principalship, you'll start the process of unpacking boxes and putting your new office together. There will be a chair in that office that is all yours. In fact, it took me a long time to even let someone else sit in my chair. But as time goes on, you will find that it isn't about the color of the upholstery or the placement of the chair, it's about the decisions you make, the conversations you have, and the relationships you build during your reign in the chair.

You may not have many opportunities to deal with storms or events beyond your control, but your staff will always look to you for the solutions to problems and the guidance they will need to deal with any and all classroom concerns. Why? That's right—because you and you alone sit in the chair.

Understanding the leadership capacity needed for becoming and remaining an effective principal reaches far beyond recognizable or standard definitions brought forth by well-known researchers. Your personal leadership style and belief systems were formed from childhood events and a walk that only you could take. Servais and Sanders (2006) contend that our belief systems were formed early in our lives, were modeled by those around us, and grew from our life experiences.

As you reflect on your particular place regarding the principalship, understand that you may still be in the process of learning about what kind of leader you will be, or you may be looking for a new chair. Your personal leadership style did not develop overnight, nor was your belief system created by you alone. People and situations that came in and out of your life were somehow connected to special moments that will remain with you forever.

These people who left imprints in your life not only touched your heart but left behind a legacy for you, a legacy that birthed your need to help others and affect their lives in a particular way. You know who you are because of them. You know what kind of leader you want to be. Because of the belief system that guides you, you will be able to guide others. You have no choice. Make each day count.

DEVELOPING YOUR PERSONAL LEADERSHIP CAPACITY

Deciding to become a principal took courage and conviction, knowing the duties and responsibilities associated with the job. As a classroom teacher, you may have watched your principal fight daily battles, rejoice at the success of a child, or defend a decision. Your outlook on the principalship is all that really matters, and it is directly linked to your abilities to lead. This chapter gave you insight on how leadership theories affect what you do, as well as the personal belief system you follow. With this in place, how can you further develop your personal leadership capacity?

1. Keep learning. Join professional organizations that foster leadership. Continue to seek the knowledge that will impact your decision making, communication, and character as a leader. Attend staff development opportunities with your teachers. Research new methods of instruction. Let your staff and faculty know that continual learning is expected.
2. Volunteer to help with special projects at the campus and district levels. Let others see the natural leadership abilities you have.
3. Encourage collegiality among your peers. After a principals' meeting, have lunch with other principals. Plan for it, arrange it, and enjoy it.
4. Accept who you are, the beliefs you hold, and what you do not believe in. Convey this continually as you walk your halls, talk with your teachers, and establish the goals of the school.
5. Admit it when you make a mistake. The Earth will not stop moving. The sun will not drop from the sky. As they say, you are only human. Admitting a mistake will help build your character and show the staff you are only human.
6. Have fun. You are in a place full of children who will love you unconditionally if they feel safe and dignified. Their smiles and achievements will only prove what kind of an instructional leader you are.

WHAT WILL MY PRINCIPALSHIP SAY ABOUT ME?

In deciding who you are and accepting the life events that shaped you into the person you are, you also have to accept how your actions and words affect others. If and when you leave the principalship, what do you want staff, the parents, the children, or the main office to say about you? When I leave the school, I want people to say:

"Every decision she made was made for the welfare of the children."

"I knew I could trust her."

"She was fair."

"She worked just as hard as we did."

"I knew she always cared about my child."

"I never gave her a task she couldn't do."

If you are in your first year as a principal, you have to consider what leadership traits you will need to actively build positive relationships with all those involved in the education of the children and the culture of the school. Not everyone will like you or the decisions you make, but it is here that your personal belief system will be of value.

- Your principalship should be based on ethical behaviors that support your personal belief system.
- Your principalship should be seen in such a way that it is felt campus-wide.

USING YOUR 20/20 VISION

At the very beginning of this chapter, it was suggested that there are three primary groups of principals reading this book: the Wannabes, the Newbies, and the Veterans. Their reasons for choosing this book to read revolve around where they are in their professional careers as campus leaders. No matter what point you are at, what are some strategies, practices, or suggestions that could ready you for the world on the other side of the desk? Who better to advise you than recognized leaders? Here is a checklist that you might use to be prepared for the start of your path in leadership.

- ☐ I know what kind of school leader I want to be.
- ☐ I am ready to be a school leader.
- ☐ I have supportive people to help me.
- ☐ I have created my non-negotiable list of beliefs.
- ☐ I have created my "I Don't Believe In" list.

LEADERSHIP INSPIRATION

The quotes below also deliver a message of leadership that you can adopt for your belief system.

"Education is not the filling of a pail, but the lighting of a fire."—William Butler Yeats

Set people on fire because they see you on fire.

"Getting things done is not always what is more important. There is value in allowing others to learn even if the task is not accomplished quickly, efficiently, or effectively." —R. D. Clyde

Be strong enough in your leadership capacity to allow others to learn from and with you.

"Education is the ability to meet life's situations." —Jon G. Hibber

Accept the situations that made you strong and able to persevere. Embrace childhood events you may not have understood then in order to help others now.

"Let us think of education as the means of developing our greatest abilities; because in each of us there is a private hope and dream which, fulfilled, can be translated into benefit for everyone and greater strength for our nation." —President John F. Kennedy

Simply realize your own potential as a great and influential person.

"Life can only be understood backwards, but it must be lived forwards." —Søren Kierkegaard

Whatever made you accept the principalship, whatever life event created in you the ability or desire to lead, here you are. You will set the stage to be the example of effective leadership on your campus.

MY WISH FOR YOU

May your principalship be designed around your personal strengths and beliefs.

May your personal strengths and beliefs speak volumes for your ability to lead.

May your ability to lead create a successful educational experience for all.

May the children show you leadership skills you never knew you possessed.

ADDITIONAL RESOURCES

Reading Material

Canter, L. The caring administrator: Positive resource guide. Santa Monica, CA: Lee Canter & Associates, Inc. 1080.

Cottrell, David. *Monday Morning Leadership.* Dallas, TX: CornerStone Leadership Institute, 2002.

Creighton, Theodore. *Leading from Below the Surface.* Thousand Oaks, CA: Corwin Press, 2005.

Maxwell, John C. *Developing the Leader within You.* Lakeland, FL: Maxwell Motivation, Inc., 2005.

————. *The 21 Indispensable Qualities of a Leader.* Lakeland, FL: Maxwell Motivation, Inc., 1999.

Roberts, Wess. *Leadership Secrets of Attila the Hun.* New York: Warner Books, 1985.

Walters, J. Donald. *The Art of Leadership.* Nevada City, CA: Hansa Trust, 1987.

Internet Resources

edweek.org
The *Education Week* site provides principals with the most current news relating to school practices and policies.

www.aasa.org
The American Association of School Administrators provides several pieces of information that directly impact school leaders. It also provides information concerning opportunities for professional development.

www.nassp.org/s_nassp/index.asp?CID=1138&DID=54609
Educational studies and professional development opportunities are only two of the benefits of this site, established by the National Association of Secondary School Principals.

www.naesp.org
Another helpful site for leaders at the elementary level. The resources provided by the National Association of Elementary School Principals at this site are endless.

www.nea.org
The National Education Association offers a wealth of information for school leaders such as the possibility of grants, methods for data retrieval, and research studies that impact the role of school leaders.

2

WEARING A RED CAPE DOESN'T MAKE YOU SUPERMAN

There she stands, her red cape flowing in the breeze on a spring afternoon. The school dismissal bell is about to ring, and soon the children will leave for the day. She is ready at her car rider post to assist the children safely into their waiting cars. As they leave the building, the children move quietly toward seats in their assigned areas and promptly begin pulling out books, paper, and pencils from their backpacks so they can start their homework.

The parents are cautiously and calmly moving their cars in an orderly manner toward the designated pickup areas. Every teacher who is assigned to car rider duty for the week has reported to his or her post on time and is wearing a "Here I am to help you" smile. As the line of cars begins to dwindle and the last child is placed safely into his or her car, another day of car rider duty is finished. She thanks all of the staff members on duty and sees them clasp their hands together as they exclaim, "Thank you, Super Principal. We couldn't have done this without you." With her hands on her hips, the red cape billowing around her, Super Principal has once again saved the day.

Or . . .

There she stands, her red cape flowing in the breeze of the pungent exhaust fumes coming from the cars in the pickup line. The bell is about to sound the end of another day, and soon the hordes of screaming children will hit the side doors of the school like linebackers hitting the opposing team's front line during a Friday night football game.

The children have been told many times to sit in their assigned areas, but they never seem to get to that area without hitting or screaming at other waiting children. Countless letters, reminders, and even a map of the parking lot have been sent to the parents, fully describing where and how car riders will be picked up to ensure the safety of all the children.

In spite of that, mothers are parking in restricted areas or racing through the two lines of parked cars to get to their child first. As she stands in her high heels and pearls thinking of the hours of paperwork that await her on her desk, she notices that no other teaching personnel have made it to their assigned duty spots. With her handy radio in tow, she calls for the school secretary to make an announcement on the intercom, "If you are on car rider duty this week, I'd get out there if I were you."

The children are becoming restless and beginning to irritate each other. Spitballs are seen flying through the air. One lands on the cheek of a younger child, who automatically begins to wail loudly. As the last car leaves the parking lot, she turns to find every teacher gone and several children remaining. When she opens the door and places the last child in his car (an hour after dismissal), the mother emphatically apologizes for her lateness because of a doctor's appointment with the younger brother. She explains that the little brother is having stomach problems—and sure enough, projectile vomit spews from his mouth and lands squarely in the center of the shiny silver "S" on the billowy red cape.

As the last car begins to pull away, Super Principal realizes that not only does her red cape have a horrible vomit stain on it, but it is trapped inside the door of the departing car. She stands with her hands on her hips, half of the smelly cape blowing in the afternoon breeze, and exclaims, "Thank God another day of car rider duty is over!"

So much for the real world of Super Principal and her mighty cape.

The real world of the principalship does not always include breezy spring days and adoring fans. Hero worship will only go so far. When you begin to examine the true nature and responsibilities of the principalship, you will come to understand that genuine strength and courage are not found in the folds of a flowing red cape or by simply embroidering a shiny "S" on the front of a suit. This chapter will ask you to realize the importance of your personal strength, the responsibilities of holding a position of power, and the knowledge you will need to guide your school and your staff. With these mighty abilities, you will become a superhero for your campus.

THE POWER OF THE PRINCIPALSHIP

According to an Internet source, "superhero" usually refers to a comic strip or television character who is known for amazing talents of courage or strength that enable him or her to fight evil and evildoers. These fictional men and women possess extraordinary powers that exceed mere mortals. They usually wear very descriptive costumes that are indicative of their persona.

For instance, Superman has a red cape and can fly. Batman has an unbelievable array of weaponry attached to a black leather utility belt. Even Wonder Woman wears red, white, and blue and carries a rope that when placed around someone elicits only the truth. There is no question that superheroes are readily noticed. However, there is just one small consideration that I want you to be constantly aware of: They're not real. They are fictional, man-made, and sheer fantasy. Your goal of becoming Super Principal, the next fighter for right and good in the world of academia, begins the moment you take your first steps on your very own campus.

To understand what it takes to be a superhero at a school, let's examine their sources of power. For instance, Spider-Man has the ability to shoot extra-strength webbing from his wrists that attaches to any surface, allowing him to detain the bad guys or quickly fly from crime scene to crime scene rendering aid to the helpless. Batman has an entire arsenal of gadgets that are used in a variety of ways to prevent crime, not to mention a bulletproof, tight-fitting, spandex-looking hero outfit that would be really cool if I weighed 120 pounds or was six feet tall.

We cannot forget the many extraordinary powers of the X-men. They seem to possess a power for every need that arises. One of them can call on the elements of weather to change dreadful situations, while another one can move people or objects by simply using telepathic thoughts. It appears that being a superhero involves self-realization of the powers you possess and using them to save mankind.

Not only are these fictional characters flashy dressers and a little out of the ordinary, they also have similar traits that endear them to us. First and foremost, they do what is right, at the right time, for the right reasons. They live by strong moral beliefs and are never tempted by evil thoughts. A strong sense of duty and responsibility guides them as they keep a constant vigil to protect and serve those under their care. Without all of the fancy costumes or extra abilities, these powers are the same powers you possess as a school leader.

And if school principals are so powerful, where does that power come from? Is there a hidden power pack in the bottom drawer of their desks? Do they carry a magic potion of creamed spinach in their briefcase that causes bulging muscles to appear in an hour of need? The powers associated with the principalship come from the position itself—while another sense of power simply lies within the individual.

Many school boards across the nation set in policy the requirements and the duties of campus leaders. In conjunction with those duties, the school board gives the authority to complete those tasks to the principals. In the state of Texas, as determined by the Texas Association of School Boards, the duties of the principal include the following:

1. Recommend personnel for employment or nonrenewal
2. Create a school vision that includes specific goals and strategies
3. Maintain the school's budget
4. Supervise personnel and instructional programs
5. Supervise all campus improvements
6. Keep all records current
7. Assume all other assigned administrative duties

These are only a few of the many responsibilities facing campus principals. In order to accomplish these and more, a principal had better have some kind of extraordinary strength or skill.

The Texas Association of School Boards also establishes the qualifications of principals who hope to serve as a campus leader. First, they must have at least two years of teaching experience. They must also hold a valid master's degree from an accredited college or university. Finally, they must have successfully completed all the necessary state certification assessments that are associated with becoming a principal.

Knowing what I know about the principalship, there may be a few more qualifications that were omitted from this list of requirements. First, our superheroes must have additional sight in the form of an invisible eye in the middle of their foreheads and another two eyes on the back of their heads. This allows them to know all and see all.

Additionally, their hearing must be so acute that they can hear the beginnings of a fight from two corridors away. Their sense of smell must be so sensitive that it can lead them to a potential fire in the cafeteria or a bag of burning microwave popcorn in the teachers' lounge. Finally, they must possess superhuman strength that allows them to talk with the superintendent on the phone, discipline a child sent to the office with a mere glaring stare, and respond to an e-mail from one of the teachers—all at the same time.

So let's get a picture of this person in our minds. He or she has multiple eyes, a set of floppy ears, a bulging set of nostrils, and six fingers on each hand. I am not sure this is how Superman, Wonder Woman, or even the Incredible Hulk started out as superheroes.

While these attributes are necessary, there is still the question of your source of power beyond what a school board gives you. The position itself brings a sense of power to the person who sits in the chair. You are the boss, the manager, the supervisor, the foreman. You are in charge and because you are in charge, you have the power to make decisions about instruction, schedules, and personnel. The staff will look to you, as the campus leader, to make those decisions. How and when you use that power is what will define your principalship and your status as a school hero.

When I began my first principalship, I understood that because I was the principal I had the power to relocate teachers to any classroom. The usual practice was to cluster grade-level teachers together in close proximity, especially if the children would be changing classrooms and moving to different teachers during the course of the day, to save time and resources.

On one hallway, three of the four grade-level teachers were clustered; the fourth teacher was on the opposite end of the hallway from the others. Being new and somewhat naïve, I thought that by grouping all of the grade-level teachers together it would lessen the amount of travel time for students between classes. Since school had not started yet, I began calling teachers to let them know of the upcoming changes. Almost everyone agreed. The most interesting conversations began when a few of them asked me if I had called Lulu the Loner.

Lulu was a teacher in this particular grade level, but her classroom was at the other end of the hallway. She had been in that room for years and liked her room a lot, even though her classroom was far away from the other grade-level classrooms. After being asked several times if I had called Lulu yet, I began to worry about what I would say to Lulu and how she was going to react. Call it bravery or sheer stupidity, but I assured all the teachers that everything would turn out just fine.

When I called Lulu, she told me without hesitation that she did not want to move, that that was and had always been her classroom, and that she was very upset that she had to move. I explained to her the benefits of the move and how the children would best be served by the grade-level teachers being clustered together. I wish I could tell you that she cared. Not really.

What I did not know at the time was that the thermostat for some of the classrooms was in that room and she liked having control over the room temperature. Her old room also had carpet, where most of the other ones did not. Little did I know this would be the first of many power struggles that I would have during my first year as the principal on that campus.

The decision to move the teachers was in the realm of my power as the instructional leader of the campus. I did not have to wear a T-shirt that said, "I'm in charge and you are not."

By the way, she changed rooms—kicking and complaining, but she moved. I didn't know it at the time, but teachers were taking bets on who would win the Great Move Debate, me or Lulu. Score one for being stupid and brave!

In another instance, a teacher forgot about the respect given to the position of the principal. In most school districts, it is customary to have a deadline when all monies in the school budget are to be spent. The deadline is usually set in March or April of the school year, to allow the district's bookkeeping department to clear any purchase orders or late deliveries for that year. At a principals' meeting, we were asked to announce to all staff members the deadline date and tell them that if they wanted to order any materials it had to be done before the end of March. No requests would be accepted after that date.

For many years on this campus, this practice was not observed. After telling the teachers of the stop date many times, I did not allow any more purchase orders to leave the office. Despite my request, one of the teachers somehow managed to send one off.

At another principals' meeting, the superintendent, realizing that several teachers had disregarded the request, instructed the principals to collect any materials that had been ordered after that date and return them to the supplier. Following her directive, I asked the teachers to send those materials to my office. After the request, one of the teachers came storming into my office, slammed down a bucket of counting blocks, screamed, "You wanted them—here they are," and turned and promptly left my office.

I simply sat there in amazement. The rational side of my principal persona wanted to believe she was just having a bad day. The patient side of my principal self wanted to give her time to cool down and then talk to her in a calm and understanding manner. However, this wasn't the day for either of those personas.

She had entered my domain, screamed at me, and then proceeded to tuck tail and run. I was simply following a directive I had been given from the superintendent. The teacher had gone too far, and I was in one of those moods to let her know about it.

I leaped up from my chair, threw open my office door, and with clicking heels headed after her. She was still in the hallway trying to return to her classroom, when I called to her and said, "I need to see you back in my office now. This is not a request. Now!" I waited for her at my office door and when she entered the room, I slammed the door, sat down in my chair, looked her straight in the face, and said, "Who the °&^°° do you think you are and just who do you think you are talking to?"

You will find that many of the memories I share with you are intended to teach you about the real world of the principalship that is found beyond the books and classroom doors of colleges and universities. Throughout this book, I will try to share words that you can use to inspire and uplift your staff and students. Unfortunately, this is not one of those times.

I was mad, not because she showed disrespect to me but because she was disrespectful to the position that I held. When she returned to my office and I asked her that all-important rude question of my own, she broke down in tears. Just that morning she had received some devastating news that left her vulnerable and brokenhearted. I just happened to be the first one who got in her way.

One of the many super powers you will need to acquire when you begin your principalship will be that of discernment. I have always tried to live by a "twenty-four-hour rule." If a decision has to be made and it is not one that involves emergency measures to be taken, wait twenty-four hours and see how things turn out. If you are angry at a parent, a teacher, or your immediate supervisor, wait twenty-four hours before you speak words that cannot be taken back or forgotten. Take time to watch and observe certain situations that exist on your campus. Have enough insight to know when to speak and when not to speak. Following this simple rule will make you a stronger principal and a hero to someone.

On one such occasion, our campus was participating in some after-school professional development activities. At the same time, I had recommended a teacher for employment who I feared would not be brought to the school board. There were some factors that I did not know about until after the interview process had been completed. This teacher was excellent and would have been a great asset to our campus; however, during the interview the teacher had not shared some valuable information with the committee. After talking with the superintendent, I found him to be very supportive but apprehensive about taking the teacher's name to the board.

At this same time, the teachers were taking a break from the professional development activity, and I was in my office with the assistant principal talking about the teacher's situation. All at once, a teacher knocked on the door, stuck her head in, and asked if she could leave early. She had completed the rest of the group activities and wanted to go home. I told her I would be with her shortly because I had a situation that I needed to personally address. She said OK and closed the door.

A few minutes later, there was a knock on the door and there stood the same teacher. She asked if I knew how much longer I would be because she was ready to go home. I reminded her that we were required to attend the professional development for three hours and we still had some more work to do. She backed out of the doorway and closed the door. The third time she knocked on the door and opened it, my twenty-four-hour rule did not kick in.

That third knock did it. When she opened that door and asked again if she could go home, I proceeded to tell her I didn't care if she stayed or left. I just didn't want her to knock on that door again. I had a serious situation that I was dealing with and if she wanted to go home, then by all means go. My twenty-four-hour rule of waiting to respond to an angry or aggravating situation disappeared with that third knock. She did not come back into the office. She just sat at her table, in her group, crying.

I had a great deal on my mind at that time, but hurting the feelings of one of my teachers was not acceptable. If I had taken the time on her first knock to ask why she needed to go home early knowing we had planned the in-service activity for that evening, I would have found out that it was her son's first birthday and her family was waiting for her to join in on his party. No wonder she was upset and crying. Not only had I yelled at her, she couldn't be with her family to celebrate.

The next morning I searched for her and of course apologized for my rude behavior. That is when she told me about her son's birthday. I told her if I had only known I would have made other plans for her to earn her in-service hours. She was also looking for me to apologize to me for coming to the door so many times and making a pest of herself. I should have remembered my twenty-four-hour rule. I should have thought to ask her why before I jumped her. So please, learn to give yourself some wait time before you make a teacher cry and miss her firstborn child's first birthday.

As you begin to learn about the powers that have been given to you by a school board and understand the personal sense of power the position holds, you must also be aware of the misuse of that power. I heard of a principal once who required his teachers to wear shirts with sleeves. Not because of the teachers' dress code, but because when teachers wore sleeveless shirts he saw the sagging skin (no joke) under their arms and he didn't like to see it. If they did not do this, they would receive a written reprimand.

Another principal, on a yearly basis, moved his teachers from one grade level to another, without asking them. Not only did he move them every year, he informed them by mail. This is not the way to inspire trust among your staff.

Superman, Batman, Wonder Woman, and the Incredible Hulk know they have powers that set them above the rest. They know how to chan-

nel their powers for the good of mankind. Think of your principalship
in the same way. I am sure that there were many episodes where Bruce
Wayne (the real identity of Batman) did not want to look up into the
night skies and see that flashing figure of a bat calling him to duty.

Maybe Clark Kent (Superman's real name) was tired of changing
clothes in phone booths and flying off to do battle with a meteor hur-
dling to the Earth. He probably just wanted to have a nice quiet dinner
somewhere and read his paper. Perhaps Bruce Banner (the real identity
of the Incredible Hulk) hoped for the day he would wake up from a
night's sleep fully clothed and without any mysterious bruises or broken
ribs.

These were ordinary characters by birth. Yet when they realized they
possessed special gifts, they became heroes for the world to admire and
respect. This can also describe you and your principalship. Find the
secret powers you have and become a hero to children. You don't need
a red cape, a shiny silver "S" monogrammed on your jacket, or a gadget-
filled utility belt. The words you use and the actions you take toward
helping a school achieve its goals or a child believe in himself automatically make you a superhero.

USING YOUR X-RAY POWERS FOR THE GOOD
OF THE SCHOOL

Let's say you come upon a scene where people are screaming and in a
state of panic as smoke billows from a burning apartment complex. A
frantic mother hysterically pleads for help. Her young son is still trapped
on the third floor of the burning building. From his window at the *Daily
Planet* newspaper, Clark Kent sees the commotion and leaps from his
desk in search of the nearest phone booth. Once he has changed his
clothes, the superhero is ready to fight the blaze, save the child, and
return him safely to his mother.

But, where is the child? How much of the third floor is destroyed
from the burning inferno? What is the best way to enter the building? In
a flash, a single beam of light streams from Superman's eyes; his X-ray
vision has shown him how to safely enter the burning building, where
the little boy is hiding, and the fire-free path he needs to take to bring

them both to safety. Once again, Superman has saved the day by using another of his extraordinary powers, that of X-ray vision.

By using his X-ray vision, Superman had the ability to see through walls where crime and mayhem were taking place. Superman broke down those brick walls, fought the bad guys, and returned justice to an ever-grateful city. Since you are already wearing the red cape and the shiny silver "S," why not learn how to use the power of X-ray vision to help the city that lies within the walls of your school?

For a few minutes, consider that city. Visitors are always traveling in and out. People are busily working, continuously moving here and there. Opportunities present themselves to attend musical or sporting events that draw in people from various cultures. The intoxicating smells of delectable foods cooking in the cafeteria fill the air. And after a busy and hectic day, your city will turn down its lights, lock its doors, and wait for the next day to dawn.

The city that is under your care is no different than the cities protected by our favorite superheroes. However, even with all the good emanating from the four walls of your small city, danger still lurks. The need for a superhero still exists.

One of the most important responsibilities you will ever have as the principal of a campus is to secure the safety and welfare of the staff and the students, and that can be accomplished by using your power of X-ray vision. Knowing this, let's see how many of the questions below you can answer.

- ☐ How many entry/exit doors do you have on the campus?
- ☐ Where are the fire extinguishers kept?
- ☐ What chemicals are kept in the custodial closets?
- ☐ Can the front door of the school be seen from the main office?
- ☐ What are the fastest routes out of the school in the case of an emergency?
- ☐ Do teachers and students know what to do in case of a fire?
- ☐ Where are the gas and water mains located?

These are only a few questions to ask yourself when you take on the responsibility of a school. Knowing the answers to these questions and more will allow you to develop a keen ability to see through walls, down hallways, or around corners. You may not always have time to change into your Superman outfit. Your X-ray abilities come in the form of being proactive, knowledgeable, and willing to do just about anything to protect the ones you serve.

In your attempt to be like Superman or any other well-known defender of justice and truth, you must also remember to err on the side of good judgment. Many times parents of potential students would visit our school to meet the teachers and tour the campus. It was not uncommon for these parents to introduce themselves in the office and ask to visit the classrooms.

On one such occasion, two women entered our school with the intention of visiting some of the kindergarten classrooms and teachers. After finding a teacher who was on her conference time, one of the women engaged the teacher in conversation while the other one excused herself under the guise of visiting another kindergarten classroom.

While visiting the classroom, one of the women proceeded to steal the wallet from the purse of another teacher in that grade level. Thinking nothing was amiss, the teacher thanked the women for coming and expressed the hope that they would enroll a child in our school. Seconds later, as the women were leaving the school heading toward their parked car, the teacher came flying down the hallway screaming, "They took my wallet."

My red cape must have been flying high that day because I jumped up from my desk and ran after the women. Here's the main point I want you to reflect on once again: When you are faced with a situation on your campus, err on the side of good judgment.

As I rushed to the parking lot, the women were getting into their car about to drive away. Without thinking, I opened the car door and asked them to return the wallet. After several adamant denials from the women, I finally retrieved the wallet. Not only was I effectively using my skills of cape wearing, my X-ray vision powers were also on high alert because something made me ask for the money that had been in the wallet. In the short time it had taken them to leave the building and enter their car, they had already emptied the wallet of all the money. I told them to leave my campus and that I would wait five minutes before I called the sheriff's office.

As they were leaving, I turned back to reenter the building and found a crowd of teachers huddled against the front fence of the school. "What are you doing?" I asked. One of the teachers proudly replied, "We had your back, T, if you needed us."

I am fairly certain I was wearing some sort of professional dress such as a skirt and jacket set or a nice dress and heels. However, I am absolutely sure that I was not wearing a bulletproof vest. I do not have nor have I ever had the ability to turn into the Invisible Woman. Neither do you.

Superman could have stopped a speeding bullet, but the only thing that can stop a speeding bullet as it heads toward your body is, in fact, your body. Being a principal who acts with good judgment requires you to look at situations and make the best decisions possible. There could have been another person waiting for them inside the car who had a weapon of some sort. They could have run me over with their car. Your personal safety is just as important as the safety of the staff and the students.

If the comic strip superhero characters were created with the intent of fighting injustice and using their extraordinary powers to save the world from evildoers, I may have been neglectful in failing to mention a little-known superhero who never has appeared nor ever will appear in the comic strips of a newspaper or a Saturday morning cartoon lineup on television.

This dynamic person is always there to assist the staff and help the students in any situation. He or she fights off angry parents with a patient smile and willing attitude, and soars over colleges and universities looking for eager new teachers. Yes, I am referring to the unsung hero of the public school sector, the fighter for the continuous learning and success of all students, the follower of all school policies and practices. There is only one person this could be, Proactive Principal.

Before school begins for the new year, Proactive Principal can be seen walking the hallways of the school with the custodian, as they make a list of the maintenance concerns that need attention. Proactive Principal spends countless hours disaggregating student data to help create the educational focus for the school, and meets with every faculty member before the first day of school to start building a positive relationship with the staff. Proactive Principal's skills are many, and no one is more prepared to be the school leader than this great and wonderful person. With an uncanny ability to know what to do in almost every situation, Proactive Principal is ready to set his or her school vision in place.

For almost every educational learning center, from an elementary campus to a high school level, the steward of these institutions must have a clear vision and a set of strategies to attain those goals. This vision of leadership includes knowing what children are expected to learn, having enough resources to enhance the educational process, and creating a safe learning environment that fosters and celebrates learning. Knowing these responsibilities, Proactive Principal can use various means of cognitive power to work for the good of the children and the school. However, this is not always an easy task to accomplish.

When Superman saved the Earth from evil space invaders or a child from being hit by a runaway train, he was hailed as a courageous hero and a defender of mankind. At the end of many television episodes of Superman or Batman, the superhero was seen atop the tallest building, hands on his waist, cape rising and falling with each gust of wind, looking off into the sunset as a grateful city lay down below. Looking up toward the skyscrapers, the common people on the street were filled with a sense that they were safe and protected.

I would love to tell you that this blind hero-worship is waiting for you when you begin your principalship. I would also love to tell you that throngs of admiring individuals will be lining up to see your next magical act. This is probably not going to happen. Unless you have acquired a principalship at a spanking brand-new school, inside the doors of your school may be waiting some situations that would drop Superman to his knees or send Batman flying back to his bat caves.

There will be some on your staff who will be in awe of your leadership abilities. For these, they welcome change and still have a passion for the teaching profession. But your vision and strategies to develop and maintain student achievement may not always be applauded as heroic, especially if it means a schedule change for some teachers who really have no interest in changing their schedules.

Not every decision you make will be popular or received with a warm, "We can do it" attitude. This is when you seek out and find the courage that you need to always, always, always do the right thing for kids. Proactive Principal knows this and accepts this truth. However, being Proactive Principal was the farthest thing from my mind.

During my first year as an elementary principal, I did not take on the persona of Proactive Principal. I took on the cloak of survival. If Proactive Principal had actually been a comic book hero, I would have bought every issue, watched the video, and become a card-carrying member of an adoring fan club. I knew I possessed the strength and courage of a tried-and-true superhero. But somewhere along the way, I lost my innate X-ray vision abilities and went blindly into the unknown. My blinders were clearly on when, acting in the best interest of the children, I

- relocated a teacher from a classroom she had been in for many years so that the children would not lose so much time traveling between classrooms when they changed teachers
- ended the practice of administering corporal punishment
- expected grade sheets from teachers every three weeks to keep me informed on the educational needs and concerns of the children

I am here to attest to the fact that there were no cheering crowds or ticker-tape parades waiting for me when I stepped in and asked teachers to make these changes. No, as a first-year principal, I would have and should have known more about Proactive Principal.

Throughout this chapter, we have discussed and focused our attention on the many skills, abilities, and gifts that superheroes possess. No matter how strong or smart, even superheroes can't always be in the right place at the right time. There may be more than one runaway train or more than one burning building.

How do superheroes know when to be superheroes? Do they have an alarm at the base of their necks that sends strong electric impulses to their brain alerting them to the possibility of danger or harm? Do they have tiny police band radios carefully concealed in their school radios that emit the exact locations of imminent danger? Not Proactive Principal. He or she calls upon the power of absolute genius to be constantly vigilant regarding the needs of the staff and students. Proactive Principal believes in his or her decisions because they always focus on what is best for the education of the students.

The maintenance staff, custodial staff, and Proactive Principal work collaboratively to keep the school safe and secure. On a daily basis, Proactive Principal's presence is felt as he or she moves in and out of classrooms and hallways monitoring instructional practices. Parents and community members recognize Proactive Principal at football games, band concerts, and the third-grade Christmas program. Proactive Principal realizes that many super powers reveal themselves away from his or her desk and outside the office doors.

Superheroes were created to be examples of strength, duty, and honor. Your days of being a superhero such as Proactive Principal are in the making. I am not sure what trials you will face or who the enemy will be. Elizabeth Dole, the wife of Senator Bob Dole, was quoted as saying, "We have learned that power is a positive force if it is used for positive purposes" (Lewis n.d.). The power of the principalship is yours. How you become a hero to your staff and the children is in your hands.

IDENTIFYING THE KRYPTONITE IN YOUR WORLD

As strong as the comic book heroes were, each one of them had a weakness or a flaw that sometimes prevented him or her from using those super powers. If Bruce Banner, the scientist, became angry, the Incredible Hulk emerged and caused untold damage and destruction, not to mention the fact that he would end up half naked in a deserted and unknown location. If Bruce Wayne, better known as Batman, lost his handy-dandy utility belt with its many crime-fighting gadgets, the bad guys were sure to win. While Superman, who was actually Clark Kent, a mild-mannered newspaperman, could leap from tall buildings or stop speeding locomotives, he was still rendered helpless in the presence of a green element called kryptonite.

When there were no situations of danger present, these superheroes led normal lives of going to work or even reading the Sunday paper. Their super powers were always with them, just as they are with you. The difference lies in the fact that they knew their weaknesses.

Superman knew he could never be around kryptonite. Batman knew he needed to keep the utility belt close to him at all times. Bruce Banner always warned people not to make him mad. They had accepted the fact that as strong as they were, something could make them less powerful. On your journey to becoming a superhero for children, you must be aware of the powers for good you possess as well as those factors that will permeate your protective armor and weaken your super powers.

Part of the essence of being a superhero is accepting the fact that there will be people and situations that may cause you to be an ineffective principal. In the beginning of my professional career as a principal, I learned very quickly that I needed to suppress my quick-fire temper and in some cases my mouth needed to be wired shut so that only a small straw could fit through the wires.

In that first year, I can recall many wonderful and joyous memories. And equally, I had many learning opportunities (a nice way to say trials and tribulations). I did not realize it at the time, but my personal kryptonite came in the form of a woman we will call Casey.

Casey had two children in our school district. Her son was moving to the junior high campus after spending two years with me in the elementary school. Her daughter was still enrolled on our campus. Every single time Casey came to school she complained in a loud and obnoxious manner about everything and anything that had happened to her children while at school. She would rant, rave, and cuss her way through the hallways until she found me. If I was not in my office, the school secretary would call me on the district radio and let me know that Casey needed to talk to me.

On one such occasion, my red cape was at the cleaners and the batteries on my utility belt were dangerously low. As Casey came barging into my office with yet another complaint, I stood up, slammed my hand down on the top of my desk, and screamed back at her, "Are you crazy?" She was so stunned she just stood there saying little or nothing. I felt just like Bruce Banner right before the Incredible Hulk takes over. I had been pushed too far. My eyes turned to a devilish yellow color, and my skin was already changing to a lovely green that Kermit the Frog would have been proud to call his own.

I can tell you I completely forgot the principal courses that I had taken in college that had prepared me to deal with difficult parents. The notes I took in the class that focused on building a strong parent and community relationship must have been in the pocket of my other suit. Casey might as well have been a walking billboard with letters painted with kryptonite.

To this day, I truly believe the sanity of that woman was questionable. However, my behavior was inexcusable. I was a superhero in training. I was the administrator, principal, and instructional leader of the campus. Proof of the completion of many years of college coursework lined the walls of my office in the form of nicely framed diplomas. Any praise or recognition I had received from other parents was lost when I engaged in a verbal battle with Casey. I let Casey's words and actions drop me from my lofty Olympian pedestal to fall to the ground as a mere mortal. On that day, my temper and lack of patience became my personal kryptonite in Casey's hands.

There will be many times that you are faced with people like Casey and situations that you least expect. Facing your weaknesses and limitations is the first step on your way to becoming a powerful superhero for your campus. So with that in mind, take a few minutes to reflect and recognize what could prevent you from taking care of your school, your staff, and your children.

Discover what your personal weaknesses are and your path to becoming a true superhero will be an easy one. These are only a few of the possible impediments that you may face as a campus superhero. I realize I don't possess a degree in psychiatry, but I certainly know what makes me lose my focus and makes me less productive. Don't be too proud of me—I know my personal kryptonite now, I didn't then.

Just another reminder: The people and situations that we identify as being our personal barriers do not change. Look at it this way. Superman always knew that if he was ever in the presence of kryptonite his strength would fail him and he would be rendered helpless. Batman knew if he lost the utility belt he would not even be able to help himself, much less Gotham City. If you know a parent is going to make you angry, limit the time you have with him or her. Have your secretary run interference as much as possible.

Once I was having difficulty with a fellow teacher. I simply did not like the way she treated children. The situation became so difficult for me that, being a good Catholic girl, I went to confession. At that time, our parish had a wonderful priest by the name of Father Julian. I remember his kindness and patience with the fondest of memories. Once in the confessional, I explained my situation. I told him of how I was becoming very resentful of this woman and it was difficult to even like her. He smiled sweetly and said,

"Always remember to be kind to everyone. That is what we are called to do."

"But, Father," I said, "I really don't like her."

"Find something nice to say about her every day—even if you have to say, 'My, your shoes are on the right feet today.'"

For beginning principals, your days will be filled with a multitude of responsibilities, some that you are ready for and some that just have to be learned. You cannot afford to be without your cape or your utility belt or crippled by kryptonite. Therefore, make it a point to be self-reflective. Identify those personal traits that make you strong and those hindrances that weaken you. I can already see the beginnings of a shiny "S" forming on your suit jacket.

BECOMING A MIGHTY MANAGER

When I was younger, Saturday mornings were filled with cartoons and Frosted Flakes. The cartoons included Tom and Jerry, Bugs Bunny, and the beloved Road Runner. One of the most remarkable characters to ever cross the screen was only about five inches tall and wore a tight-fitting costume of yellow and blue with a tiny little cape attached. He was the archrival of the criminal cat element usually found on water-fronts and in alleyways. This tiny titan fought for justice, protected the innocent, and could fit in the palm of your hand. If any crisis occurred, Mighty Mouse simply flew in and saved the day.

I can certainly understand how Superman came into being. A quiet man sees injustice and fights to correct it. Batman fought injustice by protecting his treasured city of Gotham. So I must pause a moment and wonder how Mighty Mouse became a superhero. Was there a terrorist cat population that was trying to take over a wharf or fish market? Were veterinarians' offices being continually robbed of hairball treatments? How could a mouse be a superhero?

He was certainly a handy fighter and definitely a mouse you would want on your side if and when you found yourself in a closed alleyway facing a band of marauding cats. Amazingly, he would telepathically know, like all superheroes, when he was needed, the exact location of the predicament, and where danger and kitty mayhem were taking place. Before he fought the good fight and restored the city streets and alleyways to safety, he would lift one of his tiny arms triumphantly and announce that he had in fact come to save the day.

I have to believe he was good at being a superhero because I have never seen any Kitty Wanted posters at the post office. Actually, Mighty Mouse and his mission to save the day might be exactly what you need to remember on your quest to becoming not only an effective leader but a mighty manager as well.

Thousands of books and journal articles have been written regarding the development of a personal, effective leadership style. Even chapter 1 of this book asked you to reflect on the beliefs that would assist you in becoming a true leader. With all the attention given to developing yourself as a caring and effective school leader, another consideration of good leadership is the ability to manage what you have been given to lead.

Many definitions exist regarding the concept of leadership and the abilities needed to be a productive manager. Pedler, Burgoyne, and Boydell (2004, 3) believe that "leading is more concerned with finding direction and purpose . . . whereas managing is about organizing to achieve desired purposes." An old adage questions whether true leaders are born or made. It is my honest opinion that good leaders are born from the ability to be good managers. I always said that if the principalship didn't work out, I could always manage a hotel, a restaurant, or a hospital, because all of these places employ a number of people, complaints are a regular occurrence, and if these places are to be successful, hard work and long hours are required.

Being an effective school manager will require you to gain an understanding of the daily tasks that face a principal. While some duties are seasonal, such as planning the master schedule, many are ongoing. Also be aware that many of the duties are school specific. Elementary principals are asked to create a teacher duty schedule for students who are picked up from school in a car. However, many high school students drive themselves to and from school and require no teacher to be on car duty. Teachers must be assigned classes. Fire extinguishers have to be checked every year before school starts. All school records have to be updated and moved up to the next grade level and possibly transferred to another campus.

I can almost see those little wheels inside your head spinning when you realize that while you hope to get out of the office and spend time in classrooms watching children learn and teachers teach, the mail, the schedules, the duties, and the paperwork needed by the main office do not get done by little elves. Now do you see why the strength of Mighty Mouse is needed to save the day? So just strap on your red cape, swing your little arm high into the air, and become the mighty manager you were meant to be.

If leadership entails a feeling of accomplishment, then management is surely the completion of day-to-day activities that help you become an effective leader (Pedler, Burgoyne, and Boydell 2004). Listed below are actual managerial duties a principal faces when planning for a new school year and as the year progresses.

- Keep all student records up to date (programs, emergency numbers)
- Create class rosters or sections
- Count all textbooks
- Check all safety features of the school (fire extinguishers, etc.)
- Locate all electrical closets
- Abide by all safety and health regulations
- Be knowledgeable about the individual health needs of students (e.g., asthma)
- Keep budget amounts for all areas and programs current
- Check attendance rates on a regular basis
- Meet with the custodial staff on a regular basis
- Learn where the water and gas mains are located
- Hire the best teachers possible
- Work with teachers in need of assistance
- Replace teachers who are not good for children
- Conduct meaningful staff development
- Learn to document anything and everything
- Check lesson plans for the completion of required curriculum
- Visit classrooms to ensure students are learning
- Assign teachers to duty positions
- Serve as a monitor in the cafeteria
- Monitor teachers' schedules to ensure maximum instruction time
- Know the curriculum requirements for each grade level or subject
- Create a personal time management system

- Be involved in community events
- Learn the names of the children in your school
- Complete employee time sheets
- Order ample supplies for the teachers

Are you OK? Are you breathing? First things first—close your mouth and take deep breaths. Take a few more minutes; take a moment or two to collect your thoughts. I guess you really don't want to know this is only a sketchy list of your responsibilities. Just keep saying over and over again, "I want to be a principal to help children succeed. I want to be a principal to help children succeed."

Once you attack the managerial side of the principalship, you will most assuredly be on your way to becoming an effective school adminis-trator. The completion of the managerial responsibilities listed above—and more—depends on several other factors such as your secretary's willingness to assist you, whether you have an assistant principal, how many grade levels you have, how well you delegate, and especially the relationships you build between the maintenance, custodial, and cafete-ria departments.

After examining the list above and knowing that more duties exist, you are no doubt asking yourself how one person can accomplish these and more. This is why the first year of the principalship is referred to as the year of survival or a trial by fire. After a few years, these tasks will be-come second nature to you. You will have established strong and trust-ing relationships, and you will have grown in your personal strength.

Even old Mighty Mouse didn't have this much to think about. Think-ing back to the list, did you see any assigned task that called for you to protect your school against wayward stray cats? Every morning when Mighty Mouse awoke, he had one goal in mind, to save the day. He might not know what alley or street he would have to fly to or how many villainous cats he would have to fight. He just knew that his purpose that day was to be a hero. As a mighty manager, your awareness of the du-ties that fall on your shoulders also gives you reason to be a hero, and to make your school a safe, secure learning place for children.

I don't own a red cape. I have no special utility belt. As much as I would like to, I can't fly or stop a bullet between my fingers. I have only one special power to offer a school and that is the gift of being a hero to children. Comic strip and Saturday morning cartoon characters dress up newspapers and make us wish we could shoot webbing out of our wrists and soar between skyscrapers while cheering fans applaud our greatness.

The only greatness I can offer you is the first time an elementary-age child looks for you because he is afraid and he knows you will keep him safe, or when he holds your hand as you walk him to his car at the end of the day. Or when a high school student asks you to write her a recommendation for college because you have been her mentor for four years and she knows you care. Then you won't need any fancy suit or futuristic gadgets. You will feel like a hero.

A few years ago, a former student of mine applied for a teaching position in the district where I served as an elementary principal. During his interview, he was asked to name three of the most influential people in his life. He mentioned his mother, another individual, and me.

The superintendent called me to ask if I knew him, and of course I said, "That's one of my babies." My former student told the interview committee that if it had not been for me he would never have finished school. In the eyes of this one small child, I was a hero. And nothing—no award, no prize, no gold medal, no other recognition—could have meant more to me. Keep your cape flowing and your "S" shined, and simply and continuously, be a hero to and for children.

DEVELOPING YOUR PERSONAL LEADERSHIP CAPACITY

When you begin your principalship, the idea of being a hero may not come easily as you face the many managerial duties attached to the position. And try as you might, there will be days when your survival is all you can think about. Self-doubt may even creep in and cause you to wonder why you wanted the job in the first place. Your personal abilities to lead are not always determined when everything is going well, all the teachers are happy, and you're caught up on all the paperwork.

Remember the superheroes from this chapter. They were called when danger was present. Mighty Mouse lived a normal everyday mouse life until the kitty crime element in his city became too much. Batman's normal life was filled with philanthropic deeds until a glowing bat sign appeared in the sky. Superman investigated stories for a newspaper until shrieks of alarm alerted him to impending doom.

And as for you, you will simply be walking the halls, talking with children, meeting with parents until that one event hits your world and the cape will come out and your utility belt will somehow magically appear on your waist. You will just know that Super Principal is needed. This is when your words and actions will determine your leadership capabilities. With this in mind, how can you further develop your personal leadership capacity and become a hero?

1. Choose your words wisely. Speak to others with considerate, thoughtful, and kind words. There is an old saying that goes, "People may not remember what you said, but they will always remember how your words made them feel." If the situation allows, do not respond for twenty-four hours, until you have had time to think and rethink what needs to be said and what words you are going to use.
2. Always be and act with an ethical stance. Enough said.
3. Take care of difficult situations in a prompt and appropriate manner. Superheroes never turned from confrontation and neither should you. You have a backbone and it needs to be used. Heroes do not have a choice about being heroes. You do not have a choice about being an effective school leader. You took the job, didn't you?
4. Build trusting relationships with the students, faculty, and community members. When Superman was on the scene, the surrounding crowds knew they would be safe. When the police chief in Gotham City shone the bat signal into the night sky, he knew Batman would come. Develop that same kind of trust by being there for kids, helping teachers succeed, and assuring parents that the school is a safe place for their children.

WHAT WILL MY PRINCIPALSHIP SAY ABOUT ME?

Comic books, comic strips, and Saturday morning cartoons filled children with a picture of a true hero and how justice, right, and good should prevail. They also revealed how the "bad guys" always lost to the "good guys." The superheroes were kind, strong, and fearless. Through your words and actions you too can show children what it is like to be a hero. Knowing that you will never have a television show dedicated to your managerial abilities or a comic strip showing your uncanny knack for car rider duty, what do you want said about your super powers?

When I leave the school, I want people to say

"She always made me feel important."

"I knew I could talk to her about anything."

"She always had an answer for me."

"I knew I was safe at school when she was there."

"Even when I let her down, I knew she still cared about me."

"No matter what the situation, I trusted her."

Newly hired principals don't have much of their flowing red capes yet. As each year passes, the red cape grows a little longer in length and a little stronger in color. The people you serve in the city we call a school deserve a hero who is strong and fearless, whether you are a little fighting mouse or a green monster that arrives in times of trouble. It is not the cape that you wear on the outside, it is the courage you possess on the inside that makes you a true hero for children.

USING YOUR 20/20 VISION

In this chapter, we discussed well-known famous heroes and their superhuman abilities. We brought into being our very own education hero and saver of the day, Proactive Principal, who possessed the gift of X-ray vision to serve and protect his school. While Superman, Batman, Wonder Woman, and the Incredible Hulk are strictly fictional and genuinely serve as models for good and justice, they will not sit in the chair, make a difference in the life of a child, or be called upon to lead a school toward sustainable success. This rests on your shoulders. In realizing this, how can your 20/20 vision serve you best?

☐ I realize I am the leader of the campus.
☐ I am learning about my personal kryptonite.
☐ I am building positive relationships with everyone on the campus, from the custodian to the cafeteria manager.

☐ I know that everyone has worth and I acknowledge everyone's
dignity with words and actions.

☐ I have adopted my own twenty-four-hour rule.

☐ I let others help me with managerial tasks.

Being a hero to a child does not take a person of steel or an avenging
green monster. Being a hero to a child calls for someone who is willing
to take the time and effort to make a difference in the life of a child.

MY WISH FOR YOU

May your principalship be filled with opportunities to see beyond what
you thought you and your school could achieve.

May your school vision be filled with attainable and worthwhile goals
for your teachers and the success of your students.

May the success of your teachers and students be more than numbers
on a page or scores on a test.

May you earnestly seek the courage, power, and strength in yourself
to instill courage, power, and strength in the children under your care.

May you be a hero who does not live on television or in the comic
strips, but in the hearts of children.

Ode to Proactive Principal

You will never hold a scepter.
You will never wear a crown.
You cannot leap tall buildings or fly from town to town.
Your kingdom is a small one with many jobs for you to do.
And if you really wear a red cape, they'll only laugh at you.
Yet in your hands you have more power than you could ever know,
The pleasures of seeing children as you help them learn and grow.
One thing you must remember,
One thing more I must impart.
Because you are a hero,
You, too, will touch a heart.
June 2007

ADDITIONAL RESOURCES

Reading Material

Binney, G., G. Wilkie, and C. Williams. *Living Leadership: A Practical Guide for Ordinary Heroes.* Harlow, UK: Pearson Education, 2005.

Cohen, William A. *The Stuff of Heroes: The Eight Universal Laws of Leadership.* Marietta, GA: Longstreet Press, 2001.

Harvey, Eric, David Cottrell, and Al Lucia. *The Leadership Secrets of Santa Claus.* Dallas, TX: Performance Systems Corporation, 2003.

Pellicer, Leonard O. *Caring Enough to Lead: How Reflective Thought Leads to Moral Leadership*, 2nd ed. Thousand Oaks, CA: Corwin Press, 2003.

Phillips, D. T. *Lincoln on Leadership: Effective Strategies for Tough Times.* New York: Warner Books, 1992.

Internet Sources:

www.createpersonalpower.com/e-zine_personal_09_27_06.html
This site addresses a few of the skills needed by future heroes.

www.youtube.com/watch?v=KYtm8uEo5vU
This inspirational video defines what a hero is and does. The message is easily applied to the characteristics needed by a school leader.

www.youtube.com/watch?v=60tayZ3Lbi4&feature=related
This musical video brings you face to face with real heroes.

BUILDING A SCHOOL VISION, OR HOW I LEARNED TO PLAY WITH LINCOLN LOGS

Once the metal lid was pried off, the tall, cylindrical container would issue forth a wealth of reddish-brown wooden logs in a variety of lengths. In this cylinder lived a prized set of Lincoln Logs. Each of these logs had carved notches at the ends that made it easy to connect them. Creating wooden masterpieces held the attention of many small children as they played with these for countless hours. Young Frank Lloyd Wright designed differing log cabins of vast beauty by simply adding a door or an extra window somewhere. The end product exemplified the determination and abilities of the apprentice architects.

The sturdy shapes could withstand any natural disaster (except for the foot of an angry brother when he realized your Lincoln Log structure far surpassed his). But because of the notched ends to the logs, the interlocking grid system ensured that each log would stay firmly in place, regardless of Hurricane Bubba. Not one nail, not one screw or bolt, held the structure in place. Those notches supported the other logs and proved to be a vital part of the final structure.

Granted, you, as the principal, may not be building an actual log cabin on your campus, but you are building the vision, goals, and culture of your school. You will be the one responsible for placing each log carefully in place so that the end creation can withstand any storm that comes its way. You will do this by connecting the goals of the campus to the needs of the students, teachers, and school.

Every stakeholder will know and understand how your vision for the school builds a strong, safe, and successful place for learning. The log cabin you and your staff build will have its own culture and climate and be held together by the efforts and contributions of all. You, as the principal, are the architect.

KNOW WHAT KIND OF CABIN YOU NEED

In your university preparation courses, you were expected to know and understand educational jargon such as stewardship, transformational and transactional leadership, and instructional leadership. Truthfully, there will be a limited number of times that you face a situation and actually say to yourself, "OK. Now for this particular instance, I need to use my transformational leadership abilities." That just is not going to happen.

Much of the theoretical framework you learned in your graduate studies is there to give you a basis for making a decision or solving a problem, not for actual real-world situations. It does serve the purpose of helping you discover the type of school leader you want to be. Knowing what kind of leader you want to be also assists you in the development of the vision and goals for your campus.

Almost every company or organization, whether it's McDonald's or Exxon, establishes a mission or vision statement and a set of goals to share with their employees and customers. These are posted on websites, at the entrances of buildings, and sometimes on correspondence that leaves their offices. When you were standing in the line at McDonald's waiting for your fish sandwich, did you happen to look at the wall where the company's goals are posted and then stand there in awe and utter amazement at what the company hoped to do for you?

Most school districts are required by law to submit district and campus improvement plans. These plans are initiated based on the educational and instructional needs of the students. Resources, assessment measures, and action strategies are also aligned to meet those needs. The principal, faculty and staff members, and community representatives work collaboratively to develop the campus vision and a set of goals and strategies to achieve that vision. If you are a first-year administrator, how do you know where to start?

Think again about the Lincoln Logs. Opening the Lincoln Log canister was easy. The lid came right off. The logs always spilled straight to the floor and there was no instruction manual to follow or batteries to buy. One day you might build a house and the next day you might build a bridge. Whatever structure you wanted to build, you had to start somewhere, you had to have some kind of construction plan in your mind. Creating campus improvement plans is no different than creating a fancy cabin out of those Lincoln Logs. Begin slowly by answering three simple questions.

1. Where is our school right now in regard to academics and student success?
2. Where does the school need to go to improve student and teacher performance?
3. What are we willing to do to improve the school's academic performance and increase student learning?

And you thought this was going to be hard.

It's not so hard, really. Before you sign a contract, before you walk down your school's hallways for the first time, or before you speak to even one staff member, decide how you want to lead that school.

Make some decisions about how successful you want the school to be in a year, in three years. Consider the effectiveness of the students' educational programs that are in place. Review the class schedule to ensure that the maximum amount of time during the day is spent on instruction. Pay attention to the personal relationships that exist between staff members and how those relationships affect the students and the culture of the school. Think about all those Lincoln Logs lying on the floor, just waiting for you to pick them up and begin building something phenomenal.

As you begin to reflect on the statements mentioned above, you have already started the process of building and creating the school's vision. For the most part, you should always try to include others when making decisions, but the vision for any school or business begins with its leader.

You get to build the log cabin *you* want to live in—the log cabin that others would want to live in.

In the first chapter, I asked you to think about those beliefs that you hold dear about the education of children, the dignity and worth of all, the impact of successful learning strategies. Whatever those beliefs were, use them to build and establish your personal vision for the school. Just start with "I believe" statements:

"I believe it is my responsibility to . . . "

"I believe everyone on this campus should . . . "

"I believe the children on this campus deserve . . . "

"I believe the teachers on this campus should . . . "

How easy it would be if Madame Olga, the psychic who performs every year at the county fair, allowed you to peer deeply into her crystal ball and through a cloudy apparition you would instantly realize the goals you and your school need to succeed.

Using your prior knowledge about developing goals and mission statements, let's review what they are. Educationally speaking, a goal becomes the focus of what people are working toward (Snowden and Gorton 2002). Equally, a mission is a quest that you have to achieve or aspire to.

With this in mind, let's say that after you collected and reviewed all your school data, you discovered your school was having a problem reaching the 95 percent attendance rate required by the district and the state. A strategy such as the implementation of a Perfect Attendance Recognition Wall may be just the thing to help you achieve the goal of improving the average daily attendance of the students. From there, you can utilize the three guiding questions: Where are you, where do you want to be, and what are you willing to do to get there?

How does this process look in terms of our Lincoln Logs? All we knew when we sat on the living room floor with those reddish logs surrounding us was the fact that we had the opportunity to build anything we wanted. The structure could be a one-story cabin, a two-story house, or anything our imaginations could invent. The end product would be something constructed from all the logs.

Once we were through, there would be an interlocking structure that could stand on its own. Our creativity and the work of our hands together helped to construct an architectural work of art—or for your purposes, a school that will be a successful learning place for children.

When you accept a principalship, you also take on the responsibility to guide and lead that school toward continued improvement. Believe me when I tell you that if you don't have a vision for what you want, if you don't already have some ideas regarding the learning atmosphere that's taking place on the campus, you are in trouble.

I am not referring to the kind of trouble that occurs when you run a red light or forget to mail your credit card payment. I am talking about the kind of trouble that prevents anyone or anything from growing or progressing, the kind of trouble that lasts for years when students experience gaps in their learning or the school climate becomes poisonous. Wow, what cheery little thoughts. Unfortunately, I have seen too many school leaders not succeed because they did not know how to build a school vision for success.

Regardless of the economic status of your families or the neighborhood where your school is located, creating a set of educational goals for your campus is quite simply a to-do list. This list becomes such an integral part of the school's daily life that parents are talking about it at the ball field on Saturday morning during the Little League game. When people at the ballpark talk about something you've done or said, you have their attention. If you didn't know already, most of the school's problems are solved during T-ball games.

The school's vision begins and ends with you and what you want for your children and your teachers, whether it is a simple statement such as "We believe in all children and their learning" or a longer one like "In order to provide for the academic growth and maturation of the students in our school, the staff and faculty are committed to provide the best instruction possible to create lifelong learners." My advice is to keep it simple. The point with a vision statement is that it starts with you and moves to everyone else starting on the first day of school.

For example, you make several announcements that ask the students to take care of the school because the appearance of the school affects the culture of learning that you and the staff are trying to develop. As you walk the hallways, you see some paper and candy wrappers on the floor. If you believe that a clean school does influence the culture of learning on the campus, you bend down, pick up the trash, and throw it away. Several students see this happen and start believing you mean what you say. Or, you see the trash in the hallway and walk right past it.

Several students see you not pick up the trash and think you don't mean a thing you say.

When you attain your first principalship and a friend asks if there's anything you would like to have for your office, I want you to ask for a set of Lincoln Logs. Take the container and set it somewhere in your office to always remind you that what you build at your school must be strong and able to withstand anything that you may face. I want those logs to signify that you have the chance to be a master carpenter and build a strong and successful school. And on those days when the business of school has you weary and worn, take out those Lincoln Logs and have some fun.

USING THE RIGHT CEMENT

One of the more interesting facets of playing and building structures with Lincoln Logs was the fact that once the right pieces were joined together, the notches at the end of the log would connect and hold the entire structure in place. From that strong foundation of fitted logs sprang cabins, houses, fire stations, and other grandiose structures.

When you embark on the building of a strong and successful school framework, you as the campus leader must ensure that all the pieces of the school support each other just like those notched logs. After we were through playing with the Lincoln Logs, we took them apart and placed them back in their container. No afterthoughts were given to what was built that day because we were already on our bikes racing down the street or settled down in front of the television to watch *Speed Racer*. But when you are trying to establish a vision for your school, you can't just go ride your bike when things get tough.

Your school needs a principal who knows how to build a house of learning that will last long after the first day of school. After you develop your personal and educational goals for your school, it's time to look around the school for other sources of cement that will help you keep the school together.

During the first week on your campus, stand at the front doors and imagine you are a parent or a child entering the school for the very first time. What do you see? How do you feel? A familiar school adage says,

"When you enter a school you can just feel what kind of school it is before you visit one classroom or talk to one person." This falls in line with other more memorable adages such as "You'll know him when you meet him" or "I just knew this was the dress for me."

Think about your refrigerator. Compared to the other things I have asked you to think about or imagine, this one is fairly simple. When your refrigerator is sparkling clean and the new box of baking soda is in place, every time you open the door you are hit with a fresh and clean smell. However, if you left the plastic container of brown stuff in there a little too long and the box of baking soda is actually growing a green furry mass on it, when you open the door to the fridge, you know something is just not right. This is the same concept for a school and its culture.

When you open the front doors of your school, are the hallways clean and well kept? Do decorative bulletin boards give you necessary information as a parent or a visitor? Does the office staff greet you in a warm and friendly manner? Or does the school need a new box of baking soda and that plastic container of brown stuff thrown away? Not only are you responsible for the learning that takes place on the campus and for the success of your students, but you are also the one who has to bravely open the refrigerator, find the smelly thing, and throw it away.

You are, in essence, the new box of baking soda. This connection between people, school culture, and success happens when you decide the direction the school will take and the effort needed to bring it about. Easy, huh? Actually, it is. You are the glue. Through your leadership endeavors, your positive personality, and your high expectations, the school environment becomes a place of learning, hope, and success. Are you wondering if you need to carry a bottle of Elmer's glue or a roll of masking tape around with you as you walk the halls and visit classrooms? Wouldn't hurt.

One way to start using your cement magic is to examine the teachers in each grade level and how they work with each other. Some teachers are more productive in a team situation, while others work best alone. This may not always be possible, especially at the middle school or high school levels. When you see a grade level or a department that is working well and is successful, leave it alone. A principal once shared with me that he really liked to move teachers around every year; it gave them an opportunity to see other teachers' perspectives. Let them do a book study or attend an educational conference, but do not mess with a good thing.

For those grade levels or departments that do not seem to be cohesive, try to treat each one of them as unique individuals. If you think that by inviting them for Sunday brunch at your house they will change the way they feel about each other, I'd like to talk to you about some wonderful beachfront property for sale in Montana that could be turned into a great water park.

Once I worked with two very different kindergarten teachers; one we will call Sally Sunshine; the other we will call Attila the Hun. See where this is going? These two women did not like each other. Their teaching styles and classroom personalities were very different and they did not hide the fact that they were never going to get along with one another.

One afternoon after school, as they were loading their children onto the buses that would take them home, the two teachers had a verbal altercation. There they stood, screaming at one another with their children watching; in fact, every student that rode a bus home saw my two teachers screaming at one another. When I heard what had happened, I asked both teachers to meet with me in my office the next morning at 7:30 a.m.

As requested, the two teachers presented themselves in my office promptly at 7:30 a.m. I began the conversation by telling each of them that I wanted to hear what happened in their own words. Sally Sunshine started telling me what happened and Attila kept interrupting her. Sally Sunshine asked Attila to please let her finish what she had to say and not interrupt her again.

I intervened and assured Attila that she would have an opportunity to give her side of the situation in just a few minutes. This was about 7:35 a.m. By 7:36 a.m., Attila had risen from her chair, told me she didn't have to take this, and turned to leave my office. At this point, I told Attila that if she left my office, I would write her up for insubordination. As she moved toward my office door, she shot back, "Do what you have to do." In turn I shot back with, "You got it."

In a few minutes, Attila the Hun stormed back into my office and informed me that she was going to need a substitute for the rest of the day. I told her that would be no problem and one would be called immediately. I guess she thought about what it would look like if she left school that day because in a few minutes she stormed back into the office and said she had reconsidered needing a sub and decided to stay at school that day. I told her that the sub had already been called and I had decided to honor her request that she leave the school that day. The choice was no longer hers, it was mine. However, the situation was far from over.

When she announced she was leaving my office and didn't have to listen to anything, I had told her I was going to write her up for insubordination. I had to follow through. I documented what had happened between the two teachers, her behavior while in my office, and my warning about what would happen to her if she left my office.

She filed a grievance against my decision that made it all the way to the school board. During the school board meeting regarding this issue, one of the school board members asked her, "When Mrs. Tareilo told you she was going to write you up for insubordination if you left the meeting, what did you think she meant?" The teacher promptly answered, "I didn't know what she meant by insubordination." Needless to say, the board found in my favor.

I knew these teachers would never be buddies, share lesson plans, or even eat with each other at lunch, but I assured them that while they did not have to like each other, the children in their classes had better not see another display of discourteous or rude behavior transpire between the two of them ever again.

In fact, I probably said something along the lines of when the students see them together, for whatever reason, they had better get the idea that Sally Sunshine and Attila the Hun were Siamese twins that had been separated at birth. That's how close they had better appear. Their behavior toward each other had better be, should be, and would be friendly and professional, or I would document their inappropriate behavior and use that documentation on their end-of-year evaluations.

WHEN THE CABIN IS DONE . . . WHAT GOES INSIDE

After putting the Lincoln Logs together so that they form a remarkable four-walled, cabin-like structure, and after putting on a roof and a wrap-around porch, your building day has come to a close. Before you, there stands a structure that would rival the pyramids of Egypt. However, there is one more decision you have to make. What do you want to put on the inside that matches the beautiful construction on the outside of the cabin?

This is the same premise of building your school vision. When you walk into your school for the very first time, I hope your mind is just racing with ideas to improve this, keep that, and make some adjustments here and there. From these thoughts, you begin the process of vision building. However, I cannot get away from drawing your attention back to what is needed inside your school to make it a successful and nurturing place for children.

The landscaping surrounding your school may be stunning enough to merit making the cover of *House Beautiful*. The school may be located on top of a lush green rolling hill and be a spot on the scenic tour of your town. But it is what happens on the inside of that school that makes the most difference.

First, I want you to look at your staff, from the members with the most years of service to the ones with the fewest years of experience. Visit with each one personally to get an idea of each one's passion and dedication to the students you will serve. From these sessions, you will get a true feel for your teachers' commitment level as well as insight into their demeanor.

During this meeting, assure the teachers that you want to help them in any way you can and repeatedly tell them your vision for the school and the children. End the meeting by asking everyone the same question, "So, now that we have talked a little about you and your teaching, I'd just like to ask you one more question. What percent commitment can I have from you to support the educational vision for this school?"

If your teachers are very smart, they will answer that they are behind you and the school vision with 100 percent commitment. If they answer with any other response, let's say 80 percent commitment to the school vision, you might consider reminding them that if the surgical staff at a hospital only used 80 percent of an anesthetic, many people would feel a great deal of pain during surgery. I certainly wouldn't want my child to be at that hospital.

Or, if I made a deposit at a bank and only 80 percent went into my checking account and the other money was divided between the bank tellers, I would have insufficient-funds checks all over town. I certainly wouldn't start a college fund for my grandchild at that bank. The vision is not about their agreement with you; it's about their agreement to help in an endeavor to provide the best educational experience for the children at that school.

I must take a soapbox moment here. If for some reason you are reading this book and you have no intention of being the type of school leader that we have been talking about or are worried about accepting all the responsibilities that are associated with the position, I want you to do one of two things.

First, I want you to consider dropping out of the educational leadership preparation program in which you are currently enrolled. Maybe you would be more suited to selling real estate. Maybe just from the first three chapters of this book you have a new appreciation for the principalship and have decided it is really not your calling.

Or, I want you to make the conscious decision here and now to become the committed and supportive leader that your campus and your students will need to become successful. Campuses and their stakeholders do not need an indecisive, uncommitted, or misdirected leader. Decide now. Put the book down, call your advisor, and find out what courses you need to get your real estate license if you do not see yourself in the role of the principal. It is certainly not for the fainthearted.

Once you have had the opportunity to talk with each of your staff members, start exploring the school. Move in and out of classrooms. Look at the furniture, the carpet, and the chalkboards. If you can stand a few feet from the entrance to the bathrooms and smell the bathrooms, this is definitely an area that needs your prompt attention. The inside of your Lincoln Log cabin must reflect what your goals are for learning just as much as any other area you choose to address.

Recently, I visited a large high school. The front of the campus was absolutely beautiful. The entryway was well landscaped, and there was a very well-kept commons area for students. However, when I walked up to the second floor to meet with a teacher, I noticed that the walls in every hallway were empty of any student work, decorations, or sense of the school's culture. I expected to find the same care that I noticed on the outside of the school to be on the inside of the school as well. I was wrong.

This type of miscommunication of expectations is what I hope you avoid when developing your vision for the school. You and the teaching staff must work together in an effort to build the best Lincoln Log school you can. When you put the right people together in the right places doing the right things for children, nothing, and I mean nothing, can break down what you have created.

DEVELOPING YOUR PERSONAL LEADERSHIP CAPACITY

As the campus leader, you are also a master builder who possesses the skills and tools to build a vision of success for that school and then set that vision in motion. Master builders carefully study the structural design, floor plan, and layout of a building to determine what kind of framework is needed to support that building.

Creating a school vision requires principals to follow the same premise. Building a vision for the success of your school and students means you examine all the elements of your school involved in the learning process, ways to assist teachers, and how those pieces fit together. Consider the following when you become a school leader and begin developing your personal leadership capacity:

1. Expect that building a school vision will involve some change. Prepare yourself and your staff for ways to handle the change that is needed.
2. Use teams of teachers and other staff members to help you create that school vision.
3. Be prepared to be a strong and purposeful administrator who can lead the school toward achieving that vision.
4. Be fearless in your attempts to build and create a school climate that is inviting and risk-free for all the students.
5. As a true leader, don't be afraid to rebuild or modify your vision statement.
6. Constantly ask yourself what your school needs to succeed and then create a culture of success in order to achieve those goals.

WHAT WILL MY PRINCIPALSHIP SAY ABOUT ME?

Building a school vision does not require brain-draining thought or fingernail-biting decisions. It merely starts with a belief about what you want for your school and how to engage the staff in the achievement of those goals. Someone has to be brave enough and strong enough to put the vision in motion, and because you are the school leader, you are the chosen one.

Knowing this, imagine you overhear this conversation. As you are walking by the teachers' workroom before the first day of school, you hear a few teachers talking about the first faculty meeting you had with your staff. They are discussing the part where you mentioned that your first priority was going to be the establishment of the school's vision, and that you wanted and needed their help.

Teacher 1: When she said she wanted our help to build a school vision of success, I thought I was going to scream. How many times have we heard that?

Teacher 2: She did say we were going to be involved in the process. Maybe she means it?

Teacher 1: Honey, you are a first-year teacher and you have a lot to learn.

Teacher 3: Well, she did present a lot of school data for us to consider. We have never had that happen before.

Teacher 2: I like the way she is focused on the students and I think she has some good ideas.

Teacher 1: I'll believe it when I see it.

Teacher 3: Have you been in her office yet? Did you happen to see that set of Lincoln Logs sitting on her desk? What's up with that?

When you decide to leave that campus or even retire from the principalship, what do you want the teachers in the workroom to say about you?

"I knew she was strong enough to see us through the changes we had to make."

"He always made sure to include us when we planned the school's yearly goals."

"I always felt she knew exactly what we needed to do to help our kids."

"I liked the way he used data and research to help us make some decisions."

"Since she came, our school is such a great place to work."

USING YOUR 20/20 VISION

Playing with Lincoln Logs is so much fun and requires very little mechanical skill. Logs of different sizes are put together, piece by piece, to create a strong and sturdy building. The notches at the ends of the logs guarantee that when the logs are connected the structure will not fall apart. The process of building a school vision requires you to be the one who puts all the right pieces in all the right places so your school stays strong and endures. The school and the children need a principal who has the courage to let others help him or her build a vision for success, and that person is you. The list below will help you become a Proactive Principal when building a vision for your school.

- ☐ Various sources of data are collected and disaggregated to identify school needs.
- ☐ A teacher survey is conducted to help you determine teachers' perceptions about the learning climate on the campus.
- ☐ Teacher teams are utilized to work collectively to create a school vision.
- ☐ Several methods of communication are incorporated to ensure all the stakeholders know and understand the school's goals.
- ☐ The goals established in the school's vision statement are monitored continuously.
- ☐ Evidence of the school's success at achieving the goals is constantly shared with the students, the staff, and the community.

MY WISH FOR YOU

My wish for you when it's time that a vision must be built is that you keep a flame of passion deep inside you lit.

My wish for you when choosing those that touch your children's lives is to choose the ones who care and help at least one child to thrive.

My wish for you as you build your school with Lincoln Logs or stone is that each person makes even the smallest feel welcome and at home.

My wish for you as you build a school that allows each child to succeed is that the school you build will give each child more than they'll ever need.

My wish for you as you begin this trial to build a school that's strong is that the gifts you bring to children last their whole lives long.

ADDITIONAL RESOURCES

Reading Material

Blanchard, Kenneth, Thad Lacinak, Chuck Tompkins, and Jim Ballard. *Whale Done! The Power of Positive Relationships.* New York: Simon & Schuster, 2002.

Blanchard, Kenneth, and Don Shula. *Everyone's a Coach: Five Business Secrets for High Performance Coaching.* Grand Rapids, MI: Zondervan, 1995.

Dungy, Tony, and Nathan Whitaker. *Quiet Strength: The Principles, Practices, and Priorities of a Winning Life.* Loveland, CO: Group Publishing, 2007.

Klemash, Christian. *How to Succeed in the Game of Life: 34 Interviews with the World's Greatest Coaches.* Kansas City, MO: Andrews McMeel, 2006.

Krzyzewski, Mike, and Donald T. Phillips. *Leading with the Heart: Coach K's Successful Strategies for Basketball, Business, and Life.* New York: Warner, 2000.

Internet Sources

humanresources.about.com/od/involvementteams/a/twelve_tip_team.htm
Through this site, twelve steps are introduced that could assist new principals in the development of efficient teams.

www.managementhelp.org/grp_skll/teams/teams.htm
This site provides numerous links with countless suggestions to build strong and committed teams.

management.about.com/cs/adminaccounting/a/teambuilding_2.htm
From team-building suggestions to team-building activities, this site will help administrators focus on strengthening relationships.

www.mdk12.org/process/leading/vision.html
This article explores how building a school vision supports instruction and school improvements. It also provides strategies for principals in the development of a school vision.

cnx.org/content/m14078/latest/
The Connexions Project, through the National Council of Professors of
Educational Administration, provides an in-depth guide to establishing
a school vision.

4

ONCE A TEACHER,
ALWAYS A TEACHER

On a calm day when the campus is running smoothly, the teachers are teaching at their best, and the students are wrapped in the throes of meaningful learning, look slowly at the wall in your office that holds your certificate of graduation. The beautiful script that states the college you attended crests over the block letters of your name, and for a few minutes you feel like an accomplished learner. The diploma on the wall proves it.

You worked long nights and most weekends writing papers, studying for tests, or completing assigned projects. Missing family celebrations and becoming sleep deprived were all-too-common occurrences. With the master's degree earned and the principalship attained, you have achieved a pinnacle in education that many have not. Whether you believe this or not, you are considered a smart person.

The faculty of the school actually expects you to be the Great and Powerful Oz—the one with all the answers, the guru of educational knowledge, and the possessor of enough common sense to make Thomas Paine look ignorant. So, why do some people in the principalship act foolishly?

There, I said it—controversial as it may sound. I said what needed to be said about some principals, who say and do things as if they came out of a "teaching" coma and became a principal. Some people who possess a principalship, who hold the position just like you, say things and do things as if they had no prior knowledge about the teaching profession and all it entails.

As the principal of a campus, your role as the instructional leader far surpasses the diplomas on the wall. You are now, and will always be considered, the keeper of the knowledge or, better yet, a teacher of teachers. Those on the campus will seek you out because you are supposed to know all the state and federal laws that govern the school system or know where to send inquiring staff for answers to unbelievable questions such as "Is the gizzard of a chicken the filtration system for its body?" or "How can you tell if a cantaloupe is ripe?"

When you became the principal, you automatically grew another appendage to carry a "bag of tricks" that has all the answers to solving problems, defusing angry parents, or providing budget money for new supplies even when Peter is so poor that Paul has to steal from someone else (and that isn't looking too good, either). When all of this happens, and it will, you must throw on your wizard's hat, grab Madame Olga's crystal ball, and become a teacher once again.

REMEMBER WHEN YOU WERE A TEACHER

I can clearly remember standing at a gas station at a local convenience store years ago when a perfect stranger at the other gas pump casually said, "You're a teacher, aren't you?" How did this perfect stranger know that I was a teacher? Did I have a look on my face of exhaustion and despair? Was there Odor of Child perfume filling the air where I stood? Maybe I had inadvertently carried a small child away from the school in the grille of my car. I, of course, said that I indeed was a teacher. The stranger then gave me one of my most memorable compliments when he said, "I could tell."

As a classroom teacher, I loved watching learning take place. The interaction between my sixth-grade students and the subject matter caused heated discussions, a desire to learn more, and sheer joy. Remembering my years in the classroom conjures up the many students who passed through the doors of my sixth-grade classroom. The child who was so smart he would never take notes for a test during class but later pass the test with flying colors. The young girls who fought the desire to enjoy math class because reading was the subject girls were supposed to love more. The excitement of the small groups as they designed, planned, and constructed a new zoo complex or created meals for their families using recycled restaurant menus and only twenty dollars. I always wanted my classroom to be filled with the expansion of knowledge and engaging children in the learning process. If I felt this way as a classroom teacher, why should I feel differently when I became the principal who was responsible for twenty-three classrooms and more than five hundred children?

No matter the profession or occupation, there is always an end product, and that product is judged or ranked based on the taste, success, or quality of that product. Think about it this way. If a gardener spends all morning in his front yard, mowing the grass, raking the leaves, and cleaning out the flower beds, by the end of the day he will be the next winner of Yard Beautiful. Anyone who drives by his house will see the accomplishments of all his hard work and the sign in his front yard proclaiming what he won.

If a seamstress buys three yards of woolen plaid material, places a pattern on the material, cuts outs the pieces, and proceeds to sew a garment worthy of a display window at Macy's department store, anyone who walks by will see the end product. With these analogies in place, think about the teachers on your campus. What should their end-of-the-year product look like?

Meaningful instruction and successful student learning are the two primary reasons your doors open every day. I cannot begin to tell you how many times I have heard a parent tell a child, "I send you to this school to learn, not so you can have fun" or "I want you to have the education I never had."

So day in and day out, teachers constantly work with students in the various subjects to help them acquire new skills, maintain skills already learned, and use previous knowledge to process that learning. Teachers may never see how their end product turns out or how their efforts influenced that child's life until the end of the school year—or even after they graduate.

Let me tell you about two of my end products. First, let me tell you about Edward. One day, the principal called me to her office to inform me that our school was about to receive a child who was being kicked out of a neighboring school. The other school's principal called my principal to let her know that Edward was incorrigible, that his mother followed some obscure religious belief that allowed her son to miss school whenever he wanted to, and that they had done all they could do. Edward was now ours.

Sandy McEntire, my principal, had decided to place Edward in my classroom. And to be proactive, we were going to meet him at the front door with tough love and let him know that at our school he would be expected to follow all the rules and learn something new every day. Based on the reports from the other school we were expecting some feral child to walk through our doors, and if that was the case, we were ready for him.

The bus carrying Edward pulled up in front of our school. McEntire (for some reason many of us went by our last names and still do) and I stood ready. When the doors of the bus opened, there stood Edward.

As he walked down the stairs of the bus and toward the front doors of our school, we turned to each other and said, "This child is the next Tasmanian devil?" Edward was one of the most beautiful children I have ever seen in my life. He was a very small-framed child with huge brown eyes and the longest eyelashes imaginable. But even his fine features did not compare to the light of his smile. When Edward smiled, his entire face lit up. I knew I would love this child forever, and I still do. By the way, Edward never caused me, our classroom, or our school one day of trouble.

One day I was sitting at my desk when I received a call from the superintendent's office. They were in the process of interviewing an applicant for a new administrative position. They called me because the applicant had listed me as a reference.

The associate superintendent asked me if I knew anyone by the name of Edward. I immediately went into my teacher mode, "Oh my gosh, that is my baby." During the interview, Edward was asked to name three people who had most influenced his life, and he had mentioned me as one of them. He told the interview committee that I had been the reason he had stayed in school. He had never forgotten me. Now, that is a little better than winning Yard Beautiful.

Another child I want to tell you about is Carl. I was Carl's elementary principal for three years. Carl was not athletic and tended to push the envelope whenever he could. His mother and I grew to be great acquaintances since we saw each other on a regular basis. Almost every week, Carl and I would meet in my office about something; either he did not complete his homework assignments or he said something inappropriate to a fellow student.

At every campus where I served as elementary principal, the fifth-graders were the senior grade level on the campus. Therefore, at the end of the school year we always had a fifth-grade graduation ceremony. The teachers would call out the student's name; the child would come to the stage, take the graduation certificate, and shake my hand. Because I believe it is important to know every child's name and a little something about them, I would say something specific to each child as he or she crossed the stage. It was Carl's turn to come to the stage. As he shook my hand, I leaned down and said to him, "You'd better stay in school and you'd better invite me to your high school graduation."

I recently saw his mother at a neighborhood grocery. She informed me that this was Carl's senior year and she needed my address. Carl had remembered what I said when he crossed the stage in the fifth grade. He informed his mother that he wanted to make sure I was at his high school graduation to see what he had done: He had stayed in school. In fact, his mother told me he wants to be an underwater welder. When I sit at that high school graduation, and I *will* be there, I will not be seeing a young man cross that stage, but an eleven-year-old Carl who gave me a wonderful gift. He remembered me. As a teacher, it was my responsibility to make a difference in the lives of the children in my classroom. As principal, it is your responsibility to make a difference in the lives of your teachers so they in turn can make a difference in the lives of their students.

The importance of your role as instructional leader for the campus cannot be overlooked. You are not afforded wait time to see if the finished product (the child) uses what he or she learned at your school to make a living, become something better, or even be the best gardener in the Yellow Pages. Your classrooms must reflect the educational expectations that support the goals your school has developed. The principalship and its related duties give you several opportunities to know the strengths as well as the needs of the teaching staff on your campus.

Just as every child and what he or she needs to learn differs on your campus, so will the teaching staff. Once you begin moving in and out of classrooms, watching the interactions between the students and teachers, and learning more about their teaching styles, you will gain a vast amount of knowledge on each individual teacher. More importantly, you will learn when teachers need help as well as when to praise them for all their hard work.

I am not sure what happened to those principals who forgot about their own personal teaching careers or what it was like to work with children every day, try to have a family life, and then grade papers late into the night. Many times when I would leave the school, I looked like a pack mule ready for a trip through the Sierra Madre mountains. Each arm carried a bag of papers needing to be graded, a lesson plan book that needed refining, and some kind of paperwork needed by the main office. Many nights, I would lug those bags out to the car, get home, face household and family responsibilities, and then feel tremendous guilt because I had been too tired to even walk to the car and retrieve the bags from the trunk.

Now, granted, I am a Type A personality with a little bit of anal retentive disorder thrown in, but to feel guilty about not working on school stuff when I got home, this should have qualified me for the cover of the next issue of *Psychological Disorders "R" Us*. When I visit campuses now, I still see teachers lugging out the many bags, and I know they are packing for their own trip to the mountains.

Elementary teachers are some of the most committed and dedicated teachers I have ever known. In the middle of July, the phone calls would start. "When can I come to the school to work in my classroom? Will the copy machine be on? Do you have our class lists ready? How long can I work in my room today?" Some teachers would actually have camped out at the school if I had let them. However, their dedication to preparing that perfect atmosphere for their students made them tired before the first day of school.

It was my general practice to write each one of the staff members a "Welcome back" letter and mail it before the start of school. Attached to the letter, I always enclosed a schedule of when the school would be open and the nights I planned to stay late. Many nights a little group of us would stay well after midnight, sharing pizza for supper, and having moments of true camaraderie. I was not the principal, I was just another teacher working late to make sure the children's first day back would be something to remember.

However, there was one rule that I followed to the fullest: Teachers could work any day or night for as long as they wanted, but on the Friday before the first day of school they had to leave the school by 5:00 p.m. and they could not return until the first day of school. I hoped this would give them a chance to be with their families, help their own children get ready for school, and relax a little before school started again. Most of the teachers who grumbled had already spent countless hours preparing their rooms, decorating their bulletin boards, and making copies of papers they needed for the first day of school.

I had to actually escort one of my pre-kindergarten teachers from her building complaining that she still had so much to do. The last task I saw her do was filling up an empty two-liter soda bottle with different kinds of beans. This was a task that could wait. As a matter of fact, many teachers later told me that while it made them angry at the time, having to leave probably saved their sanity and allowed them to focus on something else other than their classroom.

Another simple consideration for your teachers that requires absolutely no money centers on the most loved of all duties, after-school car and bus duties. For many years, I struggled with assigning teachers to these duties in a fair and equitable manner. I developed charts with the teachers' names and carefully drew stick figures to keep count of the number of duties each teacher had.

Some of the staff had certain health issues that needed to be taken into consideration as I assigned them to after-school duties. If they had health conditions that intensified in the colder months, I assigned all of their duties during the spring semester. Many of the teachers had young children and preferred to do their bus duty in the afternoon instead of the morning, when they were busily making lunches, dressing their children, and getting themselves ready for school. By simply talking with the teachers, I was able to try to fit their real world to their school world.

Many people not in the teaching profession have no clear comprehension of what a teacher does. Oh, they understand their children go to school, listen to teachers talk, and have some kind of homework at the end of the day. Very few really understand the teaching profession. This was very evident when Davis's father came to school one day.

Davis's father was a Texas Ranger. Yes, a gun-totin', ten-gallon-hat-wearin' Texas Ranger. One day he decided to visit my classroom. He happened to arrive in the classroom about five minutes before lunch-time. You and I both know what is happening in an elementary class-room at this time. Children are putting away their books, gathering their lunch kits, and yelling that they have to go to the restroom.

In he walked, a very tall and foreboding-looking man, still wearing his gun. I asked him to take a seat while I prepared the children for our lunchtime. He watched the entire process. As the students lined up for lunch and we proceeded toward the cafeteria, he looked at me with awe and said, "I could never do your job." This man, a Texas Ranger, a man carrying a gun, could not be a teacher. I have never forgotten that visit and I hope that you as a principal will never lose sight of what it is like in the teaching trenches.

I would be remiss if I did not add a little something about classroom discipline. If you are not fortunate enough to have an assistant principal who can help you in this area, you will be the primary disciplinarian on the campus. Many secondary schools have assistant and associate prin-cipals who are invaluable.

On my last assignment as an elementary principal, I was very lucky to have an experienced assistant principal who took on most of the disciplin-ary issues on our campus. There were some teachers who would send a student to the office for rolling a pencil down his desk or turning her head around during circle time. No matter what the size or grade level of the campus, you and I both could put a name and a face to these teachers.

Then, there are some teachers who never send a child to the office. These teachers have wonderful and exciting lessons, actively engage their children in the learning process, and handle the small things on their own. That does not mean they deserve less of your attention when they have a real need.

Take for instance, Mrs. Wilson. Her teaching style allowed for active participation of the students, yet order was maintained at all times. When-ever I walked down the hallway, she was always teaching or somehow involved with her students. She very rarely called upon me or the assistant principal for assistance. However, when she did call for help, I went im-mediately to her room. Because she always handled most of her discipline issues, if she asked for me, I knew it was something important. Make sure that all your teachers know you will be there when they need you.

On those days when our assistant principal was not going to be on campus, I would arrive early, settle paperwork issues on my desk, put my purse on the floor, change from my real people shoes into a pair of tennis shoes (yes, with my hose on), and prepare myself for the day—because I knew what was coming.

All the discipline issues would be at my door as soon as the children's day started. I actually had a pedometer that measured my steps and on those days, I logged an average of four thousand steps. (Just a note: I wore the pedometer on the first day of school and at the end of the day I had taken over eight thousand steps, approximately four miles.) These are the days I chose to be in the hallways and classrooms more to show my presence and be proactive—just in case we had a rash of pencil-rolling or head-turning delinquents.

The French-born historian and educator Jacques Barzun wrote, "Teaching is not a lost art, but the regard for it is a lost tradition" (Teachers Quotes n.d.). These dedicated men and women on your campus depend on you to never forget their importance. Yes, some need to be nurtured and given opportunities to grow. Some need to simply know you support and respect them. Sitting in the pink chair in an office of your own does not change what you really do for a living. You are really a teacher. I hope you keep the tradition alive.

I'M NOT SURE, BUT I'LL ASK

Do you have any idea how many prototype light bulbs Thomas Edison threw away before he finally raised his hand high in the air and glee-fully exclaimed, "Eureka, I think I've got it"? Nine thousand. Yes, nine thousand (Foo 2007).

Now, we are not talking about some fluke inventor who discovered the pizza-cutting wheel or the remedy for male-pattern baldness. Edison tried nine thousand ideas, concepts, suggestions, and prototypes before reaching success with a light bulb that shone longer and brighter than any of his previous attempts. With his nine thousand attempts under his belt, Edison exclaimed, "I am not discouraged, because every wrong at-tempt discarded is another step forward."

In his lifetime, Thomas Edison applied for 1,093 patents for his in-ventions (Foo 2007). Just picture Tommy Edison at his desk putting a filament here, moving a filament there—nine thousand times. Surely he asked himself and others around him a barrage of questions throughout the process. If Thomas Edison, world-renowned inventor and scientist, had questions about what he was doing, your principalship will be no different. During the course of your role as a school leader, you will find yourself inundated with a multitude of questions on a daily basis, about nine thousand of them.

When you think about the role of the campus principal as being the instructional leader for the school, you should face the reality that you are expected to know what to do, when to do it, and how to do it—whatever it is. In some instances you will find yourself at a crossroads. Staff members will constantly come to you with a variety of questions that need answering—and if the truth of the matter be told, as a fledgling principal, you have your own set of questions that need answering.

- What time should I get to school every morning?
- What time should I leave school every day?
- When are the state reports due?
- How do I write a set of school improvement plans?
- Is there a different way to spend federal money?
- How much authority does the fire marshal have?

On a personal level, you begin to wonder whether, if you ask a question, you will appear incompetent. Will the questions you ask be intelligent and relevant, or make you appear ineffective? From the standpoint of answering questions for your immediate supervisor, a teacher, or a parent, you truly need to give a coherent and correct answer to the questions they ask.

From my experiences, I found three general categories of questions: (1) the questions you will ask; (2) the questions you should not have asked; and (3) the questions that you really wanted to ask. Whatever the case, no crime was committed, no earthquake ripped a small country in two, and the sun did not set in the east just because you did not have an immediate answer for someone.

The simplest response to uncertainty is, "I'm not sure about that, but I'll ask." Sam Keen, American author and philosopher, said, "To be on a quest is nothing more or less than to become an asker of questions" (Lewis 2006). This is such an eye-opening description of the way you should view the art of questioning: as a quest.

An old Chinese proverb says, "One who asks a question is a fool for five minutes; one who does not ask a question remains a fool forever" (Thinkexist n.d.). Many school districts call a planning meeting for all principals, supervisors, and program coordinators at the first of the school year. After a few of my own "five-minute follies," I learned to listen more closely to the conversations in the room and wait to see if anyone else had the same question I did. I learned to be patient and let others speak first. If my particular question was not asked, I wrote it down so I could ask it later in private, either to a fellow principal or one of my supervisors.

Another example of questions not asked occurred during a budget meeting. Because school budgets are open records, anyone has the right to see campus and district budgets. At one budget hearing, the district's budget was passed among the attendees at the meeting. As I looked through the budget, I found that my salary was less than the salary of the newly hired, no-administrative-experience, primary principal's salary.

With five more years of experience as a principal, I was sure this was a typographical error. When the meeting was dismissed, I asked the board secretary about the difference and she had no answer for me. In fact, the superintendent leaned over and asked the secretary, "Can't you answer Tareilo's question?" To this day, I can still see the look on the secretary's face when she replied, "No, I can't." Very quickly the budget was retrieved from the audience and the board meeting was moved to executive session. At that moment, I should have asked about the difference in salaries. Instead, I let the information fester and that later caused a much greater scene between myself and the superintendent.

Another night at a school board meeting, I was blindsided by a question from the board. The meeting was moving along nicely and out of the blue one of the board members asked me if I had taken a wall down between two of my classrooms. Actually, I had taken down a wall because two of my teachers wanted to do some team teaching in their grade level. I called the maintenance department and made sure the wall that I was taking down was not a support wall. Since it was not a support wall and my teachers believed the open-classroom, team-teaching concept would be more beneficial to the children they taught, I had the wall taken down.

However, I did sit there a little taken aback by the question. I knew the only way the board would have known about the disappearing wall was if a teacher on my campus had informed her friends on the school board about what I had done. I knew exactly which teacher it was. I proceeded to inform the board of the teachers' request, how the students were performing in the open classroom, and extended to them an open invitation to visit the classroom any time. What could have been a gotcha moment for me turned out to be a very positive experience.

For some reason, the preparation of school administrators leaves out a very important issue, that of teaching campus leaders how to have crucial conversations. These conversations are not always pleasant and many involve some element of conflict. However, certain questions must be asked, and principals must be prepared and readied to ask those difficult questions.

When a parent calls you at 9:30 at night and is dealing with a crying child because Mr. or Miss I-Forgot-You-Were-a-Child said something hurtful, you assure the parent that this particular situation will be addressed first thing in the morning. When you arrive on the campus, you head toward that teacher's room to talk with him or her about the situation. If the students are already in the classroom, you ask to see the teacher outside of the room. You simply say, "I received a phone call from little Janie's mother last night. What else should I know about this situation?"

Now to be quite honest, that was normally the way I handled that kind of situation. I would simply go to the teacher and ask him or her, "Janie's mother just called. Is there anything I should know?" or "Can you give me any reason why the superintendent wants to meet with me in his office concerning a phone call he received from Janie's mother?" See, I can be nice—but then again . . .

Over the many years serving as a principal, I learned how to suppress my volatile temper. I am one of those people who, when angered, take on either the nature of a mad Chihuahua puppy snapping at someone's ankles or a 180-mile-an-hour hurricane headed for shore. I tried to always ask questions in a calm manner; however, there were times when being calm and kind did not serve my purpose.

One such event occurred on an early-release day. Our district calendar allowed for a few half-day school holidays for the students. On those days, we were instructed to provide staff training or professional development. Because the students left school those days about 12:45 p.m., our schedules for music and PE had to be rearranged.

Normally, the PE staff provided a "B" day schedule, which allowed all the teachers to have a shorter conference time. One of the teachers came to my office to complain that she would not be receiving her required amount of conference time. I explained to her that while she would not have a regular conference time, the students would be leaving at 12:45 p.m. and the superintendent would most likely allow the teachers to also leave for the day. Since this happened early in the morning, I proceeded with my day and did not think another thing about the conversation. However, not liking the answer I gave her, the teacher e-mailed the superintendent with her complaint.

Around 11:00 that morning, our school secretary came running to the cafeteria where I was on duty to let me know that all school secretaries had just received a message from the superintendent's secretary telling them to locate their principals, have their principals go to their computers, and wait for a very important e-mail from the superintendent.

Sure enough, a message from the superintendent quickly appeared. He proceeded to inform all the principals that teachers would *not* be allowed to leave when the students left that day. He had received an e-mail from a very concerned teacher that she was not afforded her full conference time because of a shortened PE schedule. In order for her to have her lawful conference time, all teachers in the district would be required to stay until their usual dismissal time at 3:30 p.m. He apologized for not taking that issue into consideration with his original plans to release all personnel at the same dismissal time as their students. We were to immediately announce this change to our staffs. If he changed his mind, he would certainly let us know.

I sat at that computer dumbfounded. Did I call and ask if it was one of my teachers? Remember the section on the questions that should not be asked? This was one of those kinds of questions. I could not believe that the actions of one of my teachers had caused every teacher—not just the teachers on my campus, but every teacher in the district—to have to remain at school and not be allowed to leave early.

I decided to have one of those crucial conversations that involve conflict. I leaped from my chair, threw open my office door, and headed toward her room with hurricane debris following me along my path. Let me assure you, I was not nice, I was not kind, and I could be heard snapping like a Chihuahua as I headed to the teacher's room. When I reached her classroom door, I found her sitting at her desk in an empty room. I closed the door, looked at her with the most venomous snarl I could muster, and asked her if she e-mailed the superintendent about her shortened conference time.

When she said that was what she had done, I exploded. "Do you have any idea what you have done? Did you not think about anyone but yourself? Because of your actions, every teacher in this district has to remain on their campuses and is not allowed to leave early. What were you thinking?" She stammered around for an answer, began to apologize, and even started crying. Anyone who has ever worked with me or for me knows that I care nothing for tears of this nature. I left the room with the same angry posture that I had when I entered the room, except that the teacher was frantically looking for bandages to cover the dog bites on her ankles.

When I returned to my office, the secretary informed me that many of the other principals had called and were asking if I knew any reason why the superintendent would change his mind about the early dismissal for teachers and saying that he sounded very upset in his e-mail. Do you think I returned any of those messages?

As the students were leaving the school to go home, the superintendent's secretary called our secretary to let us know that, after considering the situation, the superintendent had changed his mind and the teachers were now allowed to leave the school when all their children had left for the day. To this day, only a few people from the district know it was one of my teachers that caused the problem.

I would also like to take a moment and share with you my idea of the twenty-four-hour rule I tried to apply at all times. I live in a continual state of biting my tongue. Words that I really want to say float around inside my head waiting for my mouth to open so they can fly out and my size-8$\frac{1}{2}$ foot can slide inside.

Since the duties of the principal regularly involve communicating and talking with people from all walks of life, I certainly cannot meet people with the heel of my shoe dangling from the corner of my mouth. So, I learned quickly that I really did not have to respond immediately to all questions or statements posed to me. The twenty-four-hour rule taught me to reply to some situations in the following ways:

- "I do not have an answer for you at this time. Let me get back with you before the day is over and I'll see what I can find out."

- "Since I do not have all the facts, please give me until the morning to answer that question."
- "I know you need an answer as soon as possible. After I look into the situation, I will call you first thing in the morning."
- "If you really want me to answer you in a positive and calm manner, you need to back off and give me twenty-four hours."

With all of this said, you truly need to answer questions for teachers, parents, and supervisors in a timely manner and in the best way possible. Providing an answer, no matter what it is, in a timely manner reflects on your ability to address and solve problems.

Take, for instance, one of the times a parent wanted to file a grievance against me. A mother was questioning a practice at the high school regarding cheerleader tryouts. While on car duty, a teacher noticed a mother was moving in and out of the parked cars with a clipboard in her hands. It appeared that she was asking parents to sign a petition that asked for certain practices and policies regarding cheerleader tryouts to be reexamined. While I might or might not have agreed with her, our school board policy stated that this type of name gathering for a petition could not take place on a school campus.

I saw her the next day and explained the policy to her and told her she could no longer collect signatures, in any form, while on the campus. This did not make her happy. She proceeded to become very agitated and directed that agitation straight at me. My internal snapping Chihuahua retorted back, "I do not know why you are so mad at me. I actually agree with you, but I am not afforded an opinion on this. As an employee of the school district, I have to follow policy, and the policy states you may not circulate a petition on a school campus." I guess she also graduated from the Chihuahua School of Snapping, because she asked how she could file a grievance against me. Oh, well . . .

Your principalship should reflect the sentiments of American author and humorist James Thurber, "It is better to know some of the questions than all of the answers." Whether the questions come from a teacher needing help with a student, from a parent who does not understand a policy, or from the superintendent who needs an explanation about a phone call he or she received, you need to put on your thinking cap, fire up the data bank, and communicate the answers in the best and most logical manner.

Your reputation as an instructional leader and a problem-solver grows stronger each time you accomplish this task. And if you cannot answer a question immediately, you can always say, "I'm not sure, but I'll ask."

PROVIDING SUPER SERVICE

Taking care of a school is really no different than being a waitress at a very large and very busy restaurant. At a restaurant, almost immediately, waiters and waitresses come to your table wearing a friendly smile and offering to bring you a beverage of your choice while you have a chance to look at the menu. Once the meal is delivered to your table, the waiter or waitress asks if there is anything else you need.

The wait staff becomes your constant companion for the next hour or so, watching your table with eagle eyes, knowing the precise minute the water glasses need filling. As a reward for exceptional service, a monetary amount is left on the table for their hard work and thoughtful service. Even though administrators will never get a trip to Tahiti with the money they find in their tip jars, providing super service to the students, the staff, the parents, and the community remains a key factor in your success as a school leader.

You need to accept the fact that as the principal of a school, you are the manager on duty and every single child, staff member, and parent is your customer. It is very easy to remember to treat your children and parents in a friendly manner. Unfortunately, some principals forget to treat their teachers with the same courtesy.

Before the first day of school, I always left a little something and a personal note on my teachers' desks. One year I left a carnation and a note that simply told them how important they were to me. One year I left a tiny flower pot that held a small package of seeds and asked them to "grow something special" that year between themselves and their children. Another year I glued matchsticks tied with a ribbon to note-cards. The note inside the card read, "I know you are going to light the world on fire this year for our kids."

These small tokens for my teachers let them know how much I cared for them. Later, a teacher shared with me that every year she knew there would be something on their desks the first day of school to remind them how special they were to me. She always looked forward to opening her door that morning and looking on her desk to see the new little wish I had placed there.

A very important aspect of providing super service to and for others lies in the understanding that you must keep your word. Your credibility as a leader is at stake. If you tell a parent that you will check on Little Billy because he left the house with a fever, then make it a point to check on Little Billy and call the parent back. If a teacher asks to be the next one in line to receive the bigger room at the end of the hall, make sure she gets the room. Whatever the situation, when you keep your word, others will keep theirs (Gee and Gee 1999).

In the business world, the customer is always right. That is not always the case in the world of education. On several occasions, parents would ask if they could visit their child's classroom. Sometimes they wanted to stay all day. A mother walked in with her child one day and asked if she could sit in her son's classroom for awhile. The teacher, being a super service kind of teacher, said of course.

The teacher thought she would only stay a short while. The mother stayed all morning. She stayed during their reading time, all through their math lesson, and was on her way to PE with the class when the teacher decided I should be involved. The teacher had already thanked the mother for coming and told her she would be welcome to visit anytime.

Thinking the mother would leave, the teacher proceeded with her children to the gym. A few minutes later, the teacher came to my office and told me of the situation. About the same time the phone on my desk rang. It was the PE coach letting me know there was a parent in the gym instructing the other children to play with her son.

As I headed to the gym to solve this problem, I was trying to formulate some positive remarks to say to the mother. When I reached the gym, I found the mother and asked her to come with me. Outside in the hallway, I thanked her for coming and assured her that her son would be fine and that we appreciated her visit but we had to get back to the business of school. This made the teachers happy and also made the mother feel appreciated.

Friendly service should also be the focus of the secretary or administrative assistant who sits in the front office. I am very fortunate to be able to say that every school secretary I ever had could not have been more friendly or giving to the teachers and our parents. Unfortunately, that is not always the case.

In visiting other schools, I have often encountered rude and inconsiderate front office staff. This impression is a lasting one. In one school, the secretary kept the key to the teachers' supply cabinet, and the teachers had to ask her permission to get supplies. Gee and Gee (1999, 39) contend that we should all forget our "own immediate concern and focus our complete attention on serving the customer." Your leadership challenge is to remember that everyone you come in contact with—a child, a teacher, or a parent—deserves "super service" from you.

BEING THE KEEPER OF THE FLAME IS A HOT JOB

Many crests, rings, and motivational banners associated with educational institutions or related educational concepts portray a copper or brass lamp that resembles the one from the story about Aladdin. Usually, the tip of a flame can be seen coming from the spout.

This emblem signifies learning and accomplishment. Imagine further for me, if you will, that you are the holder of said lamp and it is your primary job to keep it filled with oil so that the flame never burns out. This flame will light your way and that of anyone who follows you. Now, having painted that Kodak moment for you, I want you to invest in a very thick oven mitt that resists the heat from a lamp that has fire shooting from its tip.

This lamp signifies knowledge, learning, and success, and your responsibility is to make sure these elements are part of your school. Some of this can be accomplished by providing meaningful and needed professional development for your teachers.

I am not referring to the "before-school-starts meeting" where everyone sits in the cafeteria on "kiddy" seats and listens to the reading of the faculty handbook. Ask your teachers a few very simple questions when making decisions regarding in-service activities or professional development opportunities.

"What can I do to help you become a better teacher this year?"

"What can I do this year to help you reach even the most unreachable child?"

"What do you want to learn this year that will improve your instructional ability?"

This is not rocket science or quantum theory physics. It is just you trying to find out what kind of oil your lamp needs.

Other ways a principal learns to keep the flame of learning alive is by providing the resources necessary for teachers' instructional needs. On one campus, a school bond passed and we were going to be able to build a brand-new campus for elementary students. Contractors visited the superintendent, who in turn asked our teachers to respond to this question: "If you could have anything you wanted in your classroom, what would it be?" I can almost see the little cogs and wheels turning in your head.

Some teachers took great thought about what they would really like to have in their classrooms. They drew pictures of classroom designs that incorporated the different learning styles of their children. In one corner of the new room they wanted a hanging rack for Books in a Bag that they used for their auditory learners. They wanted two sinks in the room, one at an adult level, and the other one at the children's level. These teachers took their time and planned for themselves and their children. If the teaching thing did not work out, they could have easily had the next hit show on any design network. Their lamps burned brightly.

Then there were some teachers who considered the question and began looking through home decorating magazines and decided they needed a ceiling fan and a nice eggshell white color for the walls. If there were going to be windows looking into the classroom, there would need to be a way to hang curtains. Not a lot of light coming from this lamp.

But as the principal of the school, your lamp must burn the brightest. The oil burning in your lamp must be a high-premium, long-lasting, burn-forever kind of oil. So many authors have written about the importance of the principal as the instructional leader on the campus—hence, the Keeper of the Flame of Knowledge. I could write volumes about what you will need to know about effective and meaningful instruction, how to help teachers improve in their craft, and what student success should look like. So grab your oven mitts, pour the best oil in your teachers' lamps, and prepare to burn brightly.

I want you to imagine this scenario. You have just acquired your first principalship. The superintendent has handed you the master keys to the

school, and you cannot wait to visit your school for the first time. As you
are driving up the driveway to the school, you notice that there are no
lights on and the building is completely dark except for the EXIT lights
emitting a shadowy red haze. Before you even get out of the car, you know
you are going to need some source of light to tour your school.

Because you are a prepared principal, you happen to have an oil-
filled Aladdin-looking lamp on the floor of your car (it could happen).
Removing the lamp from the car, you move toward the front doors of
the school. The only thing you have to show you the way is the lamp
with the smallest of blue flames coming from the spout. However, the
minute you put the keys in the lock and push the doors open, that flame
grows a little brighter. By the time you walk the halls and realize the
school is really yours, the flame is burning brightly and it's time to pull
out the oven mitt.

There will be some days when the light coming from your lamp is only
a small flicker of a flame. You are exhausted or have fought many battles
and are truly worn to a frazzle. Teachers' needs and concerns have been
at your door all week. You have been inundated with parent questions
or countless central office meetings. The cafeteria even ran out of corn
dogs and the last classes had to eat the Manager's Special. Though your
lamplight may not resemble a raging bonfire, you must still keep it burning. You have to be the one to light the way and set the example for other
frazzled and exhausted staff members. Your lamp can never go out.

Whether it is an instructional issue, a teacher concern, a budgetary
matter, or a cafeteria problem, holding that lamp means you are the possessor of all knowledge regarding the school and the learning that takes
place inside. In researching information on the "lamp of knowledge," I
found a website called "The Oil in My Lamp." A teacher by the name
of Miss Settles (Settles n.d.) created a webpage of her virtual classroom.
This page opened with bright colors, clearly stated directions and objec-
tives, as well as several additional links including the following:

> Knowledge is the property of all people. Knowledge is to your mind as
> oil is to an old lamp—keeping your mind filled with innovations, positive
> thoughts, and open for new information, will ensure that when an oppor-
> tunity presents itself, you will be able to see it. A wise mother advised her
> children, 'Always keep oil in your lamps.'

Miss Settles clearly knows what it means to keep a lamp lit and filled with knowledge. Her underlying meaning also relates to how important it is to be prepared and ready for questions that may arise, situations that will need your direct attention, and a lamp filled with enough oil to light your way.

DEVELOPING YOUR PERSONAL LEADERSHIP CAPACITY

Early in the chapter, a reference to the Wizard of Oz was made. This reference referred to a place where one man was considered great and powerful by many because he made wise and thoughtful decisions and even seemed to sense what everyone needed. In the movie, the wizard is seen as a fire-breathing, angry, and loud-speaking being. But at the end of the movie, the wizard is revealed as a plain and soft-spoken man who sees the potential in others that they did not see in themselves.

What a great testament for a true leader: to be able to see the greatness in others when they can't see it in themselves. Therefore, your capacity for becoming a leader who holds a lamp that burns continuously is to have enough oil to

1. Light the way for others as well as yourself
2. Never forget to applaud the successes of your teachers, no matter how small
3. Remember that sometimes it is better to smile and walk away from a situation if you are going to say or do something that does not reflect a professional behavior
4. Ask questions in order to learn something new
5. Be courageous enough to remain a teacher at heart

WHAT WILL MY PRINCIPALSHIP SAY ABOUT ME?

I have always had and will always have the deepest respect for teachers. In my years as a classroom teacher, I worked with some of the most remarkable men and women, who were committed to their profession. During my principalship, I had the privilege of supervising teachers who quite literally lit up a room with their lamps. Even though you might keep your lamp hidden somewhere in a desk drawer or on a shelf in your closet, I hope it is always at your fingertips ready to be lit. When your lamp is filled with oil and burning brightly, I expect people to say that:

"He helped me create a classroom discipline plan that really worked."

"I could tell she was upset with me, but she just said we could talk about it later."

"Have you ever noticed how much he offers to help us?"

"She is the first principal we have had who included us in planning for in-service days."

"You can tell he was a really great teacher because he is a really great principal."

USING YOUR 20/20 VISION

Not all principals have a lamp with a blazing flame of blue coming from the spout. Some have a lamp with a flame so small it couldn't toast a miniature marshmallow at a wienie roast. But you're not going to be that kind of a principal. You're going to be the kind of school leader whose flame is always burning. I know that you can't really carry a lamp around the school with a flame coming from the tip, so barring getting a lamp tattoo, keep these lamplight strategies close to your heart as you prepare to be a teacher of teachers.

- ☐ Regularly visit classrooms to ensure your teachers are on fire for learning.
- ☐ Learn to praise in public and address concerns in private.
- ☐ Provide continuous and purposeful learning for yourself and your staff members.
- ☐ Commit yourself to doing random acts of kindness for others.
- ☐ Create a "twenty-four-hour rule" for dealing with difficult situations.
- ☐ Build professional relationships with your staff members in order to help them fill their lamps with the oil that will light their ways.

MY WISH FOR YOU

The age-old story of Aladdin's lamp involves a young man who happens upon an old lamp lying in the sand. When the young man, Aladdin, picks up the lamp, he wipes off the sand to get a better look at his new treasure. As he is rubbing the lamp to get it clean, an ominous dark blue cloud streams from the tip of the lamp and turns into a large and somewhat scary genie.

Aladdin asks for and is granted three wishes by the genie, with the understanding that once the three wishes are fulfilled, Aladdin will grant the genie his freedom. Imagine that you are Aladdin and you have three wishes coming to you. These wishes can only be for the success of your school. What three wishes would you choose? Here are mine for you.

My wish for you is that you never forget how hard teachers work and that you are and will always be a teacher.

My wish for you is that you always know where to go and what sources to use to help your teachers learn something new, and that that knowledge helps at least one child succeed in some way.

My wish for you is that your kindness toward others is the oil they use to light their own lamps.

ADDITIONAL RESOURCES

Reading Material

Gee, Jeff, and Val Gee. *Super Service: Seven Keys to Delivering Great Customer Service . . . Even When You Don't Feel Like It . . . Even When They Don't Deserve It*. New York: McGraw-Hill, 2009.

Kozol, Johnathan. *On Being a Teacher*. Rockport, MA: Oneworld Publications, 1996.

Liesveld, Roseanne, and Jo Ann Miller, with Jennifer Robison. *Teach with Your Strengths: How Great Teachers Inspire Their Students*. New York: Gallup Press, 2005.

Rath, Tom, and Donald O. Clifton. *How Full Is Your Bucket: Positive Strategies for Work and Life*. New York: Gallup Press, 2004.

Welch, David A. *Decisions, Decisions: The Art of Effective Decision Making*. Amherst, NY: Prometheus Books, 2002.

Internet Sources

712educators.about.com/od/teachingstrategies/tp/sixkeys.htm
Successful teachers have several characteristics in common. This article provides the top six characteristics of effective teachers, which also reflect effective leadership.

www.virtualsalt.com/crebook5.htm
From this site, administrators are provided definitions, strategies, and a formula for helping in the decision-making process.

www.bls.gov/oco/ocos007.htm
The United States Department of Labor provides this website, which is filled with updated and statistical information on education that all administrators need to know.

www.joelonsoftware.com/articles/customerservice.html
This website offers seven remarkable ways to ensure quality customer service that any administrator could use to make his or her school a special place.

marketing.about.com/od/relationshipmarketing/a/crmtopten.htm
At this site are ten tips for becoming a caring and attentive school leader for the staff and the community.

5

"MY MAMA SAID . . ." LOVING
THE KIDS DESPITE THE PARENTS

Recently, we celebrated New Year's Eve and the awakening of another potentially terrific year. As is the custom of our daily newspaper, the first child born in the new year is pictured on the front page being held by the happy mother and father. It is very evident that these parents love and worship their new little bundle of joy. In fact, the mother has already made up her mind that nothing known to mankind will ever harm, malign, or in any way endanger her beloved child, if she has her way.

The umbilical cord that attached mother and child during the gestation period stretches from wherever his mother happens to be to the child's school, to his or her first dance, and even all the way to the college of the child's choice. Realizing that this phenomenon occurs between a mother and her child, you already possess a great wealth of knowledge when you begin your principalship and begin dealing with parents on a daily basis.

Where can I possibly begin to describe the importance of the relationship that you build between the parents and yourself as the principal? For the most part, the parents you encounter will be only too happy to help you help their child. They will genuinely care about the education their child receives and want to be an active part in that educational process.

When you meet this kind of parent, I want you to learn to appreciate every act of helpfulness they give you and cherish their support as a small gift of confidence for you, your school, and your teachers. This kind of parent brings joy to your day. Unfortunately, joy will not always be the gift some of your parents bring to your office door.

Here and now, remember this: You do not get to choose the parents who come with the children in your care. If this were the case, I would have chosen more Martha Stewarts, a few more Bill Gateses, and a couple of extra Colin Powells.

There will be some instances when you actually pray that gypsies will come in the middle of the night and steal the children away just so they can have a better life than the one they have. But remember this, you can't change the way some parents act or treat their children. You can't make them care about their children if they don't want to. What you can do is guarantee that for 170 instructional days, while their children are in your school, they will be loved, cared for, and kept safe.

PARENTING 101

I wish I had kept a journal of parent stories that happened over the twenty-four years I spent in public education as a teacher, program director, and principal. Those journals would be filled with memories that brought tears to my eyes and ones that regrettably filled me with anger and disgust. I have testified at custody hearings, had a mother arrested in my office, initiated trespassing warnings to parents, and helped mothers and fathers bury their sons and daughters who were taken too soon. I even had to watch a father steal his children from my campus.

In regard to dealing with parents, I can assure you that no two situations will ever be the same. In fact, some of the circumstances you will have to deal with should be the next exhibit at Ripley's Believe It or Not Museum, simply because they are just that quirky and unbelievable.

At any moment, you could turn to your computer and choose a search engine, type in the words "parent involvement," and a multitude of sites would appear. Page after page of websites would be available to you that detail suggestions for including parents in their child's education, ideas on how to encourage more parental involvement at school, and hints on how to engage parents to help their child with homework or reading assignments.

However, you won't find the websites that you will really need when dealing with difficult parents. These might include sites dedicated to how to teach a parent to tell the child no, how to make the child take responsibility for his or her own actions, and—the best one yet—how to prevent a principal from saying or doing something unprofessional when dealing with a parent. I really should have saved that site as one of my favorites and burned the information into my memory.

For your first faculty meeting with your staff, I want you to create a PowerPoint slide show that reflects all kinds of families. One picture would be of traditional mom and dad with the kids and the family dog at the park having a picnic. Tell them that this picture of a family represents just one of the family types you have at the school.

On another slide, show a picture of a mother and her children, while telling the teachers that some of your children will come from single-parent homes. For the next couple of slides, show a same-sex family and a racially mixed household. Make sure that all of the people in these pictures are smiling and appear happy. Now that you have painted a Norman Rockwell moment for your staff, present another set of slides that depicts another type of family.

Let your first slide in this grouping show the picture of an economically disadvantaged women sleeping in a car with her children. Show a slide of a man being arrested for spousal abuse as his children stand by watching their father being taken away in a police car. Impress upon your teachers that not all families are made up of Ozzies and Harriets. Not all families have a mom and dad. Not all families are held together by the same beliefs and practices that you have or believe in. Teachers need to be made aware of how vital it is to know about the makeup of their students' families.

When I started in education, I could actually say to a child, "Is your mom or dad at home? I need to talk with one of them." Years later when I became a principal, I had to change that saying to, "Who is at your house right now that I can talk to?"

I had to deal with two moms or two dads who were raising blended families, instead of one mom and one dad. I spoke with grandparents who were raising another generation of children. I had to watch as some of my children were taken away by Child Protective Services in order to keep them safe from abusive or neglectful parents.

As you already know, school is often the best and safest place for a child to be; therefore, you and your staff have to continuously be champions for children. In the case of Daniel, I had to step in and have a crucial conversation with his mother and her boyfriend.

Daniel was a child who had many problems in and out of school. Almost every week, Daniel was sent to my office for some outrageous classroom outburst or disturbance. After trying to deal with Daniel at the campus level, his teacher and I had decided it was time to involve his mother. I asked her to come to my office for a conference concerning Daniel and his behavior. When his mother arrived for the meeting, she had also invited her boyfriend. When they entered my office, I noticed that the boyfriend was carrying a leather belt with him.

Introductions were made and we started taking about what kind of problems Daniel was having at school. I explained that if Daniel's behaviors were not corrected, he would be suspended from school. After a few minutes, I could tell that the boyfriend thought corporal punishment was the answer to handling all of Daniel's problems. As we talked, I became more and more concerned for Daniel's welfare. It was very evident that Daniel's safest place during the day was definitely with us at school and that I would not be sending him home for a suspended time.

The more I sat there the angrier I became. At one point, after being told in great detail what was going to happen to Daniel as soon as he was taken home, I became Daniel's guardian angel. I looked directly at the couple, and without blinking an eye, told them that if in the future I saw one mark anywhere on Daniel, I would call Child Protective Services myself. The mother and boyfriend looked as if I had just taken that belt from the boyfriend's hands and smacked them both with it (I really wanted to).

How could I possibly insinuate that this fine, upstanding couple would ever actually use the belt that they brought to school, to the principal's office, as a means to discipline a child who was in trouble? When I said that I would call CPS, I said it with a straight face and a snarling Chihuahua look. From then on, I made it my personal mission to watch over Daniel with an extra set of eyes.

Just as we don't get to choose the students who come to our school, we do not get to choose the parents. Unfortunately, there is no educational course that teaches a person how to be a caring and loving parent. In the course of some of my parent meetings over the years, on more than one occasion a parent would tell me, "You don't get to tell me what to do. I am his mother and you're not." To which I would reply, "Then act like one."

Sometimes we as school leaders have to step in and protect a child. When it came to the welfare of my children at school, no one, not even a biological parent, was allowed to shirk his or her responsibilities to help or better a child's educational experience. (For my next profession, I should really consider being a sales representative for a major laundry detergent, with all the soapbox dancing I am doing.)

LEARNING ACCEPTANCE

He wasn't an old man, but his hard life had left him wrinkled and stooped. His hands were greasy and blackened by the many years he had spent working on machinery. The clothes he wore smelled of oil and were stained from his many labors. When he walked into our building to pick up his sick child from school one day, he bowed his head, kept his eyes lowered, and tried to become invisible. However, on that particular day, I was determined to make him feel like he belonged.

Josh's dad was one of the kindest and most caring men you could ever meet. He had little monetary worth and was constantly looking for work, usually as a mechanic. When Josh became ill at school, his dad was the one we called to pick him up.

No matter what he was doing, Josh's dad dropped everything and came to school. I happened to see him walk into the office to sign Josh out for the day and I headed toward him. I introduced myself again as the principal and held out my hand to shake his. He said, "You don't need to be shaking my hand; they are pretty dirty." I simply replied, "So are mine. I have been working with children all day" and kept my hand extended. You can't buy the look of gratitude that came from his face.

She was not what anyone would call a pretty woman. She was overweight for her height and clearly had not bathed in a few days. When she asked to speak with me in private, I invited her into my office, closed the door, and asked how I could help her. She proceeded to tell me that she knew her daughter had more potential than she was showing her classroom teacher and wanted me to intervene. This soft-spoken mother quietly said, "Chelsea is smart. She is smarter than anybody in our family. I don't want her to end up like me. Can you help me, Mrs. T.?"

I assured the mother that I would meet with Chelsea and her teachers on a regular basis and that we would all work diligently to ensure Chelsea would be successful in school. At the same time, I asked the mother to stay active in Chelsea's school experiences and make sure Chelsea stayed in school. It took a great deal of strength and courage for that mother to speak so openly and frankly about her limitations and the worry she had for her child.

These two parents are only a small sampling of the parents who might visit your office. Unless the district hasn't paid the school's water bill, there will be plenty of soap and water to wash your hands after a visit from Josh's dad. And when Chelsea's mom leaves your office, I am fairly certain that tropical-scented room spray can make your office smell fresh as an island paradise.

The point is that parents like Josh's dad and Chelsea's mom are just as important as any other parent you serve. No, they don't always present themselves as well as others might, but their concern for their children is no less important. When you can shake a man's hands that are caked in grease or sit in a room with someone who doesn't have the best hygiene practices, you have learned the art of acceptance.

When César Chávez said, "There is no substitute for patience and acceptance," little did he know he was writing words for principals to live by (thinkexist.com n.d.). When dealing with parents, their needs, and sometimes their odd behaviors, this quote should be tattooed on the inside of your eyelids or plastered on a billboard encircled by flashing red lights. Many parents are so involved in their child's life that they may bring some unique challenges into your life as the principal.

We have already discussed the many responsibilities associated with the principal's job. Because you are the principal, you also have the authority to make decisions regarding personnel, instruction, and classroom placement. What you can't decide is who the parents of your students will be or what they will do.

Being the principal of a rural elementary school brought several opportunities for growth, as I learned to deal with the parents of my students. On one such occasion, our nurse discovered that one of our children had head lice. Our school's policy stated that when a child had live lice activity (that means the lice are alive and crawling on the child's head), the child was sent home from school until the nurse cleared him or her to return to class. This usually took a few days.

Finding the live activity on the head of one of our students, the nurse followed our procedures and called the child's mother to inform her of the situation. Shortly after the phone call home, the mother and grandmother arrived at school and I received a phone call from the nurse saying that she needed me.

When I arrived at the nurse's station, the mother and grandmother were still very upset that the child had lice. It must surely be the school's fault because the child had never had a case of lice before this year. After we talked for a bit, the mother calmed down, but not the grandmother. I continued to try to defuse the situation in a calm and professional manner, but this particular grandmother was not pacified with my professional demeanor.

All of a sudden the grandmother yelled, "What do you know about lice? You're sitting there with your diamond rings and your fancy suit. What do you know, Ms. High and Mighty?" Somewhere amidst the screaming grandmother, the apologetic mother, and the stunned nurse, I actually heard a camel's back break in two as the last straw fell into a basket it was carrying.

The calm and professional demeanor that I had tried unsuccessfully to use to help calm down this grandmother diminished as my anger began to take over. I forgot all about the many times I had told the teachers to sit and listen patiently as a parent vented through a concern. Many times parents aren't really mad at teachers, they are just mad at the situation and they really don't know what to do to make it better. So, they react with accusatory remarks. Well, I quickly forgot those little pearls of wisdom.

I stood up, looked the grandmother in the face, and fiercely said, "For your information, my girls and I have all had lice. I had to do exactly what we are asking you to do. I had to wash all our sheets in bleach. We had to wash all our combs, brushes, and bows in the dishwasher. I had to buy house spray to use on the furniture just in case that's where the lice were. I sat in my kitchen and picked lice off my daughters' heads for hours. In fact, I keep a bottle of prescription medicine in my cabinet

because I get lice from my schoolchildren on a continual basis. So, don't
you dare tell me that I don't know what you are going to have to do to
get rid of the lice. I already know."

With that speech and my vented temper out of the way, the grandmother looked at me with a different pair of eyes. If the principal of the
school and her own children had a case of lice and lived through it, so
could she.

She apologized for her behavior and her unwarranted comments.
The grandmother's anger was not directed at me; it was directed at the
situation and I just happened to be the person delivering the message.
She wanted to make sure that I knew her home was clean and that her
granddaughter's health was very important to her. This may be the only
time having lice myself worked out to be so beneficial.

IN LOCO PARENTIS

In every school, in every state, the practice of in loco parentis is accepted. This term literally translates into "in place of a parent." During
the time a child is at school, the school acts as a parent of the child with
regard to the child's education, safety, and general welfare.

As a principal, your involvement with this issue requires you to create a successful learning community, carefully watch and guard for the
safety of the students, and meet the needs of every child just as the
parents would do if they were at the school during the day. In your attempts to do this, you will meet and deal with a variety of parents, their
requests, and their expectations.

Please do not misunderstand me. I have had the pleasure of meeting
some of the most phenomenal and caring parents one could imagine.
Not all of these remarkable caregivers were the biological parents; some
were foster mothers and fathers, adopted aunts or uncles, and grandparents raising their second-generation offspring. Their unselfish acts and
the importance they placed on their children often made me feel inept
with my own parental abilities. In my many years, good or bad, right or
wrong, I consider some of my parents as true gifts. At the same time I
say that, some of them were just plain crazy.

Our school required students to wear standardized dress. This dress
code required a certain color of shirt with a khaki- or blue-colored pant.

Also, the standard dress code for length and appropriateness still applied. Monday through Thursday, there were no exceptions.

On Fridays, the students were allowed a free dress day. If a teacher noticed a child not in dress code, the teacher was asked to send that child to the office. Once there, the student called home and was directed to ask someone to bring an acceptable change of clothes.

When Laurie came into the office that day, I knew immediately why the teacher had sent her to the office. Laurie was a fourth-grade student who was a little larger than some of the other girls her age. When I saw Laurie, I asked her why her teacher had sent her to the office. She told me that her teacher wanted me to see her skirt. The teacher thought her skirt was a little short—and sure enough, it was not only a little short, it was very short.

I told Laurie the skirt was too short for her to wear at school and she needed to call her mother to see if she could bring her a change of clothes. Laurie called her mother for the extra clothes and her mother told her she was on her way. I asked Laurie to sit down on the bench in the office and let me know when her mother arrived at school.

I didn't have to wait too long. In just a very few minutes, from my office, I heard our secretary talking to someone who was screaming at the top of her lungs. As I stepped from my office door, I saw Laurie's mother ranting and raving about our dress code and how they did not have as much money as everyone else who went to that school. I asked her to come into my office to talk with me while the secretary called Laurie to join us.

Once inside my office, Laurie's mother became very agitated. She proceeded to tell me that her child was just as important as every child on that campus and that just because Laurie was a little overweight for her age, we shouldn't pick on her about her clothing. I tried to assure the mother that wasn't the case.

We always tried to treat every child the same way and we completely understood the fact that some of our parents experienced financial burdens that couldn't be helped. I thought I was handling the situation in a fairly calm and caring manner. Even though she had made a spectacle of herself outside my office door, I had continued to treat her with a sense of collected kindness, until she threatened me.

During Laurie's mother's tirade at me, she screamed, "Wait until my husband hears about this. He's going to come to this school and take care of you personally." I stood slowly from my chair and said, "Did you just threaten me?" When I said that, it took her a few minutes to come to her senses. She took a few steps back away from my desk and just glared at me as most certifiable, admitted patients at a mental hospital usually do.

I told her the conversation was over and that I would be contacting our superintendent. I informed her that from that moment on, she was banned from the school, and if she came on school property again for any reason, she would be charged with trespassing. I also informed her that she was to leave our campus immediately. She did so, screaming and cursing.

I did two things. I called the superintendent's office and let him know what had happened. He asked for the mother's name and assured me that a letter confirming what I had told her would be mailed to her immediately. I then called her husband, told him what had transpired, and asked to meet with him personally. He agreed and said he was on his way.

When Laurie's father arrived at school, I did not know what to expect. If he was anything like Laurie's mother, maybe my third phone call should have been to the police station to ask for backup. As it turned out, Laurie's father was one of the kindest, calmest, and nicest men you could ever meet.

I told him about his wife's outbursts and accusations. When I told him that she had threatened me, he just sat there in disbelief. He continually assured me he was not a threat to me or the school. While I believed him, I told him I would not change my decision to have her banned from the school. Since the mother was the main source of transportation to and from school for Laurie, she would be allowed to continue to pick up Laurie from school, but she could not leave her car or enter the building for any reason.

I explained to the father that many of our end-of-the-year activities and our famous Field Day were fast approaching. Because of her behavior, her verbal threat, and the subsequent no trespassing order, Laurie's mother would not be allowed to attend any of those events. Basically, Laurie's mother could not set foot on our campus or be anywhere our children were until further notice. Permission to visit the school or a school-related event would only come from the superintendent's office, and Eskimos would start selling suntan lotion before that happened.

Our Field Day event was considered one of the highlights of the year. The school rented a covered arena for the entire day. Parents and community members were always invited. The PE staff and many volunteers arrived at the arena by 6:30 in the morning, just to decorate the many rows and seats with balloons and various posters. Everyone always had a great day.

Laurie's mother did not believe me when I said she could not attend any school-related event. As I was standing in the middle of the arena floor watching the students participate in their activities, Laurie's teacher, whom I had informed about the happenings in my office, came running across the floor of the arena to let me know that Laurie's mother was in the stands.

The teacher raised her arm and pointed her finger toward the section where Laurie's mother was sitting. As soon as she pointed out her location, I started moving toward that part of the arena with my usual Chihuahua-snapping, ankle-biting walk. Undoubtedly, Laurie's mother noticed me coming her way, saw the look in my eyes, and realized that even PetSmart did not sell a leash strong enough to hold me back.

She jumped from her seat and ran quickly out of the arena. I'm fairly certain she was not afraid of me as much as she was afraid of what I would do. I had told her I would have her arrested if she came to our school or any school function and I meant what I said. I was prepared to call the police department and have her arrested right there in front of everyone, if necessary.

For the most part, parents genuinely care about their children and what happens to them while they are at school. There exists a wide chasm when defining that care. There was a mother once who wanted to sit in her car all day just in case her son needed her. She assured me she wouldn't bother anyone, but it was her son's first time away from her and she wasn't sure he could make it without her.

Even though her son was surrounded by an entourage of caring and loving adults, played with a herd of little friends, was learning to read and write, and appeared to love school, she was still going to sit in her car. I tried to assure her we would take excellent care of her son and that she had nothing to worry about, but she didn't believe me. After a few days of sitting in her car, she realized her son was happy at school and decided to give up her watchful post and wait at home for his return.

Then there are those parents who, in my opinion, shouldn't have the responsibility of caring for a gnat, much less a child. For your safety, I should issue the following warning for the next few paragraphs. WARNING: If you read beyond this point be prepared for killer soap bubbles and dangerously high levels of lather. The soap-boxing that is about to take place could be hazardous to your health.

In every crevice of my heart, I firmly believe that children should be well taken care of, kept well fed and clean, and supported by a person or persons who genuinely care for their welfare. The economic standing or the color of one's skin does not determine care like this. The kind of care I expect children to have comes from the simple love one imagines to find between a parent and his or her child. I really don't believe that is too much to ask from a parent.

When this level of care does not exist, I tend to become angry and from somewhere deep inside, that all-too-familiar, small, snapping Chihuahua puppy leaps to the surface and is poised and ready to attack. Another thing that always angered me was when a parent used our school as leverage for behaviors.

For example, Mariella had been misbehaving at home. Her mother came to see me and asked me if I would take away some of her privileges at school, such as PE, music, and recess, until she started to behave better at home. When I told the mother I could not deny Mariella those privileges because they were part of her daily curriculum, she became very upset with me.

She said that she was Mariella's mother and as her mother, if she didn't want her to have those privileges, she wouldn't. I told her that what was happening at home between Mariella and her mother really did not impact what the school was required to offer Mariella during the day.

Mariella was an excellent student and a very sweet girl. She always appeared to be a happy child but was often shy or quiet. For weeks, her teacher had been planning an educational field trip to Houston to visit one of the museums. All of the children were excited about the chance to go out of town for the day. The cafeteria had prepared sack lunches, coolers were filled with the children's drinks, extra snacks were packed for the children, and they were ready to go.

On the day of the field trip as I was talking with the teachers, Mariella's teacher informed me that she had not made it to school yet. Because of the day's schedule, the buses needed to leave on time, and Mariella wasn't there. The buses waited for a few more minutes and then pulled away from the school without Mariella. About an hour later, Mariella and her mother walked into the school. It appeared that Mariella was still not behaving at home, so the mother had decided to punish her by not letting her go on the much-anticipated field trip.

I just stood in the middle of that hallway in shock. I looked at down at Mariella's face, and I could tell she had been crying. The mother was trying to prove a point to Mariella and me. She had asked me to take away Mariella's school privileges and I had refused. So the mother was enacting her parental right to not give Mariella permission to be involved in the extra school activities by denying her the right to take the field trip.

I realized I could do nothing for Mariella at that point in time. I told the mother that the decision to allow Mariella to go on the field trip was entirely hers and that we would take care of Mariella for the rest of the day while her entire grade level was on the field trip. Oh, did I leave out that other bit of information? Mariella was the only child in fifth grade who did not get to go on the field trip.

When the mother left the school, I took Mariella in my arms and told her how sorry I was that she was not allowed to go on the field trip. I assured her I would do everything I could to make her day special. For that day, Mariella became our office aide. She took notes to teachers in their classrooms. She worked with the librarian by shelving books and helping other students check out books. She went to PE and helped the teachers with the younger students. All in all, even though she missed the field trip, she still had a great day.

Mariella's mistake was that she told her mother about her day. When Mariella's mother found out about her day of fun, she told me, in no uncertain terms, that when she had denied Mariella the right to go on the field trip, it was a punishment and I had no business interfering in her decision. Her mother intended for Mariella to have worked all day on extra school assignments. She wanted her to come home from school with her hands gnarled and aching from all the worksheets she had to do.

I proceeded to tell her in my yapping Chihuahua style that when Mariella was at home she was her mother's responsibility but that when she was at school, Mariella was my responsibility, and I would not punish her at school for something she had or had not done at home.

I would love to tell you that Mariella was able to participate in other school events, but she was not. The mother was so mad at me that from that point on whenever we were having any school event, a musical, field day, or a special visit by our winning high school football team, Mariella's mother intentionally brought her late to school or kept her home so Mariella would miss the entire event. The mother may have had the last word on Mariella's extracurricular activities, but Mariella and I knew that when she was at school, I would always make her feel special and important.

Remember the story about the little girl with head lice? Because that campus was in a rural setting, we often had several cases of head lice at one time, especially in the same family. One morning, a third-grade teacher stopped me in the hallway and asked if I had a baseball cap. I told her I didn't know but that I certainly would check and see. At that point I had no idea why she needed a baseball cap, but since I always tried to provide for my teachers, I started looking for a baseball cap.

In a few minutes, a little fellow from her class knocked on my door and asked to see me. His teacher had given him a note especially for me. When I looked at little Henry, I instantly knew why the teacher needed a baseball cap.

Undoubtedly Henry had acquired a case of head lice and the mother, not knowing what to do, simply cut out chunks of Henry's hair where she had seen the lice. Henry's head looked like a patchwork quilt that would have won a blue ribbon at any county fair. The note from the teacher simply said, "Help."

I asked our school secretary to inform the teacher that Henry would be with me for awhile. I called Henry's mother and asked her if she would mind us giving Henry a baseball cap. During the conversation, the mother shared with me that all of her children had been sent home from school with live lice activity. After pulling lice from the heads of her other children, she was just "too worn out from picking out those "&°%#&°° little bugs," so she just cut them out of Henry's hair in clumps.

Looking at Henry with his patchwork head, I knew what he was going to face that day. Children, in their cruel and often mean ways, were going to laugh at him, call him names, and hurt him in ways that only children can. Teachers and other adults would stare at his head and try to hide their pity or shock. I couldn't stand the thought of that happening to Henry.

Because the district was rather small, the high school was only a three-minute walk from our elementary campus. After calling the high school campus and talking with the boys' head baseball coach, I found out that he did happen to have some baseball caps and would be happy to give one to Henry. When we arrived at his office in the high school, the coach was very gracious to us and asked if Henry would mind wearing one of the baseball team's caps. Needless to say, Henry beamed with happiness.

Magical moments like these are so precious that I wish I had just the right words to paint a picture of that day for you, of Henry's patchwork scalp and the smile on his face when the coach placed that cap on his head. For a few minutes Henry wasn't the kid with lice whose mother had massacred his scalp. He was just a little boy with a new baseball cap who felt an extreme sense of pride and belonging.

When you face the many trials and tribulations of being a principal, days like this are priceless. My name may not appear on the next list of candidates for the Nobel Peace Prize, but on that particular day, I knew I had done something very right.

Yes, Henry missed some class time. Yes, I was off campus and not filling out some kind of required paperwork, and yes I was breaking a school rule by letting Henry wear his cap inside the school. But after all these years, I can still recall the light that shone in Henry's eyes and the look on his face when Coach put that cap on his head. One of the reasons I became a principal was for times like these and for all the other Henrys who would come into my life.

In your principalship, you are going to meet a lot of parents and many who stand in the place of parents as caregivers. I had to learn that most parents are really trying to do the best they can.

Sometimes their stories are so heart-wrenching that the only comfort you can give them is to listen. Some were facing some very difficult life decisions. Mothers shared that they were being beaten and were looking for a place of safety for themselves and their children. I have watched a grown man shed tears as I denied him the right to see his son because of a court decision regarding custodial rights. I have cried and ranted behind a closed office door when parents left my office and I knew I was helpless when it came to their particular need or problem.

So, what words of advice can I give you that will make the journey with your parents an easy one? How will you know the right thing to say to ease some of their pain? How will you fight for the educational needs of one of your students when the parent doesn't want to be bothered with the school's problems?

Try to look beyond your own expectations and understandings. Not every child is treated the way she should be. Not every child has enough food to eat or a loving parent at home to listen to him read, to check his homework, or tuck him into bed at night. Some parents are doing the very best they can, and that is what you should learn to appreciate. That said, do not ever be afraid or worried if you have to step in with Child Protective Services or law enforcement officers. Take care of the children in your school to the best of your ability. That's all you can do.

ONE SIZE PARENT FITS ALL

The past few pages have shared stories about parents who may not have been in contention for an award as Parent of the Year. However, there are some parents I have met over my years as a principal that are worth remembering, and I truly wish there was a way to clone them.

In order to get the school ready for a new year, I thought I would try to find ways to decorate our older building. So I decided, a few days before school started, that I wanted to paint a maroon stripe down the center of our cinder block hallways. I thought this might add a little color to the all-white walls.

When I came up with this little idea, I did not realize that painting cinder blocks is not an easy task. Nancy, one of my parents, offered to help me paint the stripe. Two days before school started, Nancy and I stood in the hallways until well after midnight painting a maroon stripe down three very long hallways.

She graciously and most generously helped me make our school a better place. That one stripe of maroon paint made such a difference in the hallways. She turned out to be cheap labor, because all she asked for in return for painting the wall was some pizza. Nancy is only one of the many parents who helped me along the way as I attempted to turn my schools into welcome, inviting, and caring places.

Debbie provided additional school supplies to students who started school with only a pencil and some paper. Carla donated her own money so that every child would be able to go on field trips. Mike's dad landed his life-flight helicopter in the back field of our school because he knew many of my children had never seen a helicopter and probably never would. Pop stood in the middle of a highway directing traffic to ensure the safety of our students. Charlene spent countless hours helping choreograph a musical production.

Numerous parents have volunteered over the years to watch a class, help a teacher, or help me in so many ways. Parents can be the most beneficial and cost-free resources you can have at your school. I can only hope that your own wonderful Nancys, Debbies, and Pops surround you and bring a bounty of gifts to your school and your principalship.

DEVELOPING YOUR OWN PERSONAL LEADERSHIP CAPACITY

Whether you accept it or not, as the principal of a campus you represent the final voice for making decisions, you create a vision that leads to success, and you are the one they call when parent situations arise. Not all of your parents will dress the same way or speak the same language, and not all of your teachers will be prepared to handle the unpredictable parent situations that arise.

Simply accept the fact that dealing with the parents or caregivers of the students at your school comes with the territory of the principalship. Therefore, it is vital that you prepare yourself and your teachers on how to deal with parents and their many needs and wants. Offered below are only a few suggestions for how to become a strong and committed principal when dealing with parents.

- Treat all of your parents with respect and dignity, from the mayor to the mechanic.
- Try not to lose your temper when dealing with parents and the many situations they bring to the school. (This is one of those times I would like to request that you do what I say, not what I did.)
- Do small things for parents that show them that you care about their child, such as bringing an umbrella to car duty when it is

raining or letting the child charge a lunch when Mom forgot the lunch money.

- Remind your teachers on a regular basis of how important it is to keep the lines of communication open between home and school.
- Inform your teachers that they have permission to invoke the "My principal said" rule whenever they need it.
- Be an example for your teachers when it comes to dealing with parent situations; listen closely to the parents' side of a story, be patient, and finds ways to help parents help their children be successful.
- Always look for the good in the parents and caregivers of the children in your school (even though you know in your heart that some of them need time away in a nicely padded room at a vacation resort or a place with many iron bars).

WHAT WILL MY PRINCIPALSHIP SAY ABOUT ME?

Recently, I was cleaning out a box hidden under a dresser in my bedroom. We all have this box somewhere in our house. This is the box that holds old pictures, the tooth fairy's collection of lost tusks, and the handmade stuff from our children that can never see the inside of a trash can. You know that box. In this box, I found an old black-and-gold graduation invitation from one of my former students. In the invitation, his mother had added a picture of Stephen and written me a small note.

In the note, Mary Ann, Stephen's mother, thanked me for taking care of Stephen and her other children who had entered my classroom. She wrote of unselfish acts of kindness that I had shown to Stephen and his siblings over the years and said that I had been more to her than just her children's teacher.

Unknowingly, I had influenced her children as their teacher and her as a parent. When you become a campus principal there really is only one rule of thumb to follow when dealing with parents: Take care of their children by treating them fairly and with respect. When you do this, parents will gather at the ball field and say:

"I really like that principal. Whenever I see him, he always says hello."

"I know I am always welcome at the school. The principal said we could visit anytime."

"The principal called me the other day just to let me know that my Billy made 100 on his spelling test. I wasn't expecting that kind of phone call from a principal."

"I was so mad when I got to that school—but when I talked with the principal, she made me feel so much better."

USING YOUR 20/20 VISION

Having 20/20 vision when dealing with parents won't require a special set of eyeglasses. However, you might have to overlook some of their actions, overindulge them by granting very unusual requests, and learn not to overreact to some of their behaviors. I do offer some suggestions for dealing with parents as you prepare to become a Proactive Principal.

- ☐ Ask parents to provide you with current phone numbers, e-mails, and addresses to ensure a means of communication.
- ☐ Visit outside school events where parents are likely to be, such as Little League baseball games or theater productions.
- ☐ Learn the names of your parents as soon as you can.
- ☐ Be sure to add a Parents' Corner to your school's website.
- ☐ Create a Parent Center on one of the bulletin boards at school. Be sure to add the school numbers that the parents will use on a regular basis: the nurse's station, the cafeteria manager, and the school secretary.
- ☐ Listen when you need to, stop unwarranted remarks when necessary, and have the wisdom to know when to do both.
- ☐ Give the teachers permission to use your name when they are confronted with a difficult situation. Make sure they inform you of what they have said as soon as possible.

MY WISH FOR YOU

This chapter has presented several parental situations and scenarios that actually happened in my career. I can only hope that when you begin to deal with parents on a daily basis, you always remember to be patient, kind, and understanding (that is, until they threaten you or when you feel your own snapping Chihuahua about to emerge). So, my wish for you comes from a parent's point of view. I hope that when you read these words you will do so with the eyes and the heart of a parent who may one day have a child in your school.

A Parent's Plea

I give her to you every day and say a little prayer,
That you will guide her every step when she is in your care.
I give him to you every day and trust him into your hands,
That you will make him strong and wise and teach him all you can.
I give them to you every day, these precious children mine,
That with your words of kindness you'll help them grow in time.
I'll let you be their teacher; I'll send them every day,
But I ask that you will listen and let me have my say.
So do not disappoint me.
Let me always be a part.
Because you're only borrowing this child who holds my heart.

ADDITIONAL RESOURCES

Reading Material

McEwan-Adkins, Elaine K. *How to Deal with Parents Who Are Angry, Troubled, Afraid, or Just Plain Crazy*. 2nd ed. Thousand Oaks, CA: Corwin Press, 2005.

Stevens, Larry J. *Parents Want to Know: Questions for Principals*. Lanham, MD: Scarecrow Education, 2004.

Whitaker, Todd, and Douglas J. Fiore. *Dealing with Difficult Parents and Parents with Difficult Situations*. Larchmont, NY: Eye on Education, 2001.

6

I DIDN'T GO TO LAW SCHOOL, AND NEITHER DID YOU

If I could choose to be a part of any profession other than teaching, I would want to be a lawyer. However, lawyers are not always represented in the best light. In fact, many jokes portray them as weasels, worms, or worthless. Of course, that is, until you need one. In your role as the campus leader, you will take on many other duties such as counselor, nurse, and even resident lawyer. Federal and state mandates require your undivided attention regarding the guidelines and requirements of special programs offered on your campus. School board policies must be adhered to, so that any practices you establish on your campus correlate with said policies. Custody issues are moving into the school arena more and more, leaving principals and teachers at a loss about what to do.

Somewhere in your preparation as an administrator you took a course focused on school law. If for some reason you did not take such a course, I strongly recommend you do. Several educational resource centers provide training days directly related to the educational law issues that find their way into our schools. If this chapter teaches you anything, I want you to remember that you are an educator, not a lawyer. Most school districts keep a school lawyer on retainer to help in a variety of ways. Let the lawyers take care of the possibility of litigation should it arise, and you take care of the school so that you never need the lawyer.

DUST OFF THE HANDBOOK

In an effort to improve education and close the achievement gaps that were continually occurring, Congress passed the No Child Left Behind Act (NCLB) of 2001. The intent of this educational reform act was to ensure that every child in the United States would receive an education supported by a stringent accountability system for schools and students, scientific research would find its way into the decision-making process, and student learning would once again be the focus of the instructional process of a school (U.S. Department of Education 2004). Qualifications for teachers and paraprofessionals, funding issues, and professional development opportunities are only a few of the key points addressed in this act. Because this was a federal act, state and local education entities were required to follow the mandates and proceed to take action on their own.

Now of course, there is so much more attached to NCLB. The point is that you, at the principal's level, must adhere to what the district has to do that comes directly from the federal government. If the law states that every third grade must pass a reading test with a certain score, then you hire qualified teachers to make that happen, provide several opportunities for additional help, and use research-based decision making to find the right reading program for your students. If the law says that a senior in high school has to pass an end-of-the-year test in math to graduate, then you do whatever you can to help that child succeed. When a mandate is in play, you don't get to pick up your blocks and go home. You have to stay and play, whether you want to or not.

There are also other types of mandates that you need to be equally aware of, and those are school board policies. In a way, school board policies act as mandates established in your district that will affect the practices you initiate on your campus. In general, school boards receive their directives from the state educational agency. If that policy needs any revision to specifically address the needs of the district, then the school board creates a local policy based on the legal policy from the state educational agency. Got that, clear as mud? Using these policies, the district then establishes certain practices and expectations, usually referred to as the student handbook.

For the most part, many of your parents will sign a form that states that they have read and understand the information found in the student handbook, whether it's about the code of conduct or how many days of school a child can miss without being retained for school that year. Elementary students receive a smelly sticker that they can wear all day long that signifies they brought back their signed handbook page. Children in the elementary grades would kill for a smelly sticker. Older students are promised an extra ten points on their next project if they return a signed acknowledgment page.

What is the importance of the acknowledgment page and having it signed by a parent or guardian? That signature guarantees that the person who signed the paper has read and clearly understands what the handbook says about how the school will work, the discipline plan adopted by the school, and student and parent expectations while living and learning in that particular school environment.

Most of the time in elementary schools, the school handbook is sent out the first few days of school along with all the other paperwork that needs to be signed and returned to school the next day. Why the next day? You are correct—another chance to earn a smelly sticker.

My advice to you is to take that student handbook and read it from cover to cover, highlighting the most important parts, tabbing certain pages for quick referral, and then addressing those key issues at several faculty meetings. If you do this, you don't have to have a mother in your office one day at 7:45 a.m. complaining about the teacher who deducted 25 points from her child's paper for not putting his heading on the assignment. And after reading the handbook all night, you find there was nothing that said 25 points would be deducted from a paper without the proper heading.

When this happened to me, I turned to my handy-dandy tabbed, color-coded handbook and began looking for anything that could address this concern. Sure enough, there was no connection between an improper heading on a paper and a disciplinary action being taken. The particular parent had indeed read the entire handbook from front to cover. She was now a formidable opponent in the area of handbook knowledge. The issue still remained unresolved. The parent found no information in the handbook, which was based on district policies, that supported the teacher's actions. I now faced a dilemma.

It has always been my personal philosophy to support my teachers. I usually told them, "I'll support you as far as you have allowed me to."

In this particular case, the teacher was very frustrated that after she had repeatedly told the student to put a proper heading on an assignment, he was still not doing as she asked. So out of the blue, she told her students that if a proper heading was missing from an assignment 25 points would be missing from their final grade. She announced her new practice in all her classes and asked several times if the students had a clear understanding of how their grades would be affected by simply not putting a heading on a piece of paper.

When the little boy took home his graded assignments for the week, the mother noticed that one of his math assignments was a 75; however, she could not find any incorrect answers. She asked her son how this had happened. He replied, "I told you my teacher didn't like me. She took off 25 points because I forgot to put my name on the top of the paper." At that point, the mother found her copy of the student handbook, made herself a cup of tea, sat curled up on the couch, and read the entire student handbook. When she could not locate any policy that substantiated the teacher's actions, she found me the next morning.

The only thing the mother really wanted was the return of the 25 points. She argued that the teacher could not arbitrarily make up classroom practices that did not correlate with the student handbook. I assured her that was not our practice and that I would look into it. I asked the mother to give me a little time to find out what had happened. By asking her for a little time, I also gave myself an opportunity to talk with the teacher. The mother agreed to that.

After the mother left my office, I went to the teacher's room to find out exactly what had happened. She proceeded to tell me that because the students were not putting their names on their papers she was having a difficult time giving the right person credit for the completed work. Her thinking was that if a student lost 25 points, which dropped him from an A to a C, she would get the student's attention. I informed her that her edict regarding the loss of points for a lack of an improper heading did not match a policy in the school handbook, and therefore the points had to be returned to the child's assignment. When the time came to review the student handbook, this issue of an improper heading would definitely be revisited.

The teacher did not agree with my decision at the time. I was not supporting her in this situation, and I was certainly knuckling down to the whims of a parent. Whims of a parent or not, the handbook was created from the state laws and guidelines that govern the educational process. The district created the student handbook based on those policies, and the campuses were held to those policies as well. I suggested she make herself a cup of tea, find a relaxing place to curl up, and read the handbook more closely until the policy changed. The next year the issue was placed in the handbook with only a 10-point loss for no heading.

By no means will this be the only issue that transpires because of the inconsistencies between classroom practices and school policies. Just remember that it is vital that you, as the instructional leader of that campus, are fully aware of what the handbook says and that you equally remind teachers about the guidelines found in that book.

LET THE LAW WORK FOR YOU

As much as I regret having to tell a teacher that something he or she did or did not do was out of compliance with the student handbook or school board policies, I also enjoy being the person who uses the handbook to support my teachers. When the student handbook is created, this document actually becomes the lawful expectations for students and teachers. By signing the acknowledgment page, the parents and guardians agree to those laws. Let them work for you.

Take, for instance, a policy from the handbook that states the instructional day will not be disturbed, or something along the lines that the interruptions to the instructional day will be limited and in some instances prohibited. This policy will help you tremendously when a parent asks to stay in the child's classroom for the entire day. This usually doesn't happen on a secondary campus, but it does happen regularly on a primary or elementary campus.

You can honestly tell the parent that you would love for him or her to visit with the teacher on her conference time and that by all means a short visit to the classroom is just fine. And with your most caring voice, you also say, "We are so happy to have you visit our school. As you know, we don't want anything to interrupt the instructional day, and so a short visit of about thirty minutes will be just fine." You have successfully used your knowledge of the handbook as well as accommodated the parent.

At the same time, you have ensured that your teacher's day and instructional time will not be compromised by the parent's visit.

Upon entering many school campuses, you are likely to see a sign in several languages, stuck to the entry doors, that states that all visitors must report to the office upon entering the school. This message is also usually found in the handbook. It is in place to remind any visitor to the school to notify the office when they are on the campus. For the most part, this works. Except for the mother or father who does not read the sign, enters the school, and heads directly to the child's classroom.

On one such day, a fourth-grade teacher used her intercom to inform our secretary that there was a man looking in the window of her classroom. He would walk by her door and just peer in. As soon as the secretary heard this, she informed me and off I went. Sure enough, there was a rather large man pacing in front of the classroom and looking in the window. Think back to a previous chapter where we discussed a red cape. I did not have one on and I knew I was not invisible, but there the man stood.

I approached him, introduced myself as the principal, and asked if could help him with anything. He told me no; he was just there to check on his son, who happened to be in that particular classroom. I invited him to my office so that we could continue our conversation there. My thinking was that if I could get him away from the classroom and into the confines of the office, we could alert the teachers of an emergency situation, lock the classroom doors, and call the police, if necessary.

When he came into my office, he shared with me that he liked to just pop in and surprise his son. He had told his son that he planned to sporadically check on him to make sure he was doing his work and behaving at school. The father shared with me that this was a common practice of his and that his son's previous school knew what he was doing. At that point I shared with him the school's policy of asking all visitors to check in with the office before going to a classroom. I also shared with him that when he just popped in, his son's teacher had no idea who he was and began to panic. The father was very gracious, understood the safety concerns for the school, and from that day on always came by the office first.

Your knowledge of school law will also allow you to say no to certain requests because the request does not follow the handbook procedures or is in violation of a school board policy. If some organization wants to go from room to room asking your kids to join a group, that falls into the interruption-of-school-day policy. You direct the organization toward the central administration office, where someone will approve the informational flier they have; once that is done, you will disseminate the information to your classes.

This knowledge also helped me when a teacher came in from car duty one day to let me know that a parent was going from car to car asking other parents to sign a petition regarding an existing school practice she disagreed with. This is one instance when I did not leap from my pink chair to solve a situation. I simply looked up our school policy on petitions and found that in a closed system, like a school during operational hours, no petitions could be conducted on school property. If the mother wanted to stand across the street or attend a PTA meeting with other parents to ask for signatures on the petition, she could. Those were considered open systems, and that's where petitions were permitted.

This mother's usual practice was to wait in the hallway and pick up her son as he left the school. Actually, this was a pretty good plan. She would discuss her son's day with him, and if she had any questions about an assignment or his behavior, she would address it immediately before they went home. On this particular day, I stopped to speak with her in the hallway before her son's class was released. I informed her that she could not ask people to sign a petition while she was on school property, based on the closed-system policy. She did not know about the law and assured me it would never happen again. It did not. Instead she came in the next day and asked for a grievance form. She planned to file a grievance against me with the superintendent regarding this matter.

Isn't school life exciting? While I had indeed protected my other parents from an unwanted petition and followed school policies, I was now going to have to be a part of a grievance process, and those things are never fun.

Because more and more custody cases are entering our schools, principals are having to learn how to read divorce decrees, learn the difference between primary and joint conservatorships, and try to understand what visitation rights a parent has been granted from the courts. In most school districts, there are policies in place with regard to who stands as a parent for a child. For instance, as long as a person can prove he or she is the biological parent of a child and that a court has not taken away his or her custodial rights, that parent has access to any and all educational information the school can provide. A person who cannot prove this may have no access to the child's records and may not even see the child while the child is in school.

A parent once visited my office and asked to see his son, Adam. While I had never met this man, I knew he had to be Adam's biological father because he looked exactly like Adam. When he came into my office to discuss the situation, he very politely provided his driver's license to prove to me that he was who he claimed to be. However, he and Adam had different last names. I pulled Adam's school folder and looked at his birth certificate. This man was not listed as the biological father.

Discovering this, I informed this Adam look-alike that I could not permit him to see Adam during school hours because he was not listed in our records as Adam's father. The man became very angry and told me that Adam's mother had promised that if he gave her some money she would have his name placed on Adam's birth certificate as the biological father. For whatever reason, the mother had never followed through with her promise. This man was very distraught and wanted to know if he could just see Adam to say hello. I had to deny his request because of the information in our files. I did not question the fact that this man was indeed Adam's father, but our school policies were very clear regarding this issue.

Another fun time that occurred on the last day of school involved a father, who had driven all the way from Alaska to get his daughter for the summer—and the police. On the last day of school, almost at the last hour of the school year, a parent came to the office and said he was there to take his daughter for the summer and he had the papers to prove he could do that. The secretary showed him into my office to let me handle the situation.

The father lived in Alaska and his daughter spent the summer with him every year. This year he decided to make a vacation of it and took a ferry from Alaska, hit the Northwestern coast of the United States, and drove all the way to Texas to pick her up. I asked to see his custody papers, which indeed said that he gained custody of his daughter at 3:00 p.m. on the last day of the school year. He knew his rights, and he wanted his daughter immediately.

Now, we have already established that you and I are not lawyers, and I know that I am not an expert in custodial rights. When I read over the section on vacation times, I did read that he took custody of his daughter at 3:00 p.m. on the last day of the school year. I do need to let you know that at the same time I was in my office talking with the father, I asked our school secretary to call the child's mother to let her know what was happening.

Here is another example of how the law can work for you and not against you. On the first reading of the decree, it did appear that the father could indeed take the child away from my campus. However, the last day of our school year was an early dismissal day, and the children were released for the summer at 1:00 p.m. He was not granted custody, according to the custody papers, until 3:00 p.m. By this time, the mother had arrived at the school, followed by two police cars. She had anticipated trouble from the father and wanted some protection.

So, picture this: It is the last day of school for the year. Children are running to their buses. Parents are waiting in the pickup line to take their babies home for the summer. Teachers are dancing and cheering on the sidewalk as the last bus and car pull away. When all of a sudden, a mother drives into the parking lot on two wheels at about eighty miles per hour, followed by two city police vehicles.

In my office, the conversation between the father and I was still going on. I explained to him that the decree said that he may have his daughter for the summer at 3:00 p.m. on the last day of school. It was only 1:00 p.m., and I would not release the child to him. He explained he had driven a very long way and wanted his daughter. About that time, the secretary knocked on my door to inform me of the circus happening in our parking lot. I asked the father to wait in my office while I dealt with the mother. During this entire process, I had asked our counselor to take the little girl into her office until I could sort out the situation. When the mother reached the school, the counselor was informed and brought the little girl to her.

After talking with the mother and the police officers, clearing out the last car rider for the year, and waving good-bye to my students on the bus, I went back into my office to deal with Dad. I told him that our school was not the place to pick up his daughter for the summer and that I would greatly appreciate his taking the situation to another location. I may have told him that the police were there to ensure that there were no problems, when they had really been called by the mother. In the end, the father, mother, and police officers left in a caravan to the mother's home, where the little girl did in fact leave with the father that same day.

SPEED-DIALING THE LAWYER

One class on school law cannot possibly inform you of all the policies and practices that are associated with the day-to-day operation of a school. That is not the real intent of a course of that nature. The course is designed to teach you how to locate and interpret as best you can what the law or policy means for you, your teachers, and your school. Because you are an intelligent human being with a master's degree in educational administration, you are able to read the law and quite possibly apply that law when necessary. But in some instances, your ability to read and interpret the law is not enough. Sometimes you need the school's lawyer.

First and foremost, let me remind you that most of the time you will not actually be the one to contact the lawyer. Usually, the person who contacts the school lawyer is the superintendent, after a situation occurs that might end up in a litigious battle. The school's lawyer provides sound advice and works on the behalf of the district. Most of the cases that arrive on the desk of the school's lawyer involve personnel issues, sexual harassment allegations, or injury to a child. Hopefully, you will never be a part of any of these concerns.

Sometime in your career as a principal, an angry parent or a disgruntled employee might threaten you by saying he or she is going to sue you. I will never forget the first time a parent said that to me. His daughter had been a student of ours the year before and had transferred to another school. The teacher was using some of his daughter's completed work as an example of how the assignment should be completed. When the father found out about this he was enraged and called the school's office and asked to speak with me.

When I answered the phone, he tore into me with a tirade of how he was going to sue the teacher, me, and the school. Because I had only been a principal for two years, I was still trying to pacify people. I have since changed my feelings on that. I asked him what had happened, and he proceeded to tell me that his daughter's work was being displayed in the classroom by her former teacher and that I had better stop it and stop it now. Since I had no idea what he was talking about, I asked him to give me some time to investigate his allegations. After he hung up the phone, I went to talk with the teacher about this situation. She informed me that she was in fact using the girl's assignment to show how the assignment should be completed, but that if it bothered the father she would certainly stop. Then the teacher reminded me that the little girl no longer was enrolled in our school and the father had no cause for threatening her, me, or the school with litigation.

Lightbulbs flashed throughout my mind. Buzzers went off in my head. Who did this father think he was? His daughter no longer was a student at our school. He no longer lived in our school district. At first, I was furious with the father. Then, I was furious with myself for not being quick enough to stop him during his initial tirade at me. As an inexperienced principal, I only heard his words about suing me and became nervous.

I did call the father back and was very calm when I reminded him that he no longer paid any taxes in our school district and his daughter was no longer a student of ours. Therefore, he would have to present a stronger cause for litigation to me other than that he did not want his daughter's work shown in class. The teacher had also been very smart in that she had marked out the student's name on the paper, and no one knew who had completed the assignment. My question back to him was how had he learned that the teacher was using his daughter's work as an example? For that he had no answer, hung up on me, and never called our office again.

This parent had actually served a purpose. When he said he was going to sue me I called the superintendent, who called our school lawyer. The lawyer told the superintendent that there was nothing to worry about and the parent's complaints were unfounded. What I want you to realize is that from the minute the superintendent called the lawyer, he was charging our district a fee. I never understood that. I thought we could simply call the school's lawyer and he would graciously provide an answer for us. What I learned from this situation was priceless: The school lawyer is there to help, but the superintendent is the one who makes the call, not you.

When I teach the law class for the principal preparation program at my university, I usually invite a school lawyer to come to the class and share some of the most important points of law that new principals need to know. He reminds them about first amendment rights, the importance of documentation, and how to keep their schools safe from the possibility of being sued, just to mention a few topics. His intent is not to scare future administrators or make them believe they have to tiptoe around their schools for fear they will be sued; his intent is to make them think about their words and actions and, in turn, make their staff think about what they say and do. The responsibility of the school lawyer is to keep you from needing his services. Oftentimes, they are paid a retainer to not be used. As I said before, I should have been a lawyer.

My experience with school lawyers has been very limited because I actually tried to follow all the laws and policies I could. In my later years in the principalship when someone threatened to sue me, by that time I had learned I was protected from most forms of litigation. I joined several professional organizations that also protected me with a slew of legal help, advice, and protection. Fortunately for me, my obsessive-compulsive disorder makes me a stickler for following the law. However, there are some times when the spirit of the law outweighs the letter of the law.

RECOGNIZE THE SPIRIT OF THE LAW

So there you are, sitting in your office, leading the school. Your school handbook is tabbed with floppy yellow sticky notes that clearly signify to anyone that you are well versed in the information found on those pages. You know when and why to contact the superintendent if a legal issue arises on your campus. The school board policy manual is designated as a favorite site on your computer and is just a click away when you need it. You are simply waiting for the Scout badge you have dutifully earned for being such a well-prepared and law-abiding principal, when suddenly you are faced with a situation that deals more with the needs of the heart than the cut-and-dried regulations of the law.

School attendance situations require you to follow the letter of the law. Policies state that students must be in attendance a certain number of days to be awarded credit for that school year. These policies are clear and succinct. They include information regarding excused and unexcused absences, completion of assignments, and the need for medical release statements. Based on your school district, these policies set the groundwork for the establishment of school practices, such as what to do when a child is often late to school, what kind of written excuses you can accept for school absences, and how much time to allow a student to make up missed assignments. Some days, being the principal is just plain fun. For me, reading some of the excuses that parents sent to the school bordered on the ridiculous.

At the elementary level, our office collected absence notices on a daily basis. We received notes that a child was absent because his father had just been released from prison and the mother wanted the father and son to have some time to themselves. So the mother allowed him to miss a week of school. Other notes would inform us that Little Suzie's mother could not bear to be away from her and that was the reason the child was missing so much school. That note came from the minister of a church. Or my favorite: Billy was not in school today because it was the first day of deer season and they had to head toward the deer lease. Of course, all of these were considered unexcused absences.

During the first faculty meeting of a new school year, I led the teachers through a quick review of the school's practices and policies regarding many areas, but especially, school attendance. Because funding is based on the daily average attendance of students, we were always trying to ensure that our kids came to school every day. I asked the teachers to notify the office when a student had been absent for two consecutive days, and we would make the necessary phone calls to find out why the child was not at school. The teachers were also asked to inform the office if they heard any stories from the other students about why a particular child was absent. Children were always quick to tell on other students.

One memorable incident happened with Wayne. Wayne had been absent from school for a few days, and we became concerned because we could not reach anyone at his home. Some of the kids told the teacher that he and his family had taken a trip to Disney World. The teacher of course reported this to the office, and I informed her that as soon as Wayne returned to school I wanted to personally see him and the excuse he brought from home.

When Wayne returned to school, he did have an excuse. The note from his parents stated that he had been terribly ill with a stomach virus. When Wayne came into my office, the first thing I asked him was if he had enjoyed Disney World, whereupon he proceeded to tell me all about the cruise his family had taken and how much fun Disney World had been. I told him I was sorry to hear about his stomach virus and hoped it had not stopped him from enjoying the trip. This delightful little child looked at me and told me that when his parents were writing the note he just knew Mrs. T. would not accept the excuse. He was right. Knowing his parents as I did, I just knew they would take issue with the way I handled the situation, but they never called me.

Another attendance situation involved a little girl named Sarah. Sarah had missed school a great deal because she was in the process of many medical tests to determine what exactly was causing her to be so ill. She had exceeded the allowed days for excused and unexcused absences. The mother came to see me after she had received our district's letter that was automatically sent to any parent whose child had missed a certain number of days. The mother sat in my office in tears. Her child was very sick, and the doctors could not determine what was causing her illness. And to add to the situation, Sarah's grandfather was not expected to live much longer, and the two were very close. As the mother cried, she asked for my help with the attendance issue. Would it be possible to extend the number of excused days so that Sarah could spend some time with her grandfather before he passed away?

The letter of the law in this situation was clear. A child could only miss a certain number of days, as decreed by school board policy. Sarah had far exceeded that number, was sure to miss more days because of her own medical condition, and now the mother was asking me to fudge the number of unexcused absences so that Sarah could spend time with her ailing grandfather.

With all my grandfather had meant to me, how could I not consider the mother's request and forget the attendance policy? Hadn't my grandfather meant the world to me? Would this actually be the last time the two could be together before he died? I had no choice. As the mother cried for her child, the grandfather's situation, and the warning letter from the district, I knew what had to be done. I told her that she was to send the written excuses for Sarah's absences to me personally, and I would take care of everything else. She thanked me for being so understanding and hugged me on her way out of my office. While I had not followed the letter of the law, I certainly had followed the spirit of the law.

There may be times when you face the same kind of situation. Please remember that school policies exist to help and protect your school and its children, and that while those policies and practices are in place to provide structure and organization to the school day, the law has two parts and one of those parts involves helping someone when you can. I am by no means suggesting you ever break the law nor do anything unethical. Just remember to look at each situation in an individual light and sometimes let the spirit of the law lead you.

DEVELOPING YOUR PERSONAL LEADERSHIP CAPACITY

Throughout history, there have been many wise and intelligent leaders. These people have led countries, nations, companies, and yes, schools. With ethical and lawful wisdom, they have saved their respective citizens money and property rights. Why can't one of these famous people be you?

Where legal issues are concerned, you are employed by a school district. When a parent is angry at you for adhering to a certain policy that has resulted in an action regarding her child, your choices are limited. In fact, there is only one choice for you. You, as the principal of the school, as an employee of the district, have no choice but to adhere to the policies and mandates set forth by the school board. You do not get to pick or choose which policies you want to follow. Therefore, your capacity for leadership needs to include the following:

1. Try to understand the person's point of view, as well as inform the parents of what you can and cannot do regarding school policies.
2. Stay abreast of current legislation that affects the public school domain.
3. Keep the superintendent and central office staff aware of potential legal problems that might arise. Impending lawsuits never bring happiness into the lives of school superintendents.
4. Where special programs are involved, know and understand the legal issues tied to the services provided by the program.
5. Establish school practices based on school policies, not on arbitrary decisions.

WHAT WILL MY PRINCIPALSHIP SAY ABOUT ME?

When you decide to leave the campus or retire, what do you want
people to say about the way you followed the law in regard to school
policies and practices? Do you want them to remember you as someone who possessed the wisdom of Solomon, or someone who used the
law as a crutch or an excuse to say or do things on your campus? Upon
leaving the school, I would want people to say some of the following
things:

"If I had a question about what a policy meant, she always found that
policy, made me a copy, and put it in my box."

"I just loved to see him in action when a parent threatened to sue
him. He would calmly pull out the handbook, show them a copy of their
signature on the handbook acknowledgment page, ask them if that was
their signature, and then just sit back and wait."

"She always knew what was going on in the realm of school law, and I
so appreciated her letting us know something as soon as she heard it."

"He always did what was right by my child. I know he had rules to
follow, but he still made every effort to help me when he could."

USING YOUR 20/20 VISION

Much of what you do as the principal happens while you are sitting behind your desk. Most of the parent meetings you have will find you on
one side of the desk and the parents on the other. You will probably not
walk the campus with your school handbook in tow. More than likely
you will keep the tabbed copy in your office. With your 20/20 vision for
being a proactive and readied principal, use the following checklist to
ensure your success:

- ☐ I know where the school handbook is located.
- ☐ I have read our school handbook.
- ☐ I have discussed the school handbook with the staff on numerous
  occasions.
- ☐ Each staff member has a copy of the school handbook.
- ☐ I ask the teachers if any changes to the handbook are needed.

☐ I have talked with the school's attorney about his or her role in our district.
☐ I am aware of the school programs offered on our campus.
☐ I am aware of the legal implications when providing services to the children.

MY WISH FOR YOU

My wish for you is that you use the law to protect both you and your school
. And that you know just how the law can become an important tool.
My wish for you is that you quickly learn how to read essential policies
And that they keep your school safe from harm and any impropriety.
My wish for you is that on those special times when the spirit of the law wins out
That doing what is right for kids never leaves you with any doubts.

ADDITIONAL RESOURCES

Reading Material

Alexander, Kern, and M. David Alexander. *American Public School Law.* 7th ed. Florence, KY: Wadsworth Cengage Learning, 2008.

Bosher, W. C., Kaminski, K. R., Vacca, R. S. *School Law Handbook: What Every Leader Needs to Know.* Alexandria, VA: Association for Supervision and Curriculum Development. 2004.

Dunklee, Dennis R., and Robert J. Shoop. *The Principal's Quick-Reference Guide to School Law: Reducing Liability, Litigation, and Other Potential Legal Tangles.* Thousand Oaks, CA: Corwin Press, 2006.

Essex, N. *School Law and the Public Schools: A Practical Guide for Educational Leaders.* 4th ed. Needham Heights, MA: Allyn & Bacon. 2007.

Shoop, Robert J., and Dennis R. Dunklee. *Anatomy of a Lawsuit: What Every Education Leader Should Know about Legal Actions.* Thousand Oaks, CA: Corwin Press, 2005.

Internet Sources

nsba.org/MainMenu/School?Law/issues.aspx

This is an excellent site that provides current information and resources surrounding many aspects of school law that face school leaders, such as NCLB, athletics, finances, and many more.

www.findlaw.com
The information that can be found at this site includes educational laws as well as historical information regarding the laws that have been enacted that affected school governance, the welfare of students, and contractual requirements.

topics.law.cornell.edu/wex/table_education
Cornell University Law School makes this site available. Information regarding educational statutes for all the fifty states can be accessed from this website. This source also provides educational codes and policies for each state.

www.cleweb.org/
The Center for Law and Education provides educators and administrators with useful information when searching for guidance on a particular aspect of school law.

www.edlawrc.com
The Educational Law Resource site contains valuable information for any stakeholder interested in learning more about how school law impacts instruction, discipline concerns, and federal mandates.

7

SHEPHERDING THE PUPS

Recently, as my mother was taking her pooch Pixy on their customary walk, Mother noticed a scrawny little calico cat hiding under a vacant yellow house. She also noticed that not far behind the skinny little thing of a cat were four wild baby kittens. Because my mother has always been a champion for animals, she began to feed the cat, who later became known as Mother Kitty.

Mother began her Meals on Wheels program to the little yellow house on a daily basis. Some days Mother Kitty would even venture to Mother's house for dinner. This played out for several months, until Mother Kitty decided to relocate her brood to my mother's garage. Now living at Mother's house were three other cats, a dog, Mother Kitty, a small black-and-white kitten, a beautiful calico kitten, and twin yellow tabby kittens. The black-and-white and calico kittens were so pretty they were given away very quickly. My mother thought the twin yellow tabby kittens were so cute together that she did not give them away.

During one of my visits, Mother told me she was very worried about Mother Kitty. She had not seen her since that morning when she opened the garage door. Mother had called and called for Mother Kitty and she was nowhere to be found. I told Mother that I would walk up to the little yellow house and see if for some reason Mother Kitty was there.

I took off down the street, around the corner, and toward the little house. There lying on the front sidewalk of the little yellow house was Mother Kitty. Now, I do not have a degree in animal psychiatry, but it appeared that Mother Kitty was waiting for the kittens that had been given away to find her. After some gentle coaxing and cooing of my own, Mother Kitty began following me back to Mother's house. I started to Mother's house on the path I had taken. Mother Kitty followed a path of her own.

She crossed the street in front of the little yellow house, walked into the bushes next to a church, followed a line of shrubs toward the front of the church, moved down the church's driveway, crossed Mother's street, headed toward another line of bushes, slunk along the side of the house next to Mother's, and finally ended up back in the safety of the garage, where two hungry yellow tabby kittens happily met her.

When retelling Mother Kitty's path to my mother, she said, "She is such a good mother kitten. Can you imagine her making that trip four times carrying those little fat bundles? Mother Kitty knew what she was doing. She did her job and brought her kittens to me for safety. What a good mother kitten."

When I started this chapter, the story of how that mother cat followed a certain path to bring her litter to safety and then found them a safe haven in Mother's garage reminded me of how new and first-year teachers sometimes get lost, need someone to help them find their way, and are looking for a safe haven in which to live.

First-year teachers are usually filled with an excitement that can be compared to the first time a person rides a roller coaster. You know that the roller coaster ride is going to be fast and furious. Just from looking at the structure, you can tell there are many ups and downs. Unfortunately, some of our first-year teachers don't finish the ride. I can't help but wonder how many of them would have stayed in the profession after their first year if they had had a caring administrator to hold their hands as they climbed into the seat of that roller coaster ride.

Our new teachers walk into schools every year with only a college degree, a semester of student teaching, and a hopeful spirit that they have chosen the right profession for themselves. When they reach our campuses, we as administrators are responsible for their welfare and success in the classroom. If we are to truly impact the teaching profession, a principal must accept the responsibility to take a special hand in guiding these pups through the hard times, assist them as they face the overwhelming duties of a teacher, and teach them to celebrate and recognize even the smallest achievements for themselves and their students.

THE PUPS THAT GOT AWAY

During my time as a principal, I have had the opportunity to see a broad spectrum of newly graduated teachers sit in an interview process as they applied for their first teaching position. The interview time allowed the recommendation committee a chance to meet and talk with a wide variety of aspiring teachers.

Some of the candidates became teachers because they were excited and eager to help young children learn. Some couldn't wait to become a teacher so they could use their Rambo-like abilities to whip a class into shape. Many of these hopeful candidates sincerely sought a teaching position because of their genuine love for children and their desire to make a difference.

In some cases, the committee's recommendations for hiring were exactly what the school and our children needed. The teachers we wanted would most definitely become valuable members of our campus family and add to the culture of our school. However, not all of my recommendations fell into this category. I did make a few that I still regret. One of those was Maggie.

Maggie had always wanted to be a teacher. In fact, she was one of our district's best substitute teachers. Many of the teachers and the students requested her. Maggie's skills at substitute teaching were impeccable. So when she finished her undergraduate work and became a certified teacher, she applied for a full-time teaching position on our campus. Her interview went well and was actually one of the best the interview team had seen. I submitted her name for employment and she became my teacher.

The school year started extremely well for Maggie. The children and parents seemed to love her and it appeared she was doing a great job. What I didn't notice at the time was Maggie's mounting frustration and anxiety at trying to keep up with the kids, plan for her lessons, turn in needed paperwork, and still be an effective teacher.

She had been very successful as a substitute teacher, but she was finding that being responsible for an entire classroom of students on a daily basis, ensuring that their learning was a constant, and dealing with issues such as their safety and when to let them go to the bathroom was more than she had imagined. Substituting in a teacher's classroom for one or two days meant she followed prearranged plans, left discipline notes for the teacher if needed, and did not have to regularly deal with co-workers or parents. Now all of that was hers to deal with, and she was struggling.

Maggie truly believed her first and most important duty lay with instruction and student learning. This is exactly what she should have believed. However, a teacher's responsibilities toward the students and the classroom require a balance between this thinking and the day-to-day activities and commitment it takes to make that learning happen for children. Maggie had the heart. Unfortunately, she did not know how to tackle the insurmountable workload that a teacher faces.

Around the first of November, I noticed that Maggie's lesson plans were not being turned in on time and she was staying more and more to herself. During classroom visits, I watched Maggie with her children as they participated in small reading groups and as she interacted with them as they moved easily from center to center. I was very pleased to see that her children were learning. However, I also became aware of the condition of Maggie's room.

If I have not mentioned it before, I carry a dominant gene for OCD (obsessive-compulsive disorder), and I believe all people should carry this gene. I am a firm believer that children should have a learning environment that is orderly, clean, and well kept. As I looked around Maggie's room, a small line of sweat started beading on my upper lip. There were stacks of papers clumped on every available space. Papers, books, and pencils were piling out of the students' desks. The disorganization and mess I saw on her desk actually started my hands shaking, and I just knew that any moment I would need an oxygen mask.

While I applauded her instructional methods, I was appalled by her managerial techniques and the room's learning environment. After the walk-through, I asked to speak with Maggie. During this meeting I offered several suggestions on how to improve her classroom organization.

I also took the opportunity to ask about her lesson plans and how she was getting along with her fellow grade-level teachers. Maggie listened intently and agreed that she did have some room for improvement. She planned to start implementing some of those changes immediately. Regrettably, it did not happen.

Other concerns for Maggie's well-being at school began to surface. If you don't already know, there exists a teachers' networking system on every campus that is stronger and faster than the Pony Express, a flock of carrier pigeons, and an electronic mail system all rolled into one. An emissary from our campus grapevine group let me know that Maggie was not only having trouble in the classroom, she was also having trouble outside the classroom.

Every week each grade level met to talk and discuss their plans for the upcoming week. It came to my attention that Maggie was not attending these meetings. She was also eating lunch by herself in her room. It appeared that while Maggie had developed a wonderful and caring relationship with her students, she was not expending any energy on building a working relationship with her colleagues. For a first-year teacher, this was detrimental.

Once again, I met with Maggie about her need to become a part of her grade level. She assured me she would work on this and things would change for the better. By February, I knew things would not improve, and my frustration level with Maggie was beginning to show.

For principals, March is usually the month designated for recommending personnel to a school board for continued employment. For those teachers who hold a probationary contract, this is the time that principals have to make some very hard but necessary decisions. A principal must review the abilities of those with these contracts very carefully, and that is exactly what I had to do in Maggie's case.

Maggie's love for her children never wavered. She taught every day with zeal and purpose, but unfortunately the other necessary traits of being an effective teacher were missing. It was time to make some decisions about teacher contracts, and I had to make a decision to either non-renew Maggie's contract or allow her another year on a probationary contract.

The superintendent generally met with each principal at this time of year to discuss personnel issues and projected enrollment. During the

meeting, the superintendent asked me about my probationary people
and if I planned to non-renew any of their contracts. At this time I told
her about Maggie and said that I might extend to her one more probationary contract.

The superintendent just looked at me and said she would not take
Maggie's name to the school board for their approval. I tried to convince
her that Maggie just needed one more year and with my help, I thought
she would develop into a well-rounded teacher. In essence, the decision
about Maggie was already made.

Now all I had to do was tell a first-year teacher who loved her children
that I was planning to non-renew her contract. No matter how seasoned
the principal, telling someone that he or she will not have a job next year
is hard. Whenever I know I am about to face a difficult situation, I try to
schedule that type of meeting for late in the afternoon. If this meeting
goes badly and either the teacher or I become upset, most of the other
staff members are gone and no one witnesses any emotional outbursts.
Luckily, Maggie's conference fell in the late afternoon.

Upon entering Maggie's classroom on the day I planned to deliver the
news of her non-renewal, I found Maggie scurrying around trying to bring
some order to the chaos called her classroom. I asked if I could close her
door. Whenever you need to talk with a teacher about something as serious as a non-renewal, close the door. This is an act of privacy and respect
for your teachers, regardless of the manner or purpose of the meeting.

I began the conversation thanking Maggie for the effort I had noticed
in her working relationship with her peers and in turning in her lesson
plans on time. As we sat across from each other at her reading table I
noticed a glass container that had a jagged edge. She saw me looking at
the broken jar and commented that one of the students had knocked if
off the reading table and the jar had broken. She just hadn't thrown it
away yet. After seeing the jar and thinking about the potential danger
to my children, the task of telling her about the non-renewal became a
little easier for me.

I proceeded to tell Maggie that I would not be taking her name to the
board for contract renewal. At that time, I offered her the opportunity
to submit a letter of resignation instead of having the non-renewal on
her career record. I addressed her positive attributes of teaching and
her love for the students but also mentioned that there was much more
to teaching and it was in these areas that Maggie fell short.

She became very upset and started to cry. When she began to cry, I immediately assured her I intended to help her find another position. Then it turned nasty. She informed me that if I had offered her more help than I did maybe her struggles as a first-year teacher would not have been so difficult. Maybe if I had shown her where to turn in lesson plans instead of assuming she knew where they went, her lesson plans wouldn't have been late. Somehow the issue of her not meeting certain standards for effective teaching had turned into a conversation dealing with how I had abandoned her when I knew she was struggling.

After hearing those accusations, I silently started gathering my thoughts for a snippy comeback. How dare she say that I had not helped her? Didn't I make several suggestions regarding classroom management techniques? Hadn't I given her extended time to complete her lesson plans? How could Maggie possibly believe that her non-renewal was in fact a reflection of something I had not done?

Maggie was right. I sat at that little round reading table looking at the tear-stained face of a person whom I had let down. Oh, I had made suggestions about how to improve her organizational skills, but did I ever meet with her during her conference time and show her some of the tricks I had learned that made my life as a teacher easier? No, I did not.

During the first faculty meeting, I informed the entire staff that lesson plans were due every Monday morning by 8:30. But when I noticed that Maggie's lesson plans were late, did I ever ask her why? No, I did not.

When she stopped attending the weekly grade-level meetings, did I stop what I was doing, find her, and sit with her during the meeting? No, I did not. Part of the reason Maggie failed as a first-year teacher was directly due to the fact that I had failed to be the type of supervisor Maggie needed.

Reflectively, I have often wondered whether Maggie would have become a better teacher if I had been more attentive to her needs. I will never know. Have there been other first-year teachers who made it on their own? Many. Maybe with a little more help and guidance from me, Maggie would have improved. Instead of *telling* her what I thought she should have done, I needed to *show* her how to get things done.

Up until the Maggie time, I lived with the philosophy that if new teachers survived their first year without injuring a child or themselves, they would be successful. They'd last. Teachers like Maggie needed more guidance, more assistance. And to this day, I regret not helping her more than I did. After some time, I learned that Maggie had interviewed with several other school districts and never received another full-time teaching position.

While I fully accept that an earlier intervention on my part might have made a difference for Maggie, there are some first-year teachers who really do need to leave the profession and work as waitresses on cruise ships or as sheepherders in the mountains of Tibet—something very far removed from influencing the life of a child.

I just know I should have been more reflective of Maggie's needs and struggles. From that point on, I always made it a point to stay in better contact with my first-year teachers, to assign them a buddy teacher, and to be in their classrooms more as they moved through their first year.

WHERE IS THE COPIER AND OTHER NEEDED TIDBITS OF INFORMATION

On a recent visit to one of our favorite restaurants, my family and I sat in the back dining area. At a nearby table were a young boy and girl involved in a training session. Undoubtedly, they were new employees for the restaurant.

These new trainees attentively listened as the assistant manager gave them detail after detail about the training manual, company benefits, and how to take care of the customers. After the fifteen-minute training session was over, the young lady began her duties as a restaurant greeter and started seating arriving customers. The young man was handed an apron, a spray bottle, and a cleaning rag. He had just become the restaurant's newest busboy. But what happened next made all the difference to me.

In a few minutes, the waiter for the back area arrived and welcomed the new busboy. The waiter began a lengthy description of how to remove used plates from the tables, how to fold napkins, and how to set the silverware on the tables for new customers. The waiter even took the spray bottle and cleaning rag from the young boy's hands and showed him exactly how he wanted his customers to find their table when they arrived in his section.

I marveled at the waiter's patience, friendliness, and willingness to help this young man be a successful busboy. Not only did he give the young man the tools he needed to be successful, he took the time to fully explain his expectations for him. The waiter extended a helping hand just when the newly hired busboy needed one. This practice should become second nature to us as school leaders, when it comes to helping new teachers through their first year.

Many professions require an apprenticeship before declaring that someone is ready to take on the full responsibilities of his or her chosen profession. A fledgling waiter or waitress follows a seasoned server around for days before being given their own tables. Doctors complete many years interning in a variety of medical fields before opening their own practices. Those who want to be carpenters or electricians move through several steps before they become masters of their crafts. What do we do professionally for our teachers?

In most cases, they usually complete one semester of student teaching, visit a few classrooms during their undergraduate studies, walk across the stage at graduation, and are then deemed ready to be a teacher.

Newly hired teachers, regardless of their assigned grade levels, need as much help as they can get from a variety of sources. Much of their academic learning and experiences have been at the college level, infused with theoretical thinking and, hopefully, some field experiences. Now, as newbies, they have entered a place of fast-paced action, heavy responsibilities, and the need to make decisions on a moment's notice. They have entered the public school setting, which has no mercy on a fledgling teacher.

Think about it this way. Someone comes to you and asks you to teach him or her how to drive a car with a standard transmission. You explain how the clutch and the gas pedals work in tandem with each other. You demonstrate changing gears as you sit in a parked car on the flat surface of a driveway. But until that person is driving the car, sitting on an incline waiting for a light to change, and moving his or her feet back and forth on the gas and clutch pedals, will he or she have a clear understanding of what it takes to drive a car with a standard transmission?

The reality for the first-year teacher is much like that of the person who wants to learn how to drive a stick shift. His or her training up to that point has been in a college classroom with some interaction with children. The professors brought in many examples of what good and effective teaching looks like through the use of videos or PowerPoint presentations.

During their coursework, the first-year teacher wrote several papers on classroom and discipline management techniques or how to write behavioral lesson plans. However, now he or she is on a hill, driving a standard-shift car, and trying to remember which foot goes on which pedal so the car does not die in the middle of traffic.

Where does the hands-on training come from that will ensure that first-year teachers are successful? Does student teaching really provide a young teacher with the skills he or she will need to be effective on your campus? I am still amazed to learn that most student teaching time frames begin two weeks after the first day of school. Student teachers need to be in classroom with seasoned veterans a week *before* school starts to learn how to best organize their classrooms, how to send notes home to parents, and what personal techniques and practices teachers need in place to help them survive the first week of school.

Instead, student teachers arrive after all the school supplies are put up and organized, after the classroom discipline procedures are talked about, and after the veteran teacher has established his or her classroom procedures for going to lunch, taking a bathroom break, or walking in the hallways. You will have to excuse my outburst; I saw a soapbox and could not pass up the chance to jump on top of it and have my say.

Starting a school year can be a very hectic time for even the most seasoned and readied teacher. As for the principal, there are pages and pages of things to do. Custodial crews and maintenance workers are frantically trying to finish their projects. The principal is finalizing class rosters, checking to ensure there are enough books and furniture for all their students and classrooms, completing duty schedules, and checking to make sure that the three-page list of required changes left by the fire marshal is completed before one child steps foot on the campus. Needless to say, preparing for the first day of school is rather daunting.

I certainly did not have the time to explain to a newbie teacher, a college graduate, where the copier was located, how it worked, and where he or she could find the bulletin board paper, and I certainly did not have time to walk anyone around the school to explain where the gym or cafeteria was.

Oh, I made the perfunctory offers of help, but all the while I was thinking about the work I had to complete before the first day of school. Couldn't I just delegate someone to look after this pup? Surely, no one was working as hard and long as I was. Showing the new pup where to turn in lesson plans, stand for duty, or even how to bring children to lunch didn't even make it to the bottom of my very extensive to-do list. I could not have been more wrong in my thinking.

Because of the situation that happened with Maggie, I turned over a new leaf when it came to helping first-year teachers. I met with each one of them in my office on a personal basis before school started. We just sat and talked about their lives and what they wanted for themselves and their students that year. I made them a copy of a school map and pointed out the places that their children would travel to and from on a daily basis.

They were assigned a mentor teacher who I felt would really nurture and help them. And the perfunctory speech about how I was there for them if they ever needed me went on a back burner, and instead I visited their classrooms more than the other teachers' classrooms and asked how things were going. Did they have enough books? How was their classroom discipline plan working? The needs and wants of the newbie teacher did not change; my thinking about helping a newbie teacher changed.

However, I do not want to leave this chapter of the book with you thinking that I became the Mother Teresa of new teachers. I believe that I did help some new teachers get through that first year, better than I helped Maggie. Over the years, I witnessed many exciting, eager, and enthusiastic first-year teachers who were phenomenal individuals and loved and respected my children as much as I did. Unfortunately, my savior complex could not salvage all of them, and with a heavy heart, I did not renew all of their contracts.

I'll never forget my experience with one such teacher. She truly believed she was a great teacher who connected with her children on a variety of levels. Regrettably, this was not the case. As I watched the teacher-student relationship unfold, I began to see some flaws in her teaching. I talked with her about my concerns and she thanked me for my input but said she was fully aware of what her students needed.

During one classroom visit, I noticed that the children in the back of the room were not paying attention to her lecture. They were squirming around in their seats and snickering to each other. All of a sudden, she stopped her instruction and told them that she did not really care if they liked what she had to say or not. She had a job to do and she was going to do it.

When the children heard her say that she didn't care, they decided they didn't care either and continued to disrupt her lesson for a few minutes before I stepped in and stopped their off-task behaviors. Her first year of teaching proved to be a very difficult experience for her, the children, and me. She lasted only one year and decided to move on. That was a good decision.

Shepherding the new pups on your campus does require your active involvement. You will be unbelievably busy, but that is really no excuse for not checking in on your first-year teachers on a regular basis. Most of them will survive that first year and probably go on to have many wonderful years as a teacher. Some are destined not to make it that first year, no matter how much support you give them—even if you lead them by the hand to the copier and press the buttons for them.

Learn how to be a wise and caring leader who helps them find their true calling, whether it is to be a classroom teacher or a ticket taker at a movie theater. Be prepared to have tough conversations if necessary, because all that really, truly matters is the children and what they learn.

TRAINING THE PUPS

I am completely amazed by the skills and ability for learning that animals possess. Whether I am watching a rodeo where quarterhorses are racing around barrels turning on a dime or on the midway of a state fair watching a chicken ringing a bell, what animals learn to do leaves me speechless. Are they really that smart or did they have a really smart trainer who knew how to get that animal to perform?

A friend of mine recently brought a new puppy home and started the process of potty training the puppy. He was teaching him to go to the door and bark when he needed to go outside and do his business. My friend took him outside on a regular basis to establish a set potty time. He listened closely to the puppy's barking to distinguish when it meant the puppy wanted to play or when it meant he needed a potty break. There were a few times the puppy had an accident, but my friend cleaned up the mess and kept up the training.

And after a few short weeks, the puppy learned to waddle to the door, bark his little I-need-to-go-outside bark, and do his business outside. With a set regimen of training and the patience of my friend, the little puppy is fully trained. When we think about what we need to do to help our new teachers, there is really no difference between potty training a puppy and training the new pups on your campus. They both need to know how to take care of business.

Currently, I teach in a principal preparation program at a major university in Texas. Through my instruction, aspiring principals explore educational theories, school law, how to become effective instructional leaders, and much more. A main goal of our program is to educate our candidates in the many responsibilities associated with school leadership and hopefully ready and prepare them to be successful principals. The teacher preparation program is no different.

Through a variety of college courses, some internship experiences, and many purposeful assignments, new teachers receive a quality education so they in turn can provide meaningful learning experiences for children. They must prove themselves to be proficient in their particular areas of study, whether it is elementary education or high school algebra. I have to believe that this happens. I have to have faith in our institutions of higher learning that our new teachers are actually ready to face the overwhelming responsibilities of teaching a child.

If this is the way it is supposed to be, shouldn't the pups be secure in their knowledge of what to do on the first day of school? Won't they have the skills to control twenty-one energy-filled kindergarten students or twenty-five hormonal seventh-graders? Some practical instruction about the actual job of teaching, not just related theories about the practices of teaching, must exist.

I was responsible for visiting a group of post-baccalaureate students as a mentor from our university. Part of my practice was to meet the teacher and see her interacting with her students before the official visits actually started. On one of my routine visits, I learned that this particular teacher had been moved from a pull-out program class to be the homeroom teacher for twenty-one three-year-old children. At that time, she did not have any assistance in the form of a paraprofessional or parent volunteer.

The campus where this teacher worked was only for little people. That's right: three- and four-year-olds. I must admit I am a better

teacher with older children, especially high school students. I understand their mean ways and their foul-mouthed talk (not that I condone
it). They're my kind of kids. But because of my responsibilities as a university mentor, I had to visit the land of the little people a total of five
times each semester. I was definitely not in my comfort zone.

On my first mentor visit, I found my assigned teacher in the gym
surrounded by twenty-one little people. The look on her face far surpassed a deer-in-the-headlights kind of look. Children were screaming
shrill sounds so loudly that I am quite positive glasses were shattering in
the cafeteria. Some were crying because no one would play with them,
while others were pulling on her shirt telling on the misdeeds of other
students. I thought I had somehow missed the driveway to the entrance
of the school and wound up in the pits of Hades.

As I helped her corral her little charges, we started talking about my
purpose for seeing her and that I would be her mentor from the university. All of a sudden she burst into tears and told me that she had only
had that assignment for a few days and the administration office was
trying to locate a paraprofessional who could help her in the classroom.
She was having trouble keeping them busy and attentive.

I had to remind myself as I watched the children circling the teacher,
readying themselves for a small massacre and a burning at a stake, that
these three-year-olds had the attention span of a gnat. Until she gained
control of that class, her children would be carrying part of her scalp
home in their backpacks with their signed papers.

Her classes at the college had taught her several little cutesy songs
with the purpose of moving students from a large group setting to a
smaller rug setting for story time, and a little ditty of a song to entice
small children to clean up their learning centers. These students must
have been tone deaf, because they were not coming to the rug for whole
class instruction nor were they quietly moving from center to center.
This teacher was experiencing a trial-by-fire situation and was looking
very crispy.

At this point, I was fairly certain that a fully loaded Sherman tank
would be of little or no use to her. This poor first-year teacher was
not fully prepared for the impact of what three-year-olds are capable
of doing during a fifteen-minute time frame, much less a seven-hour
school day.

I tried to assure her that things would improve and if the principal said she was trying to find her some help, she was. Standing shakily against her blue classroom door, with a pleading and tearful voice she asked if we could reschedule our visit for another day. I told her that would be no problem and I would contact her later to schedule our first visit.

I am so pleased to say that over time, I saw her become a splendid teacher. The paraprofessional placed in her room provided an extra pair of hands that helped her move from being just a babysitter to being a purposeful teacher. I watched her confidence soar. I witnessed as she transformed from a frightened I-don't-know-what-to-do teacher into a teacher who genuinely came to love her little charges.

She was well organized and had something for them to do every day. Her instructional centers were interesting and lively. These are the kind of teachers the little people need—the ones who don't mind being burned at the stake or scalped.

A common thread that all first-year teachers possess is the desire to be liked. Most of them have worked very hard to fulfill their dream to be a teacher. One such teacher was Tally. Tally had returned to school to obtain a teaching certificate after working for several years as a paraprofessional. She spent countless hours working in her room to make sure everything was perfect for the first day of school. On her classroom door, she had placed a large colorful welcome sign for her children that said, "Welcome to Ms. Tally's room." Who was "Ms. Tally"?

For years, Tally had worked as a paraprofessional on a primary campus where the little people called their teachers by their first names—"Ms. Cindy," "Ms. Mary," and you guessed it, "Ms. Tally." However, now she was a teacher on an elementary campus working with older students. She didn't need to be seen as "Ms. Tally"; she needed to be seen as and called "Mrs. Townsend."

I promptly informed her that when she left the atmosphere of the primary campus and entered the world of the elementary school, the students' maturity level also changed. She couldn't be "Ms. Tally," friend and funny person. She was "Mrs. Townsend," and the students needed to see her in that light.

Tally said she never thought about her name that way. While "Ms. Tally" was appropriate on a primary campus when working with the little ones, she was actually denying herself the respect from older students that would come by being "Mrs. Townsend." The welcome sign was changed to reflect the name "Mrs. Townsend," and her children still grew to love her.

First-year teachers—the "pups," as I like to refer to them—require a great deal of help during the year. You can certainly delegate some of the responsibilities to their mentor and grade-level teachers. And many times they learn more by simply sitting back and watching the dynamics of real-world teaching as it unfolds around them.

But no matter how busy you may get, never dismiss your responsibility in training, nurturing, and supporting them. In the end, it is your decision whether they stay or leave. It is your leadership and guidance that might make a difference.

USING YOUR BEST SHEPHERDING SKILLS

It really isn't too far-fetched to think of yourself as a shepherd when it comes to working with first-year teachers. I actually found a job description for a shepherd from a Utah State Service posting: "Tend flock of sheep grazing on a range or pasture; move sheep to and about assigned grazing, prevent animals from wandering or becoming lost" (jobspace .com n.d.). All these years I thought I had served public education by hiring and helping first-year teachers, when I was really a shepherd in principals' clothing.

Picture yourself on a plush rolling hill of green grass. The beautiful sunrise has promised a day of warmth with a light wind that will keep you comfortable all day. As you look out over the expansiveness of the pasture setting, there are white dots intermittently placed here and there. You are standing guard over your flock with a watchful eye as you hold a shepherd's crook in your right hand, ready to protect the herd from any unwanted predators. Any minute now, a National Geographic photographer will start clicking his camera just for a picture of you as you majestically stand at your post protecting your sheep.

Let's face it—you thought you were in training to be a principal, an instructional leader, an organizational manager. No, you were learning how to be a shepherd. Just to prove this point, look at the job description again.

A shepherd has to be able to tend a flock of sheep while they graze. As the principal, you are supposed to take care of the teachers, the students, and the school from 7:30 a.m. to about 4:30 p.m. every day. A shepherd has to be able to move the sheep around and prevent any harm from coming to them. As the principal, you are required to keep a safe and secure school atmosphere to ensure the most productive learning environment possible. I rest my case. Serving as a school principal means you are also qualified to apply for the position of shepherd in the state of Utah.

Many years ago, a great teacher told a story about one lost sheep. In order to save the one, the shepherd left ninety-nine sheep behind and went to search for the one that was lost. When the missing sheep was found, a great celebration ensued because what was lost had been saved.

This is the type of action a principal takes when he or she intervenes and helps guide the new pups, the first-year teachers. The shepherd in the story from long ago was prepared to leave the majority of his flock to save just one missing sheep.

When you see new teachers struggling with the arduous responsibilities of the teaching profession, find them some help. When they look as if they are lost or losing their way, take your shepherd's crook and gently guide them to the sanctuary of a veteran teacher's expertise. Offer to meet with them before or after school to review their classroom practices that just aren't working, and make sure they are surrounded by a caring and giving flock of ewes that can show them the ropes or listen to them when they are worn and weary. Whatever you do, don't leave them wandering aimlessly around the pasture looking for the way to rejoin the flock.

Shepherding the new teachers on your campus means you take on such responsibilities as caregiver, guide, and protector. Some days, because of your hectic schedule, you will barely have time to breathe, much less go in search of missing sheep.

This is when the backup shepherds can help. The school secretary becomes their go-to person. Fellow grade-level teachers surround them with support as they show them how to take attendance, check backpacks, or put their grades into the designated computer system. If the new teacher is worth saving and you know that with just a little guidance he or she will become an effective teacher, find a way to save the lost one.

Just as a shepherd learns to use a crook to protect the flock under his or her care, the shepherd also uses the crook to weed out sheep from the flock that don't belong there. If one of the sheep snips and bites at the other sheep, the shepherd uses the crook to continuously move that one around so it does the least amount of harm to the other members of the flock.

If one of the sheep likes to start fights with others and disturbs the grazing habits of the flock, the shepherd uses the crook to lead it to a place where it can feed all alone and do little to interrupt the calm of feeding time for the others. And if moving that sniping or bullying sheep does not help, take that crook, wrap it around the neck of the cantankerous one, and direct it to another flock of sheep. That wooden crook is one handy-dandy tool to have around.

As I have said before, there will be some first-year teachers you can't save no matter how good a shepherd you are. You can put all the suggestions I have talked about in place and still some will need to be moved to a different school—or quite possibly, work in a different profession altogether. All I ask is that you be the best shepherd you can, using your crook wisely and nurturing all the flock.

If the principal thing doesn't work out and you feel certain you would make a better shepherd, Utah might be the place for you. The job number for the shepherd's position is #8660798. You get room and board plus $750 a month, you're on call twenty-four hours a day, and you never know what is going to happen on any given day. Sound familiar? See, I told you. You really are just a shepherd in disguise.

DEVELOPING YOUR PERSONAL LEADERSHIP CAPACITY

As stated in an earlier part of the chapter, I missed an opportunity to help a first-year teacher develop and become better at her chosen craft. She may have had some limitations in the mechanics involved in the art of teaching, but she truly possessed a teacher's heart. My hope for you is that you develop a personal leadership capacity that allows you to recognize when any teacher is struggling, especially one experiencing his or her first year.

I never want you to have any regrets similar to mine. Remember, every time you help new teachers through even the smallest of tasks or hold their hands when they have to face an angry or confrontational situation, not only do they grow as teachers, but you grow as a caring administrator. So, keep the following in mind as you learn your skills of shepherding:

1. Most of your first-year teachers are really just sheep feeding in a pasture. They just need some direction or a gentle nudge and they will be fine.

2. Understand that all first-year teachers deserve a chance. If they are worth keeping, provide them with the training and resources they need to be successful.

3. A handful of first-year teachers, no matter what intervention you provide, will not be a match for your children or your school. If you can truly say after their first year that you did all you could do, it's time to think of the flock instead of the one that was lost.

4. Meet continually with first-year teachers to ascertain their progress, their stress levels, and their continued commitment. Lead them through the tough times and hopefully in the end, a strong and effective teacher will remain standing.

5. Ask more than just the standard questions of how they are doing or is there anything you can do to help. The first year I became a principal, I would have bitten off the end of my tongue before I admitted I needed help of any kind. Some first-year teachers may feel the same way. Ask them how they are balancing their professional and personal lives, are they taking care of themselves through diet and exercise, or does their only exercise come in the form of lifting heavy school bags in and out of the back seat of their cars.

6. Don't be afraid to have crucial conversations with first-year teachers. It is better to talk with them head-on instead of waiting to the end of the year to non-renew their contracts. Temper these conversations with kind, thoughtful, and helpful words. Listen to their problems or concerns and then work with them to find positive solutions.

The campus principal really has no choice about helping the pups. As you find yourself becoming more and more involved in their teaching lives, you are training the pups in ways to ensure their success and your leadership abilities. Even one saved is worth a celebration.

WHAT WILL MY PRINCIPALSHIP SAY ABOUT ME?

One of my favorite sayings comes from Sir Isaac Newton: "If I have achieved any greatness or recognition, it is because I have stood on the shoulders of giants." This quote rings true for you and your principalship.

As the principal of a campus, you are only a facilitator. Oh, you wear many hats, you have endless responsibilities, but nevertheless you are a watcher, a shepherd in a field leading a flock of wandering sheep. Through your facilitation of the teaching and learning that takes place on your campus, teachers develop and hone their skills, and meaningful learning becomes as much a part of the school's culture as the posters on the walls or the welcome sign on the front door. If this is the case, and especially the case when you lead the pups, what do you want your principalship to say about you?

1. I hope every first-year teacher says that you supported and respected them.
2. I anticipate that every first-year teacher sends you a note of thanks when you place them with a patient and caring mentor teacher.
3. Your whole flock of teachers should tell others how your intervention either saved a newbie teacher from burning out the first year or saved a classroom of children from an inexperienced, ineffective newbie teacher.
4. Your principalship should reflect all the ways you provided a first-year teacher with help and assistance, without seeing it on a billboard reflected in foot-tall letters.

I made some mistakes in my first years as a principal in regard to the help and assistance I gave to newbie teachers. This does not excuse my lack of effort. I was trying to survive just like them. I now realize that I could have saved more than I did, and that is my dearest hope for you: that your involvement with the pups will make you a master shepherd.

USING YOUR 20/20 VISION

If I thought IKEA carried shepherds' crooks, I would send you there in a heartbeat to choose the one that fits perfectly in your hands. I would encourage you to buy the staff now and leave it somewhere visible in your home—and every day as you walked by that crook, you would think of the sheep that will one day be in your care.

Or I would send you to puppy obedience school to watch how they learn to sit, fetch, and roll over. Either way, you are still the one responsible for the success of a newbie. With your 20/20 vision for being a proactive and readied principal, use the following checklist to ensure your success:

- ☐ I have met with all my new teachers, and we took a field trip around the school.
- ☐ I have matched all my new teachers with capable and caring mentor teachers.
- ☐ I have used several techniques to support and assist the new teachers on the campus.
- ☐ My new teachers are aware of the procedures for moving children around the campus.
- ☐ I have scheduled periodic visits with my new teachers to give them a chance to talk with me on an individual basis.
- ☐ For new teachers who clearly need my help, I have offered several managerial and organizational suggestions that will make their teaching easier and more productive.
- ☐ I have provided a variety of resources to help the first-year teachers become successful.
- ☐ I have used a variety of data sources to make decisions about the contractual status of a new teacher on my campus.
- ☐ I have made the right and best contractual decision regarding a first-year teacher's continued placement on the campus.

MY WISH FOR YOU

In this particular chapter, I feel some quotes are more appropriate than any words of hope I could pass on to you. If any of them connect to the way you feel about shepherding or training the new pups, turn them into posters to line your office walls or write them on yellow sticky notes to place around your mirror as you get ready for school (see www.brainyquote.com).

- "I hated every minute of training, but I said, 'Don't quit. Suffer now and live the rest of your life as a champion.'"—Muhammad Ali
- "I have a lot of different stages in my life when training has been easy or hard. Now, it seems that I have been training for so long that it has become almost second nature to me."—Oksana Baiul
- "The people that really were important, that mattered, had a great foundation. I had no training. I had to learn while doing, and it was really difficult."—Tab Hunter
- "The world went by, and we didn't get caught up in all the other things, because we didn't have time. We had no spare time. It was always thinking about training and focusing on what we wanted, our goals."—Peggy Fleming
- "It takes a couple of years just to get the background and knowledge that you need before you can go into detailed training for your mission."—Sally Ride
- "I have no inhibitions about smoking or drinking, but I think too much of my voice to place it in jeopardy. I have spent many good years in training and cultivating it, and I would be foolish to do anything which might impair or ruin it."—Jeanette MacDonald
- "The training of the schools should be extended to the heart as well as the mind and hand."—Sheldon Jackson

ADDITIONAL RESOURCES

Reading Material

Brock, Barbara L., and Marilyn L. Grady. *From First-Year to First-Rate: Principals Guiding Beginning Teachers.* 3rd ed. Thousand Oaks, CA: Corwin Press, 2007.

Grad, Marilyn L. *The 21 Biggest Mistakes Principals Make and How to Avoid Them*. Thousand Oaks, CA: Corwin Press, 2004.

Green, Tena. *Your First Year as a Principal: Everything You Need to Know That They Don't Teach You in School*. Ocala, FL: Atlantic Publishing, 2009.

Podsen, India J., and Vicki M. Denmark. *Coaching and Mentoring First-Year and Student Teachers*. Larchmont, NY: Eye on Education, 2000.

Wong, Harry K., and Rosemary T. Wong. *The First Days of School: How to Be an Effective Teacher*. Mountain View, CA: Harry K. Wong Publications, 2009.

Internet Sources

www.educationupdate.com/index.html
This site provides updates in education on a variety of levels that are beneficial to first-year principals.

teacher.scholastic.com/newteacher/
The easy-to-do suggestions offered at this site will provide help and support for all personnel.

www.pacificnet.net/~mandel/
Many of the ideas and suggestions provided at this site originate with seasoned classroom teachers who offer sage and sound advice for new teachers.

www.encyclopedia.com/doc/1G1-19129307.html
New principals will find this site helpful as they seek additional research on general topics in education.

www.educationworld.com
A very resourceful site for new administrators to have when needing suggestions or assistance with any topic in education.

8

IT'S LONELY AT THE TOP

The principalship is the highest administrative position on a school campus. This means that people who serve in this position must possess at least a master's degree in educational leadership from an accredited university or college. The extraordinary people who decide to pursue the principalship take additional courses, participate in a variety of professional development activities, and attend district meetings on a regular basis.

They are known for their unique abilities to make quick and relevant decisions based on the needs of their campuses and children. If in fact this is the highest position on a school campus held by a professional educator, why then do so many principals experience a sense of professional loneliness that comes from serving at this level?

Being the top dog on a campus means you have your own nifty little office, possibly a designated parking space, and most probably free meals from the school's cafeteria. You carry with you a master key to every inside and outside door of the school. You are King of the Hill, Top Banana, and Queen of Everything.

Don't let these accolades go to your head just yet. If you are King of the Hill, you have to be wary of impending landslides. If you claim to be Top Banana, there is a banana split just waiting to use you, and if you proclaim yourself to be Queen of Everything, then I suggest you look up the meaning of the word *everything*. Not everything is always rosy and sweet smelling when you are on the top.

As the chief executive officer (CEO) of the school, you may find that many of your employees believe that you get more money and really don't work in the trenches like they do. Some believe that you have a cushy job. What they do not always see is what you do behind the scenes to make their lives and the lives of the children better.

When the security alarm goes off at 4:00 in the morning, the maintenance director calls you. When the fire marshal walks through the building and documents areas of concern that need to be addressed, your signature goes on the bottom line of the report. And if you are the Chosen One, why is your car the first one to arrive and the last one in the parking lot at the end of the day?

Is it because you are the big kahuna, the big cheese, numero uno, the one with the big paycheck at the end of the month? I hate to be the one to burst your bubble, but that is not it. It's because when you took on the role of the principal, the one in charge, the one at the top, you indirectly made a decision that in some instances, you would have to walk alone.

Here is a hard and fast rule I want you to learn right now: The principalship is not a team sport. While I am sure you will work with phenomenal teachers and support staffs, you and you alone are responsible for making final decisions about instruction, personnel, and budgetary issues.

At the end of my day as I looked at my desk with the many files and uncompleted paperwork that would surely face me the next morning, I used to think how nice it would be if little elves came in during the night and cleared away all those files and finished all that paperwork. Maybe one of my staff would come in the next morning and offer to sit in the chair for me that day so I could go have my nails done. You guessed it—no elves, no painted nails.

When you assume the role of principal, you will make decisions that do not please everyone or make everyone happy. Some of those decisions will be heart-wrenching and leave you with feelings of guilt or remorse. But if those decisions have to be made, if your position as the CEO requires you to make the decisions, then make them in the best interest of your school and your children.

For your own mental health, you will have to find a way to bring yourself some joy and happiness while you serve as principal. How do you accept the awesome responsibilities of the principalship and still find a way to enjoy the position? Because the day you don't want to go to your school and make a difference in the lives of children or teachers is the day I want you to go to the superintendent's office, turn in your set of keys, back out of the designated principal's parking spot, and drive straight to apply for the position of door greeter for a large department store chain. Your health and welfare must be considered as much as any other aspect of the principalship. If not, you will burn yourself out before you have even been on fire.

MAKE YOUR OWN JOY

Joy, as defined by Random House Webster's college dictionary (1991 edition), is "a feeling or state of great delight; an expression of glad feelings." With all that has been discussed in the previous chapters about the difficulties administrators face or the unbelievable stories that actually take place, most people who are studying to be a campus leader should be rapidly running to their college's graduate department to change their majors from educational leadership to business or art appreciation. I am fairly certain these two majors have little interaction with small children.

In one of my classes, after I had recounted how important it was to have knowledge of school law issues and told yet another scary story of my time as a principal, one of the students asked me what was so great about being a principal. I had shared stories that would make grown men or women cringe in fear or cause them to run screaming for their lives.

I recounted several episodes of meetings with parents and teachers that had gone very wrong and expressed my desire that they should learn from my mistakes. This student assumed that because I used personal stories to relate points of effective leadership abilities and some of those stories were scary and unbelievable, that there were only a few real reasons to become a campus leader. Nothing could have been farther from the truth.

If I have not already expressed this in the previous chapters, let me now state my feelings about the principalship loudly and clearly: I loved being an elementary principal. My joy came from being around the children, watching expert teachers touch lives through interactive lessons, or simply seeing a herd of children at recess, running and laughing, just having fun.

Even when the duties of the position were so overwhelming I could barely catch my breath, a child would come into my office and show me how he had just passed his most recent spelling test. The light that beamed from his little face was enough to make me forget everything that had gone wrong, and it ensured I would be at school the next day, waiting for the next little piece of sunshine to enter my office.

When I first began my doctorate studies, I wanted to research why there was a shortage of principals. I began calling state education agencies to gather data regarding the shortages of school leaders in their states. During one such contact, I talked with a woman named Mary.

When I asked about the lack of people in her state who wanted to be a principal, she informed me very quickly that there was no shortage of certified principals in her state. There was in fact a shortage of qualified people to serve in the capacity of a school leader. That made a difference.

I have many theories on why people who are certified to be school leaders are declining to accept a position as a principal. First, it is a hard job with very few outside benefits. Those who apply for school leadership positions at an elementary campus do not need to apply if they faint at the sight of vomit or have an anxiety attack every time they have to face an angry mother storming straight for them.

The hours are long and, in some cases, a new principal earns less than the highest paid teacher on the campus. A word of advice here: Never divide your salary by the hours you actually devote to the principalship. This may prove disheartening and cause palpitations of the heart when you find out your actual hourly wage.

Meeting state accountability standards that have state and federal consequences for schools and school districts also scares many away from accepting a principalship. Because of federal mandates, schools are required to meet certain standards; if a school fails to do so, then federal monies that support personnel and programs could be withheld. It is very hard to try to accomplish the instructional goals for a campus without the monetary resources to do so.

Then, there are the people skills that are needed to handle the various situations that occur on a campus. Let's face it—some people just do not have what it takes to defuse an explosive situation, explain why a parent has called the superintendent, or work as a team player. It is better for everyone if these people consider becoming researchers who work in a faraway place with only numbers and not people.

No wonder certified principals are looking for other employment rather than serving as a school administrator. How many people want a job where they have to make all the important decisions, serve demanding people, and work sixty hours a week for compensation that borders on the poverty level? Those who choose to be school leaders do so because of some higher calling, some need to be a servant, or quite simply because they are committed to making things better in the lives of children.

My daughter says that being a teacher is similar to doing missionary work—very little pay but lots of rewards. This is the life of a dedicated and committed principal. Accepting the principalship also means accepting every aspect of duty and responsibility that is associated with the position.

So during my principalship, in order to keep myself balanced, I sought ways to bring a little joy into my school life. And for me, that was always being with the children, and one of them was Ben.

Ben's smile lit up a room. He tended to struggle with some of his studies but he always tried his best. In the three years he was with me, Ben always managed to bring laughter and happiness into my world. Of course, on a few occasions, Ben needed me to be his principal, not someone who admired his bubbling personality.

Every once in a while, Ben would be walking down the hallway, see me, and yell out, "Hi, Ms. T.!" and proceed on to his destination. No matter what was happening in my principal's world at that time, Ben's salutation always made me smile. I have a picture of Ben and me taken on the steps of the stage at our school. He has his arm thrown casually around my shoulder and his smile is shining brightly. It must have been a joyful time for me too, because I am grinning from ear to ear.

Then there was the time that I rode a bike down the hallways. Yes, you read that right. I rode a bike down the halls of my school. Our children were about to take some very important state tests and we had organized a raffle drawing to encourage them to do their best as they prepared for the big tests. Every time a teacher saw a child use a learning strategy or show extra effort in class, the teacher would give him or her a raffle ticket.

At any given time, the students could put their tickets into their designated grade-level jars for the drawing that would take place after the tests were over. Outside the office, we displayed several items that would be given away: a small electric piano, several basketballs, and a bike.

On one of those days when I was deciding between being the principal and becoming a door greeter, I looked outside the office and there stood that bike. In my thinking (which usually got me in trouble), I really had no choice. I climbed on the bike, tucked my skirt firmly under my legs, and pedaled off.

I started in the third-grade wing, rode easily down the fourth-grade hall, and finished my cycling trip in the fifth-grade section. I waved as I passed the children and their teachers. I said hello to students as they moved to and fro on the campus. It was just what I needed. Later, when I was talking to a group of teachers, they shared with me that seeing me fly down the hallways on that bike was just what they needed, too—a little humor and a short reprieve from their hectic day.

The pressures and uncertainties associated with the state testing had made all of us a little stressed, including the children. Seeing the principal of the school riding a bike up and down the halls brought us all some much-needed comic relief.

Many of your days as the campus principal will be filled with chaotic and harrowing experiences. Phone calls, parent complaints, classroom discipline problems—all happening before 9:00 a.m.—will leave you exasperated and ready for a small holiday somewhere on a desert island. Because there are no express flights to that desert island, I suggest you find yourself a little oasis of your own somewhere on your campus. For me, this haven existed in the form of an oversized beanbag chair that was located in our special education department.

The rooms in this building offered children a bright, colorful, and friendly place to learn. The teachers in charge of this program exemplified the patience and understanding needed to work with special needs children, while at the same time demanding their best. Many of the students who entered this building needed educational assistance as well as management skills to deal with their explosive behaviors. What better place could I find to hide away from the emotional demands of the principalship?

On days when I needed some sense of calm or a place to hide from the job for just a few minutes, I would steal away to the blue beanbag chairs in the special education classroom, flop down, turn my school radio down, and for a few minutes find some peace and solitude.

Oh, there were usually teachers and children in the room milling about and interacting with one another, but that didn't bother me. These teachers and their paraprofessional assistants provided a structured and safe atmosphere that clearly showed how much they loved their children, and I knew I could rest there undisturbed for a few minutes. On occasion, one of the children would come to the beanbag chair and ask me to read a story. Who needed a secluded beach to retreat to when I had a blue beanbag chair and a child to read to? I had my own nirvana.

After a few minutes, the radio would come to life and call out, "Unit 9, unit 9." Since I was unit 9, I would reply, "Unit 9 here." The voice on the other end, usually the school secretary, would ask my location and proceed to tell me I was needed in the office. So much for my getaway. However, for a short amount of time, the self-proclaimed refuge of that blue beanbag chair restored my sense of calm and well-being and helped to strengthen me for my next adventure.

As we have discussed in earlier chapters, starting a new school year is a harrowing experience, especially for new principals. To ready myself for the job, I tried to attend a summer conference every year dedicated to the needs of elementary principals. During one of those sessions, I heard a principal talking about her favorite thing to do before school started.

Every year before the first day of school, she would invite several community church leaders into the school one evening to pray for the school and the children who were returning in just a few days. She said her spirits were so lifted by the experience that she asked them to return every year.

No matter what your religious convictions are, no matter if you call a rabbi, a priest, or a minister, I can only tell you what happened to me. When I returned from the conference, I called together a group of clergy from the churches nearest our school and asked them if they would be interested in coming to the school one evening and praying over my school.

Not one of the members of the clergy whom I called said no. They walked in and out of every classroom, laying their hands on the students' desks and asking that any child who sat at that desk would be blessed by a desire for learning. They stood over each teacher's desk and prayed that the one who sat at that desk would help each child develop a deep and sincere love for learning. Many placed their hands over me and prayed that as the leader of the school I would make wise and meaningful decisions that helped every person who entered our doors.

Whether you attend a large congregation of churchgoers or not, regardless of your convictions, when those ministers and clergy lifted their hands over my head and prayed that I would have wisdom that school year, chills went up and down my spine. After they had visited every classroom in every hallway and before they left for the night, they gathered in the middle of the school and collectively prayed for the safety and well-being of every child who entered our school that year.

These powerful men and women were standing in my school asking for divine assistance to make that school year something special for my children. Tears formed in the corners of my eyes as I watched this gift take place and silently asked for their words to find divine ears. I have to tell you not all miracles happen with a bang or an explosion. Some miracles are just little pieces of joy that find their way into our daily lives.

Not all moments that bring you some sense of joy will be as sentimental as having clergy members pray over your school. Some moments of joy will come when you get the final word or get to prove a point. Those moments tend to be a little bit more sinister in nature.

There was a teacher on our campus who tended to be a little bit of a bully and didn't really try to be friendly with too many people. I think you met her in another chapter—remember Attila the Hun? Well . . .

Because I was usually the last one to leave the campus every day, I liked to park in the last space of the parking lot, at the end of a long wing of one of my buildings. Once I left the security of the school, it was only a few steps to the front door of my car. Most of the teachers knew this was where I parked. If for some reason I was running late to school and they noticed the parking space was empty, they would leave it open for me.

One morning as I drove into the parking lot, I noticed that Attila had pulled into my parking space. She and I were both climbing out of our cars at the same time. When I saw her, I jokingly asked what she was doing parking in my spot. She looked at me and said, "I don't see your name on it," and turned to go into the building. Another teacher who had arrived at the same time as me heard Attila's comment and just stood there in amazement wondering what my next step would be. I think she could see a little Chihuahua fur starting to curl on the back of my neck.

Since you already know that I have a little bit of a temper, you may be thinking that I promptly dropped my school bags, stomped into the school clicking my heels all the way, and yelled at her in my loudest screeching voice to take her insubordinate body back to that parking lot and move her car far away from my everybody-knows-I-park-there parking space.

And if my Chihuahua fur was really in a dander that day, I would also tell her in no uncertain terms that if she ever talked to me like that again, she would park her car in the vacant lot across the street from the school until the end of the school year.

You will be very proud to know that I did none of those things. I simply replied to her, with a hint of a smile in my voice, that she was indeed correct and that my name was indeed not on the parking space. And under my breath, I said, "Not yet, but it will be."

Unfortunately for Attila, she had acquired a reputation for this kind of behavior throughout the school district. Her unfriendly manner and rude comments had not made her a teacher people knew and respected. In fact, she had alienated just about everyone she came in contact with. In this particular instance she was right; there was nothing to distinguish that particular parking space as mine.

When I finally arrived at my office, I called the maintenance department in our district and told them what had happened. I told them what Attila had said and asked if there was any way I could have the words Principal's Parking placed on the curb of that end parking spot.

When the maintenance crew realized it was Attila who had made the comment, they were only too happy to help. By the time I made it to my office, checked on the school, and called the maintenance department, it was about 9:00 in the morning. By 11:00 that morning, four-inch black letters now stated very clearly that the last space, closest to the end of the long wing, was Principal's Reserved Parking. As I left that evening, joy filled my little passive-aggressive heart because I knew Attila would never, never, never, be able to park there again.

School year after school year joyous moments will occur when you watch your students compete in academic or athletic events, when they present plays or musicals, when they graduate and leave your campus, and even when you win a small battle, like earning a parking space. The point is that you must find ways to keep a joyful heart in the midst of the chaos and struggles you face on a daily basis as the campus principal.

When the business of being in charge of running the school takes you away from the joy you have going in and out of classrooms watching children learn or even being able to sit and eat lunch with some of your faculty, then it's time to dedicate some part of your day or your week to remind yourself that you love your job.

KEEP THE SMALL STUFF

After many years in the principalship, I earned my doctorate degree and decided to leave the world of public education and become a college professor. Because I am a pack rat at heart, I had to wade through boxes, drawers, and closets filled with memorabilia that I had collected over the years.

I went through shelf after shelf packing teacher supplies I had bought, books I had collected, and years of school stuff that had been carefully hidden away in file cabinets. I was amazed at the many trinkets and tidbits I had collected over the years.

For some of the items, I could still see the face of the precious child who had given me the treasure. It wasn't until late in my career that I learned that if I wrote the name of the child who had given me the gift somewhere on the little trinket, my mind could easily recall the face of the giver. Now as I looked at all of the little notes and tidbits, I was filled with some very happy memories.

One folder I found held notes from several students saying that I was the best principal they ever had and that they would never forget me. I came across thank-you notes from teachers and parents for extending to them some simple courtesy or helping them through a particular situation.

These notes of support and encouragement filled my heart with the thought that maybe I had made a difference in someone's life. The faces of children and teachers who had written the notes flashed before my eyes and confirmed for me the fact that my years as an elementary principal had been worthwhile. These little notes weren't declarations of my greatness as a school leader; they were pieces of someone else's heart that at a particular moment in time, they had shared with me.

The kindness of others toward me sometimes went far beyond little notes of appreciation. The staff members of the campus knew I was on my way to finishing my doctoral studies and was ready to take the next step and defend my study. If I successfully completed this task, I would earn my doctorate.

On the day of my doctoral defense, I drove to the university and met with my committee. By noon of that same day, I was calling the secretary to let her know that all had gone well and I was officially Dr. Janet Tareilo. Because I had taken a personal day to travel to the university and complete my defense, I did not return to the school. Instead, I waited until the next morning to return to campus.

As I opened the door to my office, *hundreds* of blue and red balloons greeted me. They were everywhere. I could barely see the chair behind my desk. It took me several minutes just to wade through the sea of balloons.

The school counselor rushed in to take several pictures of that moment, and the kids were happily jumping up and down asking me if I liked the balloons and the job they had done to decorate my office. It was as if the counselor, who had planned the whole thing, had given the students permission to wrap my office with red and blue balloons instead of toilet paper.

Later, when I was packing my many boxes of collected stuff and preparing to leave the school for my position at the university, I dropped something on the floor and had to crawl under my desk to retrieve the dropped item.

There on the floor, in a corner of the desk, I found the remnants of a deflated red balloon. I held tightly to that flat piece of red latex and remembered the day I had opened my door and found the sea of blue and red bubbles. I knew that no matter what position I ever earned in higher education, the best thing I ever did was serve as the principal for the teachers and the students on that campus. That little piece of balloon reminded me that because I had cared for them, the inhabitants of that school had cared enough to celebrate my success with me. No store or individual sells that kind of joy.

Elementary principals are so lucky to be the recipients of trinkets and treasures from their children. By the time children reach the middle or high school setting, principals take on a very different meaning in their lives. As the elementary principal, every year I received boxes of candy on Valentine's Day, an assortment of gifts at Christmas, and some very special end-of-the-year gifts. One such gift was a red plastic rose from Quinton.

The red rose was beautiful, and Quinton had written a special note on a card that said I was his favorite principal of all time. As he handed it to me, I asked him where he had gotten such a beautiful flower.

He told me that his mother worked at a funeral parlor preparing the deceased for burial and making floral arrangements for their funerals. Sometimes she had extra flowers left over. This particular plastic flower had been an extra one, and Quinton had asked his mother if he could bring it to school for me.

That rose was displayed on a counter in my office for many years. It really didn't matter where the flower came from; the only thing that mattered was how I showed my appreciation to Quinton for his unique gift.

On another campus, a former school counselor I worked with created sunshine folders for every staff member. She started with plain manila folders. At the top of each folder, she placed a picture of a teacher. Then she proceeded to decorate each folder with flowers, decorative squiggly lines, and little pictures. During one of our faculty meetings, she passed out the folders and asked people to write a short note for that particular teacher that would be uplifting and encouraging.

When the teachers became stressed or discouraged, they could always find their sunshine folders and read the positive comments their colleagues had written about them. Their sunshine folders would bring them some momentary and much-needed joy. What I did not know was that she had created one for me, too, and let all the teachers write a little something for me. I still have that yellow sunshine folder, and opening it up and reading those comments still puts a smile on my face.

FRIENDLY, NOT FRIENDS

Becoming the campus administrator, the instructional leader of a school, the big kahuna, does not mean your personality dries up and blows away or that you can't have fun or ride a bike in the hallways. If you are genuinely a friendly person, that character trait needs to follow you as you deal with difficult people, receive phone calls from the superintendent, and welcome new teachers to your campus. Being friendly and courteous will serve you well; however, I say that with a bit of hesitant caution. I expect you to be friendly, but I urge you not to be friends.

After applying for and accepting my first principalship, I was being escorted by the assistant superintendent through the hallways of the elementary building and being introduced to several of the faculty members. During our tour of the campus, I met two third-grade teachers, Mack and Mama D.

Maybe fate or a divine lifeline sent these women into my life, but I couldn't have survived some of the things we went through if it hadn't been for them. I know I just said to be friendly, never friends. These two women stand as the exception to the rule.

Through my years serving as the elementary principal on that campus, I can truthfully tell you that I tried my best to ensure that, even though they had become my friends, I never treated them differently. They equally tried to ensure that they expected no preferential treatment from me because of our friendship. Our daughters were friends with each other and we spent many happy and wonderful times together.

After leaving that campus, I happened to meet one of the teachers from that school. After reminiscing for a bit, she asked if I was still friends with Mack and Mama D. I said I was, but that our locations and job assignments limited our times together.

The teacher then told me that she and others had known the three of us were very close friends, and they sensed that they were my favorites. She did add that she appreciated the way we still worked together as professionals and that favoritism was never really an issue. Even with our best attempts, the friendship we shared away from the school still bled into our daily practices while at school.

Would I change anything about the many friends I have made along the way? No. I would have missed out on Mack's unique sense of humor and Mama D's motherly and patient love for anyone and everyone. From the first minute I walked down that third-grade hallway, I just knew they would be vital parts of my life in and away from the school—and they still are.

When I was assigned my next position at an elementary campus, I indeed met another set of friends; we'll call them the Tribe. This group of teachers and co-workers formed an immediate family-like attachment to one another when they met. They planned outings together and after-hour dinners, and they always invited me to join them.

When the entire school was invited to game night or to a movie, I would try to attend those ventures. However, if it was just the Tribe members meeting, I graciously thanked them for the invitation but declined. I never wanted it said that I had favorites or treated people differently because I spent time with them outside of the school setting. Yet, the Tribe will live on in my memory for the kindness and loyalty they showed me during my time as their principal.

I am sure you are wondering by now, why can't you be friends with the people on your campus? Let me explain it like this. What if my friend calls me and says she is running late for school and asks if I will watch her class until she gets there? Of course, I'll do that for my friend.

If she calls me every day for a week and says she is running late for school and will I watch her class until she gets there, she is my friend, so I say, "Of course I will." If my friend forgets to do her lesson plans and asks me to give her just a little more time to turn them in, I'll be a buddy and a pal, won't I? I'll understand that she has had a lot to do and just didn't get around to doing her lesson plans this week.

Being a friend means you overlook your expectations for your staff. Being friendly means you smile when you hand your tardy teacher a gift sack with a new alarm clock inside.

As you become more familiar with the staff on your campus, there will be teachers and co-workers you are naturally drawn to. Their sense of humor may be just what you need on a stress-filled day. They may be the ones who send you a little note about not giving up or telling you to keep smiling when molehills turn into mountains. These people will be the easy ones you work with, who always do what is asked of them and place the needs of the children before their own.

As far as the ones who aren't as inclined to ride upon your bandwagon (and if you're good at the job, that will only be a handful of teachers whom even Billy Graham couldn't convert), just remember to always treat them the same as you do your Macks or Mama Ds. It is vital that in your principalship you treat everyone in the same respectful and digni-fied manner regardless of your personal feelings.

NO, LET ME

Before you read another word of this fascinating and thought-provoking book, I want you to fill in the blank of the following statement: "I want to be a principal because _____." Simply fill in the blank with your response. No one is watching you. You're not on *Candid Camera*. Why do you want to be the one responsible for every aspect of student learning, building collegial relationships, and creating a successful learning community?

If people representing other professional domains answered a similar question as to why they had entered their chosen fields, what would their responses be? Dr. DeBakey, the well-known and successful heart surgeon, might respond that the reason he became a doctor was because he understood how the heart works and he felt he had been called to save lives. Condoleezza Rice, the first African American woman to serve as the secretary of state, might respond that she entered the field of politics because she loved to travel and learn about the different cultures of the world. And if Bob Hope had been asked why he entered the world of entertainment, he might respond that he had a gift for bringing laughter and joy to others at a time when they most needed uplifting.

Do you have an answer for the empty blank? I'll go first. I became a principal because I knew that I could make decisions in a quick and timely manner, that my love for children surpassed being a babysitter, and that my desire for school success far surpassed my love of teaching. However you respond to that statement, you should be prepared to reflect that sentiment in everything you say or do as the campus principal.

Once you have filled in the blank with your response, I want you to remember something I mentioned from an earlier chapter. Remember when I told you that as the principal you are responsible for everything that happens on your campus? You still are, and that hasn't changed. I just want to touch on those things that you will personally take care of that no one will ever see you do.

I cannot remember the number of times I heard my mentor, Sandy McEntire, tell teachers, parents, and school board members not to worry about something, she would take care of it, whatever it was. No matter what the situation, she usually was good on her word. While I was a teacher on her campus, I knew I was supported and respected. I never knew of any situation that was brought to her attention that didn't get solved, even Jamie's situation.

Jamie was in my sixth-grade class and had been absent for a few days. When we finally contacted his parents, we were informed that he had not had a certain procedure done when he was born and now that situation had presented him with certain complications.

When Sandy found out about the difficulty, she called a friend who happened to be a surgeon and asked him to perform the surgery for free; he agreed if someone would pay the anesthesiologist's fee. She arranged for the procedure to take place and paid for the anesthesiologist herself. Only a handful of people ever knew what she had done to help one of her students. I can only hope that somewhere in my career as an elementary principal I did something so selfless.

While many of your duties impact the daily lives of the school and its culture, none stand out more than your willingness to give when you don't have to or take on extra responsibilities to help a staff member or his or her family.

When one of our teachers was experiencing a difficult time, the school banded together and brought enough food to fill her freezer for the summer. What no one else knew, and I hope you don't tell anyone, is that her electric, water, and phone bills were paid by an anonymous person. It's the little things that only you know about that will bring you the most joy.

On one occasion, a parent came to school and was furious with one of my second-grade teachers. This mother felt that the teacher had somehow wronged her child and wanted to meet the teacher face-to-face and solve the problem. When the mother and the teacher met with me in the office, the conversation turned nasty and the mother began berating my teacher.

Because this teacher was very quiet and soft-spoken, the mother seemed to overpower her until I stood up. When I did, I moved quickly around my desk and stood smack dab (that's Texan for "in the middle of") between the angry mother and my teacher.

Remember our chapter on being Super Principal, the one that insinuated that you should definitely look before you leap? Once again, I took my 5'9", 130-pound bulletproof body and crammed it into a Superman outfit, as I told the mother the conversation was over and sent my teacher back to her classroom.

The mother became even angrier because of what I had done and proceeded to now direct her anger toward me. I simply stood there and reminded her that I was the principal of that school and she would never talk that way to one of my teachers again, much less threaten one of my teachers. Furthermore, if she wanted to continue visiting our school, she would do so in a controlled manner or else she would not be allowed on our campus again.

I am happy to report that before she left my office, she was apologizing for her behavior and asked me if I would apologize to my teacher on her behalf. I assured her that I would indeed pass on her apology and that we all get a little carried away when we are protecting the ones we love. My shiny "S" shone brightly that day.

Later that day, the teacher sent me a little note of thanks for handling the situation and not letting the parent beat her up. When I was leaving that campus to serve on another one, this same teacher sent me one of the most memorable notes I ever received. In this note, she thanked me for always supporting her and the other teachers on that campus. Maybe I had indeed learned a little from Sandy McEntire. Recently, I found the note in an old box of school stuff. There, all alone in my garage, I smiled remembering that sometimes just reminding myself I was the school's principal strengthened me.

Most of the time, it will be fairly easy to support your teachers. I always told my teachers that I did not like surprises nor did I like feeling stupid. So if they felt there was something I should know before a situation found me, by all means call me at home or see me before they left for the day.

One morning, I was working at my desk and happened to look up and see a mother moving quickly down the hallway with that Mad Mother's March that you will quickly learn to recognize. Instinctively, I knew there was going to be trouble. I proceeded to follow her down the hallway until she entered one of my classrooms. One of my teachers was trying to explain to this very mad woman that she, in fact, had wadded up her son's paper and had actually thrown it in the trash can, calling it a piece of trash, because the paper did not have a name on it. I could almost see steam rising from the top of this mother's head. And if I am being honest, a stream of steam was forming at the top of my head, too.

I wanted to interrupt the conversation, pull the teacher out in the hallway, and ask her point-blank if she had indeed told a child his paper was nothing but a piece of garbage and emphasized her point by throwing the assignment in the trash can.

Instead, I initiated a conversation with the teacher that centered on her reasons for her actions. I was hoping they would be better than what she actually had done. It appeared that the teacher was trying to impress upon her students the importance of putting their names on an assignment (remember her?) and in order to make her point she refused to take any assignments that did not have a proper heading. Now, telling the child his paper was a piece of garbage was a little too much.

As I soothed the mother as best I could, my mind secretly went to a time and place where the teacher and I would be alone and I could ask her what she was thinking. Back in the real world, the mother was still mad, the teacher was trying to explain her point with little impact on the mother, and I was trying to figure out a way to support the teacher's behavior. I interrupted the conversation between the mother and the teacher with a favorite of mine, "Now, let me get this straight. . . ."

Using that intro, I proceeded to say, "Now let me get this straight, you have been at your wits' end trying to instill a sense of responsibility into your students. And after several of the children failed to accept their responsibility of putting their names on their papers, you, in a frustrated state, showed the students what could happen to their papers if they did not put their names on them. Furthermore, you certainly, in no way, ever meant to tell the child his assignment was a piece of trash. Do I have that right?"

The teacher agreed with me, and I could tell that the mother was beginning to feel the teacher's frustration. I probably said something to the effect that the mother probably knew better than anyone else how difficult it was to even get some children to pick up their socks or make their beds. In the end, the mother agreed to help us help her child, and that is the best thing that can ever happen when the day starts out with a mad mother on a mission.

As for the teacher, when the mother left the classroom, I just looked at her. I think she knew what I was about to say because she automatically started thanking me for helping with the parent situation and said that she might consider choosing another way to teach the children about the responsibility of putting their names on their assignments. I smiled and told her that I was certain, I was sure, and I was 100 percent positive I would not be meeting another mad mama over this same issue.

Protecting your staff members from upset parents is only one way to show how much you care about them. Many times your random acts of kindness cost you absolutely nothing. This is never more crucial than showing you care at the times when they need you the most.

The first week of school, as you well know, is so hectic for teachers and principals. Most elementary teachers want their classroom to resemble a showcase at IKEA. They want to have all their first-day papers ready and know how each one of their children is getting home.

This is also their first week back to school and their duty schedules. In order to help my classroom teachers, I usually assigned our paraprofessional and support staff personnel to that first week's duties. The extra personnel would cover bus and car duties so that the teachers could ensure their children went home on the right bus or the right person picked them up from school.

One year, the staff agreed to wear a uniform. For the first week of school, teachers had the option of wearing khaki pants and our school shirts every day. This provided a little comfort to the staff as they returned to their school routines. We did the same thing at the end of the year.

I want to introduce you to a phrase I have coined and use quite often. The phrase is "the givens." What are the givens? These are the things you should do without thinking.

For instance, opening a door for an elderly person takes no thought process: It is something you should do out of courtesy, kindness, or respect. Buying Girl Scout cookies from the next door neighbor's daughter once a year is a given. Being quiet and respectful when you enter any house of worship takes no thought; this is a given. These are just those actions or behaviors that you should do automatically without any return expectations.

When you enter your principalship, identify your own personal givens. I am supposed to support my teachers. I am expected to help and protect my teachers from angry parents. I am the principal of the campus; therefore, I am the one who keeps the school and students safe from harm.

The givens are things you are just supposed to do. It's what you do that is *not* expected of you that makes the difference to your staff and your children. It's when you say to someone, "No, let me do that for you," that sets you apart from ordinary school leaders.

My conviction for the principalship stood on the premise of a saying from Aesop, "No act of kindness, no matter how small, is ever wasted." I believed this during my years of serving as an elementary principal and I believe it still today. The givens are things we should routinely do as campus leaders to show our appreciation and respect for all of our staff members. They will return those little gifts of kindness with dedication and commitment to the school, to you, and especially, to the children.

DEVELOPING YOUR OWN PERSONAL LEADERSHIP CAPACITY

Every year, at the beginning of school, I mailed each one of my staff members a "Welcome Back to School" letter. I provided the times and meeting places for our in-service activities, their new PE/conference schedules, and a personal letter from me to them. I want you to consider this your very own "Welcome Back" letter.

Dear Reader,

In a few days, you will start your very own principalship. You already know some of what is ahead of you. You know to expect long hours, hard work, and a variety of problems and concerns, as well as many other duties that are not listed on your job description. Hopefully, your days will also be filled with the joys of leadership that no one outside the profession can appreciate, such as the smile of a child or helping someone in need.

This year you will make some mistakes, but you will only make them once, because each one of those events will provide a learning experience for you. Surround yourself with caring and selfless individuals who not only make your job easier but your school world brighter.

I wish I could be there to watch you grow and learn. Always lead by example, expecting only the best from your staff and your students, and never settle for the status quo. Anyone can do that. Take care of your school, your children, and yourself.

JLT

WHAT WILL MY PRINCIPALSHIP SAY ABOUT ME?

Because I am a very private person and try to hide my true feelings, I learned to mask certain emotions. During my mid-management courses, we were actually told to never let our staff members know what we were thinking or how we were feeling. We were to remain impassive and handle everything in a calm and stoic manner. That advice could not have been more wrong.

I am not advocating that you be always Sally Sunshine, nor do I want you to border on being Mad Max. I am simply suggesting that you remain positive and supportive whenever possible. When you leave your campus or retire from the field of education, I hope people say the following:

"You could tell she loved her job."

"No matter what the situation, he always had a smile on his face."

"She may not have agreed with what I did, but I knew she would always support me."

"All I had to do was ask and she would help me."

"She was always the happiest when she was around her kids."

"Because of him, I became a more caring teacher."

USING 20/20 VISION

This chapter has focused on how singular in nature is the job of the principalship. Having to make all the decisions, supporting the actions of others when you don't agree with them, and finding some solitude for yourself away from the many responsibilities of the job leaves you tired and worn. Having a clear 20/20 vision of the givens prepares you to accept those responsibilities and learn how to take better care of yourself and others. Here are a few suggestions for being a Proactive Principal.

- ☐ Open the Coke machine one afternoon for those teachers who are working in their rooms.
- ☐ Create a sunshine folder for yourself that will hold the thank-you notes and good wishes you receive during the school year.
- ☐ Decide on the number of hours you plan to work each day and stick to it. For instance, on Friday afternoons, plan to leave the school when the last child has left.

- ☐ Learn to close the office door.
- ☐ Establish a twenty-four-hour rule.
- ☐ Create a list of your rights as an administrator, such as, "I have the right to have a bad day now and then," "I have the right to expect every teacher to act as a professional," or "I have the right to tell you no if I think something is not in the best interests of my children." Read the list at the first faculty meeting.
- ☐ Read the book *Servant Leadership* by Robert Greenleaf.
- ☐ Never miss an opportunity to show an act of kindness, especially when others are not watching.
- ☐ Find a place on the campus for a moment of personal solitude.

MY WISH FOR YOU

My wish for you when you sit in the chair is that you never feel alone,
    And that your door is always open to make visitors feel at home.
My wish for you when you're the one in charge is that each day brings a smile,
    So that when the hard times come, you'll get through any trial.
My wish for you as you lead your school is that friendships form and grow,
    And that each one that your heart can hold brings more joy than you'll ever know.
My wish for you when you're at the top is that your servant's heart takes first place,
    In all your words and with every smile, you're a leader filled with grace.

ADDITIONAL RESOURCES

Reading Material

Bennis, Warren, Gretchen M. Spreitzer, and Thomas G. Cummings, eds. *The Future of Leadership: Today's Top Leadership Thinkers Speak of Tomorrow's Leaders*. San Francisco: Jossey-Bass, 2001.

Colvin, Geoff. *Talent Is Overrated: What Really Separates World-Class Performers from Everybody Else*. New York: Penguin Books, 2008.

Gladwell, Malcolm. *The Tipping Point: How Little Things Can Make a Big Difference*. Boston: Back Bay Books, 2002.

Ramakrishnan, Umesh. *There's No Elevator to the Top*. New York: Penguin Books, 2008.

Tahmincioglu, Eve. *From the Sandbox to the Corner Office: Lessons Learned on the Journey to the Top*. Hoboken, NJ: Wiley, 2006.

Internet Sources

management.monster.ca/7991_en-CA_p1.asp
The site addresses the issue of how leaders choose between being friendly and being friends. Additional resources are provided.

www.mouseplanet.com/8379/Being_Assertively_Friendly
The information given at this site describes how Disney asserts friendliness in all they do.

www.ivysea.com/pages/ldrex_0103_01.html
The topics of being a joyful leader and learning how to possess real leadership skills are addressed at this site.

www.forbes.com/2006/09/22/leadership-harvard-cuban-lead-manage-cx_snj_0925opinion.html
This site leads you directly to the online *Forbes* magazine, which provides future school leaders with a look at leadership in other venues.

9

TONTO RODE BESIDE THE
LONE RANGER, NOT BEHIND HIM

History tells of a young man named John Reid who, under the command of his older brother, Captain Dan Reid, served as a Texas Ranger. During a meeting with the dangerous Cavendish gang, a fight ensued and a group of Texas Rangers was ambushed. All were killed except John Reid.

He was found, after being left for dead, by a Potawatomi Indian named Tonto. Tonto not only nursed Reid back to health, but he misled the Cavendish gang by leaving an empty grave site. By doing that, Tonto perpetuated their belief that all the Texas Rangers had been killed in the ambush.

When Reid recovered from his wounds, he vowed to not only find and destroy the entire Cavendish gang, but to fight injustice for the rest of his life. From that point on, Tonto decided to stand alongside his new friend in the fight against evil.

When Tonto found John Reid near death, the story goes that Tonto said, "Others dead, you lone ranger now" (*Lone Ranger* n.d.). Hence began the legend of the Lone Ranger and his trusted partner Tonto, which led to the creation of a comic book series, a radio program, and a popular television program. At the beginning of every show, the narrator ended the introduction with the following statement:

With his faithful companion, Tonto, the daring and resourceful masked rider of the plains led the fight for law and order in the early West. Return with us now to those thrilling days of yesteryear. The Lone Ranger rides again. (*Lone Ranger* n.d.)

Very few episodes of the Lone Ranger found him dealing with criminal elements without his trusty friend Tonto by his side. Many times, he could be seen in close conversation with Tonto, as they planned and plotted for the attack that would save a schoolmarm from a kidnapper or foil an attempt to rob the town's bank.

The Lone Ranger depended on Tonto to help him solve that particular episode's problem, save the day, and still ride off into the sunset. They were a team and worked together to change their small piece of the world for the better, just like you will do with those who stand by your side as you work to make your school a phenomenal place of learning.

WHAT DOES "KEMO SABE" REALLY MEAN?

When Tonto was saving John Reid's life, he was not looking for any accolades or thinking, "Hey, if I save this Texas Ranger my name will go down in history and quite possibly I'll get to be on a big radio show. Better yet, I'll get to be on TV one day." If the legend is correct, Tonto was just doing what came naturally to him—he was saving a life. Townsfolk and bad guys may have known the man Tonto saved as John Reid, the Lone Ranger, but Tonto knew him as "Kemo Sabe."

The International Hero website translates the name Kemo Sabe as "trusted scout" (*Lone Ranger* n.d.). During many episodes of the famous television show, the Lone Ranger would refer to Tonto as his "faithful friend." The key words that defined them as people and characters were not the supposed names of Tonto or the Lone Ranger. The words that made them important people were the descriptors used, "trusted" and "faithful."

As you watched the television program, you were likely to see the Lone Ranger dressing up to play many different roles while Tonto stood guard. At other times, the Lone Ranger would be seen capturing the pilfering cattle rustlers and Tonto would be somewhere in a ravine holding their horses. It appeared that Tonto performed all the laborious tasks while the Lone Ranger received all the glory.

Yet week after week, the two rode into a town together, solved some Western dilemma, and then rode off into the sunset as a team. If you think for one minute that you can run your school and take care of the many responsibilities you have without some faithful and trusted companions by your side, put this book down, go and stand in front of the nearest mirror, look straight into that mirror, and in your loudest voice say these exact words, "What are you thinking?"

A veteran principal once gave me some very valuable advice about respecting others. He told me that just because the sign on the door of the office and the school's letterhead had my name as the campus principal, these objects reflected a name and the position held.

Just because I was the principal did not mean that I ran the school; far from it. If I wanted to be a successful school leader I had better learn and learn quickly who actually ran the school: the secretary, the head custodian, and the cafeteria manager. You have a few more Tontos to deal with than our masked friend did.

You may sit in the chair and you may be the one responsible for the entire academic success of a campus, but don't ever think that you have the ultimate power on that campus. I am here to tell or remind you that the school secretary actually runs the school and is a force of his or her own.

When you become the principal and if a school secretary is already in place, add this person's name to your phone log, assign that number a quick dial number, place his or her birthday on your calendar, and quickly learn the name of every family member he or she has, from the newest drooling grandbaby to Great-Grandpa Clyde.

In my case, Mary Lou and Phyllis, the two remarkable women who served as campus secretaries when I served as a campus principal, were invaluable to me. They served as my office guards warning me of impending angry parents, discipline problems that were coming my way, or when a flock of teachers was heading toward my door.

Many times, when my head was down and I was trying to concentrate on some needed paperwork that had been due the day before, they would simply close my door and tell folks I was in the middle of something very important and could not be disturbed. I knew them well enough to know that if the door reopened it was an emergency and my attention was definitely needed. They were so intuitive.

Their knowledge of the communities we served was endless. Phyllis was related to half of the community we served, and Mary Lou knew most of the people in our small town. With these two women helping me, I never needed a telephone directory or a city guide. They were ingrained in the school community already, and I just needed to learn how to use their unique gifts to help me save time and energy. If I did not have enough information to help me with a problem, they knew someone to call in almost every situation we faced.

I cannot relate to you the number of times they dealt with a small situation so that I could address the more difficult ones. If teachers needed some kind of office supply, they handled it. If the copy machine needed repairs, they called the service department. Their ability to be proactive and act the way I needed them to reminded me of the character of Radar O'Reilly on the television show *M°A°S°H*.

Radar finished sentences, knew when choppers were coming with the wounded, and had a unique way of getting Colonel Blake, the commanding officer, to do exactly what he wanted him to do without making any noise or complaining. Radar's subtle ways, his skills at keeping paperwork organized, and the relationships he built with his fellow soldiers made the camp run smoothly and efficiently. Let your secretary know she is respected and trusted, and you will have many years of faithful service.

I began my teaching career on a campus that was brand-new. Everything was new—the bathrooms, the cafeteria, the carpet, everything. That school was a place of beauty. In charge of keeping the school in pristine shape was the head custodian, Ms. Eunice. She loved that school as much as any child or teacher.

The floors were her floors. The bathrooms were her bathrooms, and no one came to a dirty school if Ms. Eunice was in charge. At the end of the day, when you were leaving the school and Ms. Eunice was sweeping the floors, you'd better not get in her way. She did not work as hard as she did to keep that school beautiful and clean because it was her job. She did those things because the school was her home away from home and she always wanted it to look nice.

Years later, I had the distinct privilege of returning to my first campus as the school's principal. One afternoon before I actually took the position, I walked around the school with Ms. Eunice. I was dismayed by what I saw. Now, granted, I had been gone for thirteen years—but instead of the once-shiny floors, they were now worn and yellowed pieces of tile. You could not see out of the overly scratched windows. Something had surely happened.

As we finished our walk-about through the school, I saw more evidence of how the school had fallen into disrepair. Our conversation went something like this:

JT: "What happened to this school?"

Ms. Eunice: "They stopped caring, so did I."

JT: "What do you need to take care of this school and make it special again?"

Ms. Eunice: "Someone who cares."

JT: "When can we meet and get started?"

Ms. Eunice: "Whenever you are ready."

When I think about our cafeteria and the ladies who fed my children every day, I can't help but think about that ridiculous song that was sung a few years ago about lunch ladies. The song depicted lunchroom ladies as mean, unsmiling, uncaring people. On our campus, that couldn't have been farther from the truth.

The cafeteria manager, Ms. Ruth, was there on the day the school opened and stayed the cafeteria manager at our school for almost twenty-six years. Her crew worked very hard to make sure the food they presented to the children was food they would want to have at their own homes.

Many times the ladies would make an extra pan of cobbler for my teachers and place it in the teacher's lounge, or bring in an extra pitcher of tea for them. Their kindness was overwhelming.

In order to make sure we included them in our campus activities, they were always part of our drawings for perfect attendance, they were invited to eat with us at our birthday dinners, and they were the first people I said good morning to every day. Always remember to include them as members of your campus. You'll get great goodies for yourself and your staff.

Once in my law class, one of my students asked me if it was against the law for a cafeteria lady to tell the principal that she would not feed the children after 8:30 in the morning. It appeared that the cafeteria manager had a rule that all children had to be fed by 8:30 a.m. It didn't matter if the student missed the bus or was tardy. If a child on that campus wanted to eat, that child had better be in her cafeteria by 8:30 a.m.

When my student asked me that question, I am sure I had a look of unbelief. First and foremost, a child who was late to school and had not eaten breakfast was being denied food. Furthermore, a cafeteria manager was setting the breakfast time and the principal was accepting that as a practice. My mind was saying, "Oh, this cafeteria manager and I need to meet face to face." My mouth said, "It is not against the law, but it is not a good practice to have a child go to a classroom and try to learn without having had something to eat."

Here is an excellent reason for you to take a food handler's course and get your health service card. Why? If a cafeteria manager told me she wasn't going to feed one of my children, I would legally be able to enter the food preparation area, find some cereal and a piece of toast, grab a milk carton, and feed the child. This is what made Ms. Ruth and her crew stand out above the rest.

In all my years as a teacher on the campus and then as the principal on that same campus, Ms. Ruth not only fed every child with love and kindness, she paid for their lunches when they couldn't, and she never turned a child away. Ms. Ruth became a loving institution on our campus and remained that until the day she retired.

THE GIFT OF RESPECT

The most valuable lesson I want to share with you regarding the concept of respect is not the definition of the word but the importance of how you give and show respect to others. The position of principal automatically comes with a sense of power and authority. The person who holds this position has the authority to make schedules, assign duties, and recommend people for employment.

A principal has the power to deny budgetary funds, change the class placement of students, and rearrange the teaching assignment of any staff member. However, having power and authority without respect for and from others in many instances translates into the actions of a bully. I certainly don't want you to be a bully.

Respect for the position (of principal) is automatic; respect for the person who holds the position is something that must be earned. I want you to look at respect as a reciprocal gift; you give respect to others for what they do, all the while earning respect from others as they watch and listen to how you treat people, what words you use, and how you make others feel.

From a very early age I was taught to be respectful of the elderly, say yes sir and no ma'am, speak only when spoken to, always be respectful when entering a house of worship, and always hold my hand over my heart when the national anthem was played. Hopefully, someone in your life taught you similar values.

My upbringing in this area happened not because I had shown signs of disrespect—just the opposite. Those who had a hand in my childhood taught me these lessons so that one day when I no longer stood by their sides, I would remember and have ingrained in me a way to give and receive respect.

As a principal, you will deal with children, parents, and community members from a multitude of economic and social levels. You will work with staff members from diverse backgrounds, different religious beliefs, and differing views on how the school should operate. So what will be your mantra when dealing with such diversity? The answer is very simple: Treat everyone, and I mean everyone—those you like, those you're angry with, those who have nothing, those who have more than you can imagine, everyone—the same.

At a conference years ago, I heard a story about the CEO of a company who had decided to retire. He had started the company and had been its leader for many years. During those years, he was famous for writing little notes to his employees when he saw them do any extraordinary act of kindness, help someone in a special way, or give someone the simple pleasure of seeing a smiling face.

The little notes were written on anything he had at that time, a napkin, a matchbook cover, or even a torn envelope. On the note he would give recognition to the person for their selfless action, and sign it with just three letters, JWD. He used this method to recognize his employees until the day of his retirement.

Because he had been such a vital part of the company, giving him a gold watch for his retirement seemed to lack something. The woman in charge of choosing the gift for this beloved boss was his former secretary. She asked several family members, his close friends, and even his pastor for their input. She wanted his retirement gift to be special and a true reflection of how the staff felt about him. After careful consideration, she finally knew what she had to do.

The retirement party was a grand success. Many former employees returned to pay their respects. Smiles and handshakes numbered in the thousands. Finally the time came to give him his parting gift. As he sat at the head table in the ballroom of a very prestigious hotel, his secretary slowly came down the center isle of the room holding a very large, silver-wrapped gift box. Just the size of the box alone made everyone gasp. The CEO graciously received the gift and opened the lid of the box. After a few minutes, his well-wishers were startled to see a single tear rolling down his cheek.

Inside the box were thousands of little scraps of paper, hundreds of napkins, and even more matchbook covers, all with messages of how they had watched him serve and help people over the years in the company. At the bottom line of every piece of paper in the box, after the written heartfelt message were three little letters, JWD: Job Well Done. The CEO had earned something more precious than any gold watch. He had earned the respect of those he worked with because he first showed them respect.

One of the best examples I ever had for showing respect to others came in the many lessons I learned under my former principal, Sandy McEntire. Sandy treated everyone the same regardless of their color, the clothes they wore, or where they lived. She was known in the community because of her love and dedication to the children who attended our school and because if she felt her kids needed something, they'd have it.

On one such learning excursion, I found myself going on a home visit with Sandy. Because our school was located in an economically depressed area, many of our students came to school with very few extras. However, if Sandy felt that a home visit would make a difference in a child's behavior or improve a child's grades, off we went. This particular visit found us in a rather run-down trailer, where it was very evident that the family inside was struggling with many financial situations.

As we entered the home, the mother offered us a cup of coffee. Sandy graciously accepted for both of us. I do not drink coffee and never have, but there I sat with a cup of coffee in my hands. The cup was clearly unclean and I even began to worry about what was in the coffee, but there sat Sandy moving the cup up and down from her mouth as she talked with the mother about her child's needs. During the conversation, I noticed something moving across the floor near the baseboards of the living room. Much to my horror, a rather large cockroach was headed my way.

I realize I sound rather prudish, and let me assure you I am not. When I was a child, we called cockroaches "Mr. Crunchy" because when we turned on the lights in the kitchen at night, we would try to squash as many of them as we could before the little brown bodies had hurriedly scattered to their respective hiding holes. When we scored a hit, it sounded like something was being crunched—hence, Mr. Crunchy.

It was not the fact that the house had a cockroach, it was the fact that it was coming toward me. How was I going to sit in this living room asking a woman to help us with her child in a calm manner with a cockroach crawling over my foot? But there sat Sandy, calm as you please, seeming to enjoy her cup of coffee.

Before I had a personal encounter with the Mr. Crunchy, Sandy was thanking the woman for any help she could provide, and we were back in the car returning to school. On the return trip, I asked her how she could drink from that cup all the while knowing she had seen the crunchy visitor. She simply replied that she never drank a drop of the coffee, only gave the impression she had.

And yes, she had watched the cockroach scurrying toward us, but this was the first time anyone had made contact with the mother of our troubled child and she was not missing an opportunity to talk with her. What Sandy McEntire taught me that day cannot be found on the pages of any textbook.

When she took that dingy cup with its unknown contents, when she sat on the couch in a home that was very far removed from the kind of homes we lived in, and when she accepted the fact that a cockroach could very well crawl over her shoe at any time, she was showing that mother the truest form of respect.

The cup of kindness offered to you does not have to be made of Lenox china. The small gift of a drink may be the only gift someone has to give, and where a person lives does not diminish their importance. Sandy is one of the wisest women I have ever known, and I never forgot the lessons I learned that day.

Sandy also taught me the importance of a chocolate cake. At the beginning of every year, Sandy made a chocolate cake and took it to the maintenance department, where she would offer pieces of the cake to the secretary and any of the workers present. She referred to this as "putting money in the bank." I took this same concept with me when I left the school to become a principal.

The district where I first served as an elementary principal was a small 3A school in East Texas. It was a very close-knit school community where everyone knew each other. Taking my cue from Sandy, every Thanksgiving and Christmas I baked a little something for the transportation department, maintenance workers, and cafeteria staff.

One year I would make miniature cheesecakes. The next year I would make an assortment of cookies or brownies. These were the people behind the scenes making sure my children came and went from school in a well-maintained bus with dependable drivers. These were the women who fed and greeted my children every day with a warm plate of food and hopefully a smile. I knew I could not forget them.

After I announced that I was leaving the school district, Julie, the cafeteria manager, called me to her office. As I walked through the cafeteria toward her office in the back of the kitchen area, I saw Julie and her entire staff standing there with a decorated basket filled with candles for me. Each one of the cafeteria ladies had brought a candle to put inside the basket. I was so touched to think that these ladies thought enough about me to give me a farewell gift.

They simply said thank you for not forgetting them during the holidays. In fact, I was the only one who ever thought about the lunch ladies in that way. It has been seven years since I left that school district, and honest to goodness, I am still using some of the candles that came from that basket.

Many times the people we work with, such as the school secretary, the custodial staff, and the lunch ladies, are forgotten. Some staff members only see the position someone holds or the service performed and do not see the person behind the work. Most of my experiences with support staff people have been positive and worthwhile.

Ms. Eunice did her job with grace and efficiency because every task she did reflected on her as a person. Ms. Ruth wanted to serve only the best food to her children because she knew it might be the only hot and nutritious meal many of the children would get that day. Phyllis and Mary Lou were aware that they were the first faces many parents or visitors encountered at our school, and they wanted to be as friendly as possible. Respect is such a small gift when given to the right people at the right time for the right reasons.

GIVE ME DELEGATION OR GIVE ME DEATH

I am a firm believer that experiences from our childhood leave lasting imprints on our belief systems and actions as adults. In my particular case, I had several adult responsibilities placed on my shoulders at an early age. Because of this, I learned that if I accepted a job, no matter how small or how difficult, that job was to be done and done well. Without going into too much psychotherapy mush, because I had many responsibilities as a child, as an adult, I was very able to handle many of the situations that came my way.

Pretending to be Super Woman does not turn you into Super Smart Woman. Other than the school secretaries and assistant principals I have worked with, I did not expect nor ask for others' help. If I did something myself, I knew it would be done on time and in a professional manner. Otherwise, I could easily picture Big John and Grandpa shaking their heads in disapproval if I had failed in my attempt to complete a project on time or in the right way. I don't only need a psychiatrist's couch; I need Dr. Phil on speed dial.

The student population of both the campuses I served on numbered close to 450 students. Remind me again, how many principals were there? Oh yes, one—me. Between twenty and twenty-five classroom teachers taught those children. Let's stop again and do some math: twenty-five classroom teachers to one principal. The odds were not in my favor.

Now let's think about the many times 450 students pass in and out of rooms, travel back and forth to lunch, and leave the building every day. Let's play the numbers game one more time: 450 traveling students to one principal. No one is even taking this bet in Las Vegas. I needed some help and so will you.

Asking for help is not a sign of weakness. One more time: Asking for help is not a sign of weakness. I had to say this to myself quite often. Letting the school counselor gather testing data for you does not mean you have neglected your duties as the instructional leader of the campus. Limiting the number of after-school events that you attend is not a reflection on the way you care for your children. There is one of you and many, many more of them. If someone offers a little bit of help to make your day easier, see that act as a gift and simply say thank you.

When I took the first principalship, I truly believed I had to be everywhere and know everything. Almost every Sunday, I prepared lunch for my family, settled everyone in for a nap or movie time after lunch, and headed off to school, where I would work until late in the afternoon catching up on paperwork or preparing for the next week.

I was already tired of schoolwork before Monday rolled around again. I am telling you all of this to hopefully prevent you from doing the same thing. If I had only learned to accept the offers of help and trusted others more, I would have become the duchess of delegation and worn my crown of jewels with pride.

Multitasking can be your pal, your buddy—but definitely make delegation your friend. I want you to learn how to welcome and nurture that friendship. While attending a conference, a session speaker shared about the time he spent in his classrooms, the way he worked on projects with his students, and made time to be in and out of classrooms every day. After the session was over, I asked him how he managed to be out of his office so much, and he said, "Delegation, delegation, delegation."

I continued asking him for specifics so I, in turn, could return to my campus and put some of those practices in place. He shared that his secretary opened all his mail except those things from the superintendent or marked "Confidential." He had complete trust in her to know what he needed to see and what needed to be thrown away.

The office team met every Monday morning after the last bell and mapped out their calendars for the week to let everyone know where he was going and what plans he had that week. From there, he set aside at least one day to be on his campus visiting classrooms and seeing his teachers. The only reason that plan ever changed was in case of an emergency. Otherwise, he left the confines of his office and spent quality time with his staff and his students.

This man had delegation down to a fine art. He let the people he trusted the most, his office staff, handle things as they arose. Because he was a confident leader and his staff knew his expectations, he allowed them some authority so he could be with the children.

Learn to do what he did and not what I did. Let others help you so that you can see the teaching and learning that takes place on your campus. Give yourself some time to build important relationships with the students. At the same time, be visible on the campus to help teachers with immediate needs as well as to prevent a few discipline situations.

The English journalist Anthea Turner said, "The first rule of management is delegation. Don't try and do everything yourself because you can't" (brainyquotes.com n.d.). She is right. You need to make that conscious decision before you wear yourself out, become fatigued, and fall out of love with the job.

Delegation does not translate into you cannot do your job. So let your Phyllis or Mary Lou sort through the mail and only give you what you need to address. Let your Phyllis and Mary Lou be in charge of keeping you aware of budgetary balances. Ask your Ms. Eunice to open the school doors for you if you have an early dental appointment. You will be surprised to find out how many people are willing to help.

The roles and responsibilities of the principalship are varied and many. I don't want you to think that my ability to delegate occurred overnight. My face did not readily appear on the cover of *Delegation Daily* as the new spokeswoman. Letting go of a responsibility that had been given to me was not easy. I had not been raised to shirk a responsibility. But I want more for you. I want your Sundays to be filled with family times, birthday parties, and picnics, not weekend warrior work at the school.

Once I started mastering the art of delegation, I found good ways to put it to use. The assistant principal and I started sharing after-school functions such as school plays or parent meetings. If a play was offered on several nights, he would stay for one of the performances and I would attend the other one. We divided the number of teacher observations in half and then met at the end of the appraisal period to discuss our findings. This also meant that I was only responsible for reading the lesson plans of the teachers I evaluated. Because he handled most of the discipline concerns on the campus, he was responsible for inputting the data regarding the discipline reports. If I had any concerns about the past discipline problems of a child, I would only need to pull up his or her record and the file was available. Slowly, I learned to recognize the abilities in others as I was afforded time to be in the classrooms and with my children.

As I learned to let others help me with specific tasks, I also had to learn to accept what they turned in as completed projects. I may have already mentioned that I suffer from a slight case of obsessive-compulsive disorder. Those who know me would say that it's not so slight of a case. I did learn, however, to be gracious when their completed projects did not look like something I expected. And then I heard the story of the little boy who was learning to make his bed.

One day a little boy made his bed and sped down the hallway of his home looking for his mother. He was so proud of what he had done and wanted her to see his newly made bed. The little boy found his mother and eagerly pulled her into his bedroom. His sheet and blanket were clumped together at the headboard of the bed and his pillow was slanted sideways, but there he stood all grins and smiles at what he had accomplished.

The mother shouted praises at what a good job he had done and how proud she was of him. He beamed, until she said, "I am so proud of the way you made your bed, but your sheets should look like this," and she started straightening the sheets. The mother continued, "Look at what a big boy you are becoming, but let me show you how your pillow should really look." By the end of the episode, with the bed remade, the little boy left his room without his grins and smiles.

When you delegate, let someone make a mistake. Quite possibly you did not give clear instructions. If you ask someone to finish a project you started, be clear and succinct in your expectations. Maybe there will be a few times when you have to redo something or add a specific piece, but never forget to give people credit for what they were able to do. For heaven's sake, do not let the word "but" leave someone dejected or without his or her grins and smiles.

MAKING THE MOST OF WHAT YOU HAVE

Hanging on a wall of my house is a picture of a tree with thumbprints that look like little caricatures of mice, birds, and various little figures. Below these little figures are the names of the staff members who worked with me during one of my principalships. Each of the thumbprints is as unique as those individuals I worked with.

The picture still reminds me that even though I was the principal, there were many, many people who made what happened in that school possible. Those inked thumbprints take me back to a time and a place where a phenomenal group of dedicated and caring teachers and staff members made our school a warm, welcoming, and an exciting place to learn.

For the most part, I have been genuinely blessed with teachers who brought classrooms to life and made children want to come to school every day. When budgets were tight, the teachers planned very creative ways to get the supplies their children needed. If I had to rearrange their schedules, as long as I told them in plenty of time, most were very accommodating. One of the most daunting responsibilities of a school leader is building a school community with your staff.

This was the type of place Sandy McEntire built the first year she opened our school. Many former colleagues I taught with have described that year as one of sheer magic. McEntire, as most of us called her, set the tone from the very first meeting she had with us as a faculty. She let us know that the kids would come first, that we were about to work harder than we ever had, and that if we had a problem with that we could certainly see her in her office later where the discussion of what you were not prepared to do for her children would continue.

McEntire inspired and appreciated her teachers and never let us forget we were there not as individuals, but as a collective group of people with the same focus and intent, to teach children so that they learned something new every day.

During my first year as the principal of a school, I so tried to take this philosophy with me. I read countless books on leadership and what it took to build a cohesive focused team of people. I searched for ways to say thank you or to show the staff how much I appreciated them. We addressed certain school situations and needs during grade-level and faculty meetings. I thought I had built that same kind of magic that McEntire created, until April of that first year.

You and I both know that not every one of your staff members will come on board and want to be a member of the good ship *Lollypop*, no matter how many special notes you leave on their desks or how many special treats you put in their boxes. Some people just want to stir the waters.

I was lucky that first year that I only had one teacher who really did not want to play nice. Several things had transpired between us that year, and I was almost at my wits' end. As one of the items on my agenda, I placed a little reminder to the staff about what kind of team we were trying to create. The line read something like this, "If you do not want to be part of the team at this school, why don't you apply at Eckerd's [now known as CVS]."

Little did I know what that one statement would do! One day, I was called to the office to meet a visitor to the school. There stood the manager of one of the Eckerd's located in town, whom I had known for years.

For some reason, I thought he was bringing us some toothbrushes for my third-grade classes. To this day, I have no idea what made me think that particular thought. He followed me into my office where we sat and exchanged some small talk. When I asked what I could do for him, he asked, "Janet, what have we done to upset you?"

I sat at my desk in amazement wondering why he was not talking about the toothbrushes I knew he had waiting for us in his car. What had Eckerd's done to me that caused me to be upset with the company? I really had no idea what he was talking about until he pulled from his pocket a copy of my last faculty meeting agenda.

The agenda had made its way to Clearwater, Florida, to the chairman of the entire Eckerd Corporation. What I did not know then but what I do know now is that the corporation was very proud of their company and their employees. When I wrote that line item about leaving our school and working for Eckerd's if you could not be a valuable team player for the campus, I was basically humiliating the company with my offer to send a nonproductive teacher to work for them.

To make matters worse, someone had added a note to the top of the memo, "I guess this means that anyone who can't cut it as a teacher can always work for a company like Eckerd's where skill does not matter." I am sure you are thinking the same thing I thought: Does this mean I won't be getting my toothbrushes for the third grade?

I did not even have to wonder or guess who had mailed the agenda. There was a teacher on the campus who, from the moment she found out I was going to be the principal, had done and said a few things that caused me some problems. I was sure this was the handiwork of the teacher previously mentioned.

After the faculty meeting, she had taken the agenda, written the nasty little remark at the top of the page, and mailed it to the company's CEO in Florida. The CEO received the note and sent it to a district manager in Houston, Texas, named Jed. Jed then sent it to the manager I knew, who was assigned the task of visiting me at the school and getting his bosses some answers.

So there we sat, me with my mouth gaping open and my friend needing an explanation. I proceeded to explain to him the situation and said that by no means had my intention ever been to slander the great Eckerd Corporation. I was only trying to impress on the staff that we had to act like and be a team if we were going to achieve the many things we needed to accomplish. Eckerd's had always been a strong community supporter of our school, and of course I wanted that relationship to continue. In the past, they had made several donations to our teachers and the school, including toothbrushes.

After our conversation, my friend assured me he would relay the information and the explanation to his supervisors. This was only a bump, but it was my line-in-the-sand bump. I was finished putting up with her devious and malicious acts. As soon as he left, my anger and I headed for the superintendent's office.

When I reached the administration building, the superintendent was standing in the little kitchenette preparing his lunch. As soon as he saw the look on my face he knew something was amiss. I raged toward him with blaring questions and fierce words. I am sure he thought that any minute my head would begin to rotate on my shoulders and green slime would spew from my mouth.

With as much force as an F5 tornado, I gritted my teeth and said, "I'm done. She has tried to destroy me all year, but this is the last straw." I proceeded to tell him what had happened with the manager from Eckerd's, and he proceeded to laugh hysterically—which only added fuel to the fire.

The superintendent shared that he had had many encounters with this same teacher, and he knew I would be able to handle it. He wanted me to return to my campus and act as if nothing had happened. I wanted to confront her in the hallway, call her horrible names, and turn off the air conditioning in her room.

At this particular time, I did not want to be the better person. Yet in the long run, his advice was sound and in my best interests. By doing nothing, I actually showed the staff that whatever anyone did or said about me, true or false, I would always treat everyone the same, with dignity and respect, even if they did not deserve it.

For the most part, teachers are extremely hard workers who genuinely care about their children. They actually serve as missionaries who give so much of themselves, asking for hardly anything in return. The type of staff member who causes you grief is a very small representation of the whole staff. Do not let that person get the better of you. Remain calm and positive, expect others to be respectful toward each other, be the bigger person even when you do not want to be, and you will earn the personal respect that comes with the position of principal.

One of my favorite pictures from the years of my principalship is that of a small child carrying a black trash bag up the small incline of one of our hallways. His back is to the camera and the lighting in the hallway shines just right on his small image. It was Christmas, and we had just finished our Angel Tree celebration.

Angel Tree was what we called a Christmas project where we helped families who might not be able to bring a joyful Christmas into their own homes. The counselor asked the teachers to identify children in their classrooms who they felt might not have a merry Christmas because of their family's financial situation. Once they were identified, the counselor contacted the parents to see if in fact they did need help that Christmas.

If the parents said they did need help, our counselor started asking for donations to make Christmas special for some of the children. Instead of just handing out black trash bags filled with miscellaneous toys, the counselor talked with each family and asked what they really needed. She also asked if there were any younger children in the home who might need a little something. Then she started on the task of gathering the needed gifts.

Joy still fills my heart when I think about all those teachers who, when asked to help a child in yet another way, gave freely and without hesitation. Not only did they shop for the items requested, they went above and beyond by adding little extras to make a memorable Christmas for the children.

Instead of just handing out these care packages, the counselor invited the parents to a reception with cookies and drinks. Instead of being treated to a handout, mothers and fathers had an opportunity to sit and talk with teachers, the counselor, and me. Most of the teachers participated in the gift giving and received so much more than the little toy or stocking stuffer they gave. And then there was one . . .

Remember the teacher who took my parking space? She came into my office one day during Angel Tree collection time to let me know she did not plan to help with Angel Tree and she really had some objections to my expecting teachers to buy Christmas gifts for other children. She had already planned to do a little something for the students in her class-room, and she didn't have the funds to do anything extra. By not signing up to help with Angel Tree, it would appear that she didn't care about other children who would have little to nothing at Christmas.

When she was through voicing her opinion about our Angel Tree prac-tice, I just sat there and told her that I certainly appreciated what she was doing for her homeroom students and that if her funds were short, I certainly didn't expect her to go into debt helping another child.

I may have also told her that by no means did I want her to take part in something as rewarding and selfless as Angel Tree if she did not have a giving heart. If anyone asked why some teachers had decided not to help with Angel Tree, I would certainly tell them that it is truly better to give than receive and I couldn't wait to see what those teachers would receive.

When our instructional specialist saw that teacher leave my office, she came in and saw me red-faced and growling. I was seething. Yes, seething. She reminded me of all the teachers who would give, of the counselor who had worked so hard to plan a reception for the parents, and of the many children we would be able to help have a wonderful Christmas that year. That picture of the little boy dragging his Angel Tree gifts up that little incline said it all.

The teachers on your campus who give without seeking any recognition are angels and gifts from above. They continually bring happiness and joy into the lives of children. And if one or two don't, it is truly their loss.

DEVELOPING YOUR OWN PERSONAL LEADERSHIP CAPACITY

This entire chapter has been dedicated to showing you that the prin-cipal of a school cannot do everything the position entails without the help of others. Even a little confrontation spurs action and learning.

You will also be responsible for making the entire staff feel respected and appreciated, from the teacher with the most years of experience to the custodial worker who has been on the job for only two days. By your example, the teachers and the students will learn to recognize the importance of each person they come in contact with while at school. I would like to offer a few pieces of wisdom that might help you as you build your personal leadership capacity.

1. Work very hard to ensure that each person on that campus feels important and needed.
2. Work very hard to ensure that every person who enters the school, whether superintendent or mechanic, is treated equally and with respect.
3. When you let others help you, you are actually saying to them, "I trust you."
4. If you do not do it now, always take the time to talk with the support staff of your school such as the school secretary, head custodian, and cafeteria manager. Take an interest in them and they will never let you down.
5. Learn to let people walk with and beside you, not behind you.
6. Look for those times when the heart of the school reaches out to those who are less fortunate.
7. Accept the fact that not all of your staff will give of themselves at the level that you expect. Simply applaud those who give and what they give.

WHAT WILL MY PRINCIPALSHIP SAY ABOUT ME?

In pioneer days, farmers gathered together to help others build a barn. The women prepared lunches and lemonade. The invitation to help a neighbor was extended to all during the Sunday church service. On said barn-raising day, farmers and friends joined together to help someone, and it became a community event.

That's what your principalship really is—a community event. Whether through team-building exercises or birthday parties, you have a unique opportunity to build something special on your campus. And when you decide to retire or leave your campus, I want others who have worked with you to be able to say . . .

"She reminded me so much of Will Rogers. She never met a person she didn't like."

"I knew he was not happy with me, but he never let it show."

"If and when she decides to leave this campus, I want to go with her."

"I asked him if I could help him with the new schedules, and he said he would really appreciate the help. He made me feel like my opinion mattered."

"She always knows just what to say to make you feel important."

USING 20/20 VISION

Mother Teresa probably always knew she was destined to help the poorest of the poor. Princess Diana never realized that when she visited a hospital to see patients suffering with AIDS that she would impact the whole world.

You may never know what it means to a custodian or cafeteria worker when you ask about his or her weekend, how the family is doing, or when you just have a cup of coffee with him or her. As a Proactive Principal with 20/20 vision, there are a few things you can do to enlist the help of others and show respect to all you meet.

- ☐ Learn the names of every cafeteria, maintenance, and custodial person who helps to make your campus safe and welcoming.
- ☐ Learn as much as you can about your immediate office staff: birthdays, anniversaries, children's names, favorite perfume.
- ☐ Hold Monday morning meetings with your office staff to detail the week's activities.
- ☐ Write notes of appreciation on a regular basis.
- ☐ Keep your calendar updated on a regular basis.
- ☐ Don't forget that you also deserve respect.

MY WISH FOR YOU

My wish for you is that you learn to let others give unselfish hands
 to help with any task, not because it's a command.
My wish for you is that you learn the importance of giving respect
 and no one on your campus senses a hint of any neglect.
My wish for you is that you learn that some duties can be shared
 to save you time and energy that you really just can't spare.
My wish for you is that your Tontos ride always by your side
 and that your school is filled with great success and heartfelt pride.

ADDITIONAL RESOURCES

Reading Material

Buck, Frank. *Get Organized! Time Management for School Leaders*. Larch-
 mont, NY: Eye on Education, 2008.
Hacker, Carol A. *The High Cost of Low Morale . . . and What to Do about It*.
 Boca Raton, FL: St. Lucie Press, 1997.
Hoyle, John. *Leadership and the Force of Love: Six Keys to Motivating with
 Love*. Thousand Oaks, CA: Corwin Press, 2002.
Sharp, William L., and James K. Walter. *The Principal as School Manager*.
 Lanham, MD: Rowman & Littlefield, 2003.
Sims, Bobbi. *Don't Let Them Crumble Your Cookies: It's Your Life*. Gretna,
 LA: Pelican, 1998.

Internet Sources

www.educationworld.com/a_admin/how_i_handled/how_i_handled
034.shtml
Education World provides a wealth of information for any school leader.
This particular page offers suggestions on how to recognize all staff
members.

www.educ.uvic.ca/epls/faculty/storey/Starr.htm
Through the study provided here, principals and teachers can learn
more about the importance of building collaborative relationships.

cnx.org/content/m14705/latest/
Connexions offers a lesson from a module on the importance of creating trusting relationships between a principal and the teachers. Several suggestions of how to accomplish this are provided.

www.cadetstuff.org/archives/000335.html
The concept of respect is explained through comparisons made between school leadership and earning the respect from others while in the Marines. The concepts are priceless.

www.ehow.com/how_4511431_earn-respect-work-personal-relationships.html
This site provides several links to articles that help explore and explain the importance of showing and giving respect to everyone.

10

I'M SUPPOSED TO
KNOW HOW TO DO WHAT?

School leadership encompasses both managerial and instructional tasks. Principal preparation programs are designed not only to help prepare future principals through theoretical knowledge but also to ready them for the enormity of the job of principal. As with any profession, the job qualifications associated with the performance of duties should be clearly and succinctly stated.

The principalship is no different. Before a person decides to become an effective school leader, the real requirements of the job should be listed somewhere and discussed before an aspiring principal signs on the dotted line.

Most school districts provide a list of required duties that involve the principalship. The Texas Association of School Boards offers such a list (2006).

1. Complete staff assignments.
2. Develop and successfully use allocated budget funds.
3. Evaluate all personnel.
4. Supervise all instructional methods.
5. Develop schoolwide improvements plans.
6. Care for the school facilities.
7. Perform any and all duties assigned.

The above duties are general in nature and what I refer to as "the givens." These tasks are what are expected of a school leader. A principal should be the instructional leader on the campus and recommend for employment only the best and the brightest teachers. Principals should be able to keep a budget and take care of their schools.

These givens come naturally with the position. It's the other, unspoken duties and responsibilities that fill a principal's day with the unknowns and unexpected events that make your new best candy a bottle of Tums. Taking on a principalship requires even more than it did five years ago. I also want you to realize that even though there are only seven tasks listed, this is only a fraction of what you will face during a school year. This chapter presents a different side of the expected duties and focuses on the real-world duties of the principal's job.

WHY DO I HAVE TO COME BACK IN JULY?

Many years ago when I was a newbie teacher, the teaching profession adopted a slogan that read, "I became a teacher for three reasons: June, July, and August." The slogan appeared on T-shirts that teachers wore, on coffee mugs that sat at every teacher's desk, and on school bags that teachers proudly carried on vacation or to Walmart. Little regard was actually given to the comical phrase, expect for the fact that this little ho-ho funny statement really translated into "I became a teacher so I only have to work nine months of the year." Which, as a teacher, you know is absurd.

Dedicated and caring teachers work all year long. They grade papers in the car while travelling to their vacation sites. They can locate the nearest teacher supply store simply by raising their noses in the air and sniffing for the blue tacky stuff that makes a teacher's life a little easier.

Committed teachers strive to improve professionally by attending every conference they can and visiting the exhibit halls to collect the giveaway goodies for their own classroom giveaway bags. This should also become a way of life for you as the campus leader. You'll be surprised when you find out exactly what goes on in July and August as you prepare yourself and your campus for a new school year.

As much as I did enjoy my years as an elementary principal, there was nothing like the last day of school watching as the last little child climbed aboard the bus and waved goodbye. I can remember walking slowly back to the school thinking, "Now I can rest. Now, I will be able to finally clean out and reorganize my closet. I will actually be able to take all those stacks of papers from beneath my desk and file them in their designated folders."

Summer break had officially started, and I could not wait to prop my feet on top of my desk, play Hearts on the computer, and eat ice cream bonbons all day. Well, if you can find a principalship that allows this to happen, take the job. Sign the contract today. In fact, let me know about it and I will apply.

For about two weeks after the last day of school, you will have a great deal to do in order to close out the school year. This is where your skills as an effective manager will come in handy. The list below mentions only a few of the end-of-the year duties that will need to be completed.

1. At the high school level, all graduation requirements must be completed.
2. All budgetary accounts have to be closed out and balanced.
3. Summer maintenance requests are submitted to the maintenance department.
4. All classrooms have to be readied for cleaning.
5. At the elementary level, class rosters need to be finalized.
6. All grades have to be collected and filed in each student's permanent records.
7. Permanent records for students leaving your campus need to be transferred to their new campus.
8. Textbooks have to be counted and accounted for.
9. Personnel are assigned their duties for next year.
10. Summer work schedules are aligned with the custodial and maintenance plans.

Also realize that there are state and federal responsibilities, such as the fire alarm report, the retention plan for students, and attendance records, which must be finalized before you can even think about popping even one bonbon in your mouth. Your district may also have a checklist that you are required to finish before you leave for the summer. Be sure to find out what your district expects of you as you close out the end of the year.

If you are on a twelve-month contract, your vacation time translates into about fourteen days. Use it wisely. Rent a cabin far, far away from a phone line. Buy a novel that does not require any thinking or have the words "school," "education," or "responsibility" on any page. Go fishing and sit on a dock where the only thing you have to do is throw a fishing line in and out of the water all day long. For those two weeks, wherever you end up, make sure it is very far away from ringing bells, yellow buses, and backpacks.

Stock the fridge with your favorite foods and make sure the TV remote has plenty of batteries. Become fast friends with the daytime television schedule, which requires absolutely no thought processing whatsoever. I knew a high school math teacher who spent his entire summer vacation hiking and camping. Whatever you do, from watching mindless television programs to knitting doilies for a church bazaar, be sure to rest. Believe me, at the end of a busy school year you will look and feel like a bowl of mush. July will be there before you know it, and so will all the responsibilities that come with beginning another school year.

June was perhaps my favorite summer month. I was still so filled with the day-to-day operational energy that I used during the school year that finishing the end-of-the-year tasks never became a problem; they were easily accomplished. Around the end of June and the beginning of July, I was running out of steam and ready to play and rest.

Even though I would officially take the time coming to me, I had a teacher's heart and mind and school was never far from my thoughts. When Red Lobster decided to change its menus, I just happened to be there and asked if I could have them for one of my teachers. They were very gracious and I was able to acquire enough for an entire class to use as a learning tool for math. I would call the local printing company to ask for their extras and pick up boxes and boxes of scrap paper for my teachers.

I attended summer conferences for elementary principals and collected idea after idea from colleagues, then worked on their suggestions during my time off. I was always so impressed with educators who could simply turn off school thinking like running water from a faucet. I never could. However, if you are not careful, part of you will become a little crispy around the edges on your way to complete combustion.

For seasoned principals, beginning a new school year requires little thought. They know the decisions that have to be made, they know a master schedule is needed, and they are aware of the needed supplies, furniture, and textbooks. These principals are so proficient at opening a school year that it has become second nature to them.

However, if you are just beginning your principalship, having a checklist might help save you time and energy. In my first years, I kept a notebook with monthly calendars that designated what needed to be done that month and what special events occurred during that month.

For instance, February is designated as Dental Health Month, and usually a local dentist donated toothbrushes to the third-grade students on my campus. It also happens to be a time when principals begin looking at their student projections and personnel needs for the upcoming school year. For the first few years, this notebook took the place of my diary. After I became familiar with what needed to be done to open and close a school year, I no longer needed the notebook.

With a desire to help students and teachers, a positive and eager attitude, and your handy-dandy checklist in hand, you are indeed ready to prepare yourself and the school for a new year. However, I would be remiss if I did not add a few pointers I learned along the way that do not show up on any pre-planning list.

As much as I love elementary teachers for all their hard work and dedication to their students, they turn into vicious beasts when it comes to preparing their rooms and getting themselves organized before school starts. After talking with several secondary principals about this behavior, they assured me that their teachers do not have the same killer instinct to work in their classrooms as elementary teachers do.

Elementary teachers begin calling around the end of July on a regular basis to find out, first, if their class list is ready, and second, when they can get inside their rooms to work. Because you are a wise and rested principal, you instruct the school secretary, if he or she has returned to work, to inform the teachers that their class list will be available to them the last Friday in July at 3:00 in the afternoon.

Why this time frame, you ask? Because as soon as the lists are made available to the teachers, parents will begin their yearly grapevine chat system, which is more advanced than any communications operation system used by the CIA, FBI, or NATO.

Teachers will call other teachers about who is going to be in their class this year. Parents across the city and county borders will know within a matter of minutes if their Little Janie is in the same room as her best friend, Little Susie. And before you know it, the phone will start to ring with parent concerns, new class placement requests, or why did their child get the new teacher instead of Mrs. Wilson, who has been at the school since Washington crossed the Delaware? I understand this is primarily an elementary phenomenon, but if you become an elementary principal this is something you will have to address.

Another item that will not be found on your list is the custodian's work schedule. I learned very quickly that when Ms. Eunice (our head custodian) was ready to strip and wax her floors, it was in my best interests and the best interests of my staff to close down the school, place padlocks on the doors, and send out an all-points bulletin to any teacher who might consider daring to cross the WAX ON FLOORS sign, that entering the building during those days would be punishable by death— or even worse, extra car duty.

Ms. Eunice did not play when it came to preparing her floors and her school for when her children returned for the new school year. Just like any teacher, Ms. Eunice took pride in the school and its presence. I have never seen a woman as mad as Ms. Eunice when she discovered that some teacher had decided to move furniture from one room to the next and left scratches on a newly waxed floor.

So, to save the life of a teacher and to keep your custodian from having a stroke, simply meet with the custodial staff, identify the days they need to complete their tasks, and send out that information to all staff members by e-mail, letter, phone tree, or carrier pigeon. Just do not let them in the building when the custodial staff plans to wax the floors.

On your list of tasks to complete, there will also be a missing element regarding a summer budget. This one is very simple: There is no summer budget. In most school districts, the yearly budget draws to a close sometime in March or April. Therefore, there are little to no available funds until the first of September when the school board approves a new school budget. What does this mean for you and your teachers in the summer?

Teachers possess an extra gene that other professionals do not have. This gene gives them the ability to locate teacher supply stores, going-out-of-business sales, and church bazaars better than any other working person on the planet. They find children's books for ten cents, leftover craft material, and discontinued school supplies as well as any bloodhound finds a lost child in the woods. In some instances, they will ask when they will be reimbursed for their summer finds. The answer once again is a very simple one: Regardless of how much you would like to repay them for their purchases, you cannot, because there is no budget.

No textbook can truly prepare you for how to successfully start a new school year. Every year, you will learn another valuable lesson. I know I did. I learned to mark on my calendar when the fire marshal was due. This reminded me to ask our custodial staff to clear out the mechanical closets that teachers had used all year as their extra storage centers.

I remembered to put signs on the furniture in a new teacher's classroom that read, "Do not move any furniture in this room. T."—or else a new teacher would end up with all the mismatched chairs from other classrooms, and the kidney-shaped work table that had been in the room would be replaced with a piece of plywood and four cinder blocks.

I truly love teachers—but stand out of their way when they learn that a teacher is retiring or resigning. Before the sun sets on the day they find out Ms. Smith is retiring, teachers will have scavenged in her room for an extra file cabinet, moved chairs with missing tips out of their room and replaced them with Ms. Smith's matching chairs, and absconded with all Ms. Smith's extra boxes of tissue. This will not make the person completing the inventory list for that year a happy camper. In fact, the person who usually completes the classroom inventory check is you. Before I learned to put a "Do not touch the furniture" sign on extra furniture, I spent days trying to locate missing furniture that had been assigned to particular rooms. Usually, a teacher had rearranged her classroom and now Ms. Smith's furniture was sitting all nice and pretty in another room. When this happened, I just asked the custodial staff to help me move the furniture back to where it belonged, thus keeping my inventory list in order, at least for a little while. What is the teacher going to say? "Oh, that sign on the chairs that said don't move the furniture—you weren't talking to me, were you?"

Returning in July allows you time to accomplish all the little tasks that need to be done, as well as some time to take care of your school before the hectic pace of a new school year begins. Whether it's furniture moving or placing children in their homerooms, be prepared to face a multitude of managerial tasks that have to be completed in order to make the first of school go smoothly.

SCHEDULING IS YOUR FRIEND

A major responsibility facing school leaders every year regardless of the age of the students or the grade levels on your campus is the completion of the master schedule. Whether your assignment is to an elementary or secondary campus, there must be some viable order about where teachers and students are supposed to be, when they are supposed to be there, and what they are supposed to do when they get to where they are supposed to be.

As an elementary principal, I always started by determining when conference times would take place. By doing that, I also determined my PE and music schedules. For instance, if the fourth grade had the earliest PE time one year, I would assign fifth grade the earliest PE time the next year. I usually left the youngest grade level for the latest PE times, because they learn best in the morning.

The one thing I always tried to avoid was giving a particular grade level back-to-back lunch and conference times. This practice brought an entire other set of situations for me to deal with. For instance, some teachers thought they could leave campus, take care of personal errands around town, and ask their fellow teachers to pick up their kids from lunch because they were running a little late at the nail place.

I heard of a school where this type of thing happened so frequently that the district initiated a practice that all teachers leaving their campuses were required to sign out when they left school and sign in upon their return. By carefully considering your lunch and conference schedules, you may avoid this dilemma.

For secondary schools, a master schedule program is primarily utilized when assigning students and teachers to classrooms and conference times. Also, the type of instructional program of the secondary campuses determines much of the schedule.

For example, some secondary schools have seven- or eight-period days, with a bell sounding every fifty to fifty-five minutes sending students to their next classroom. Some schools have adopted an A-B block schedule, where three classes are offered on one day for an extended amount of time and the student's other classes are offered the next day. So the students meet with their teachers on an every-other-day basis.

By using a scheduling program, students and teachers are fed into a system that automatically assigns them a time and class schedule. The problem with this plan is that when the scheduling program is completed, there may be thirty-five students in one English class and eleven in another, only four kids in Homemaking I, and sixty-five children in first-period athletics. You still need to be the final voice when deciding the assignment and class lists for the new year.

Because running a school equates to managing a small city or factory, proper scheduling is vital. A good place to start is with the bell schedule. On those campuses that incorporate a seven- to eight-period day, a bell is sounding every fifty to fifty-five minutes—and it's not just one bell. A bell rings to tell students when to leave one classroom and another bell rings to tell students that they'd better be in the new classroom. Bells are sounding time changes better than the chimes in a grandfather's clock.

Elementary campus bell schedules are simpler. A first bell rings usually with the intent to send children to their homeroom classes. Then a second bell lets everyone know, teachers and students, that the day has officially begun. And the final bell signifies a student's last chance to be counted at school on time. That last bell is the dreaded tardy bell.

If an elementary parent was asked what they disliked most about a bell schedule, I guarantee they would say the tardy bell. Because this age student does not drive yet, the tardiness of a child driven to school falls as a lack of responsibility of their parents or caregiver. The tardiness issues became so profound in our district that the elementary schools collectively decided on a common tardy bell schedule and established practices to address the situation, such as legal actions taken against the parent or guardian.

Because this age child cannot drive, when a child was habitually late we asked the student why he or she was late and wrote the reason down using their own words on a tardy slip. Here are a few that I remember.

"I was late because my mother wouldn't stop watching her movie on TV."

"My mother likes to drop my sister off at the high school first so she can see her boyfriend before class."

"My dad has to go to back to jail today and Mom said I could stay home a little longer before he has to go back in."

"My dad and mom got in another fight and my grandpa had to come get me and he drives real slow."

If the child earned more than three tardy slips in a given amount of time, a form letter generated from the school was sent to the parents.

When the parents received the letter letting them know that the next tardy slip their child received would result in disciplinary actions for the student and the parent, angry parents started coming out of the woodwork. That is when I would pull out our copies of the tardy slips and begin reading the reasons their child had given us for being late.

Most of the time, this worked to our advantage. I did actually have a parent who said that because her child was not a morning person would I consider changing the tardy bell schedule to about 8:30 a.m. instead of 8:10 a.m. I politely told her I could not do that because the tardy bell schedule was determined by the district. And besides that, my Mama said I did not have to.

Another scheduling nightmare that is of great importance is the lunch schedule. Remember the analogy of how running a school is similar to running a small city or factory? You'd better have a well-oiled procedure for feeding the inhabitants of that small town.

The age of the children you serve will help you build a lunch schedule that works around special programs, early dismissal times, and regular instructional requirements. Some principals stagger lunch periods, which results in one grade level or group coming to the cafeteria every ten or fifteen minutes.

Oh, did I forget to mention that someone has to actually be in the cafeteria directing the hungry hordes as they move toward their goal of steak fingers, mashed potatoes, and green beans? And that person is probably you. On elementary campuses from about 10:30 a.m. (yes, that early) to about 1:45 in the afternoon, the quiet cafeteria turns into a four-walled, closed room for unleashed noise, possible mayhem, and prayer time for the next bell.

Creating an efficient lunch schedule reminded me of the days when there were no traffic lights and a policeman stood in the center of a busy street and directed the traffic. By just the gesture of his hands, the policeman stopped oncoming traffic, allowed pedestrians to cross to the other side of the street, and blew his whistle to signal that another group of travelers could move forward on their way.

Keep this picture of the policeman in mind when the time comes to build an efficient lunch schedule. Look for the flow of traffic in and out of the cafeteria. Give the cafeteria staff time enough between classes to clean the tables. Make sure you assign enough people to lunch duty so that the process flows according to the schedule. Whether you are on an elementary or secondary campus, build a lunch schedule that is efficient and create a plan that moves the children in and out of the cafeteria with ease.

It's time to finally talk about the duty that will cause you the most grief—after-school duty. For any school campus, the primary reason you assign car and bus duties is the safety factor. With adults on duty, children are more likely to move into the school in an orderly fashion and at the end of the day, leave the school the same way. Therefore, you are in charge of scheduling for those duties. The one solid piece of advice that I can afford you in this particular area is to count the number of times each teacher is assigned either car or bus duty. If you do not make it equitable, you could possibly hear about it later.

In order to make the duty list equitable for all the staff members, I usually began making the schedule for car and bus duties with a tally sheet. I used a roster listing our staff members, and with the thirty-six-week school calendar in hand, started checking off names as I assigned duty, much as a restaurant host does when he or she is seating people at their tables and determining the waitress or waiter they will have. By placing our paraprofessionals on bus duty, the professional staff was assigned car rider duty. I truly did my best to ensure that no one person received more duties than the next.

Being a Proactive Principal and trying to look after the needs of my staff, I also asked them to inform me of any health conditions or personal scheduling concerns they had that would prevent them from serving on car duty. Some teachers had legitimate health concerns that made being in cold weather difficult for them.

In that case, I would assign car duty to them in the warmer months. Because of babysitting needs, some teachers asked to be assigned to afternoon duties in order to get their children to the babysitter or daycare facilities in the morning and still be on time to school. These were requests that were easily granted. And for the most part, once the school year started we fell into a nice little pattern of getting the students in and out of the building.

With as much careful planning and as many checklists as I did, as the years went by I still learned a few things about bus and car duties. At the start of the school year everyone is fresh and ready for school to begin. As the year wears on, some teachers pay less and less attention to the planned bus and car duty schedule and create one of their own.

In my *Monday Morning Minutes*, a little newsletter I sent to the staff every Monday morning, I let them know what was happening on campus that week, who was having a birthday, and when I would be gone from campus for a meeting. I also included who was serving on car and bus duties that week. Because I usually did car rider duty, I was the first to notice when someone was late or just plain absent from duty.

When I asked about this, I was told so-and-so switched days, or she left early for a dentist appointment and forgot to tell me, or he was at the copy machine just a few minutes ago. That is when I learned to carry my phone to car duty, call the secretary, ask her to look at the duty roster that was permanently affixed to the side of the intercom, and find out who was missing from duty. Then the secretary was to make a schoolwide announcement on the intercom and ask that teacher to get to his or her duty immediately. You would be surprised to find out that you only have to do that a few times and the problem corrects itself.

The point of having a schedule, whether it's a bell, lunch, or duty schedule, boils down to keeping students safe and protecting the little time you are given during a school day for important things like instruction and learning. Of course there are days when the schedule will need adjusting. There will be field trips, students leaving early for sporting or scholastic events, or—God forbid—a natural disaster or alarming weather conditions. I suggest that as you plan the day-to-day schedule you also plan for a schedule for the unexpected. You may never need Plan B, but it is always handy to have one.

KEEPING AN EYE ON THE BUDGET

Once, early in my educational career, I served as a coordinator for a district's gifted and talented program. I was responsible for testing, student placement, instructional resources, professional development, and anything else the students, teachers, or parents needed. I shared the office space with another program director, Mr. Emmitt Smith. He was a wonderful educator who believed in the potential of all students, and it showed in all he did for his program. I remember him for many reasons, but especially for a piece of valuable advice he once gave me.

In order to capture what teachers and students were doing in the program, I purchased a camera with program money. I planned on taking the camera with me when I made school visits and taking pictures of the teachers and students in the act of learning and discovering new concepts and ideas.

On one occasion, I asked Emmitt if he thought it would be OK if I used the camera for personal reasons. What he told me was priceless and I have never forgotten it. He quietly shared that when it came to using any school-purchased materials or items, "never do anything that might one day be questioned." So now I pass on to you these sage words of wisdom so that they are burned into your mind, especially when it comes to the use, distribution, and reporting of how district money is used.

The leadership and instructional importance of the principal fills every single page of this book, whether I am retelling a story or helping you plan a lunch schedule. I hopefully have presented you with examples and information that reflect how a principal should act and behave (OK—maybe some of the stories shared showed you what not to do).

But when it comes to the management of district monies, there is only one way to act: legally. In many districts, any misappropriation of funds results in immediate termination, and I certainly never want that to happen to you. So with Emmitt's advice and some legal facts in hand, start taking written or mental notes about the importance of being budget-savvy.

For the most part, school budgets are created based on a formula that provides a certain amount of money for instruction. That formula usually is different for elementary and secondary students. A principal builds a budget for a new school year based on his or her anticipated enrollment. This process takes place before the end of the current school year.

Once the proposed budget is created, the principal then forwards it on to the superintendent. The superintendent, using formulas I do not even know, examines the budget, makes recommendations of his or her own, and then takes the final budget to the school board for its approval. When the budget is approved, usually at the September board meeting, your school money is in place and ready to use.

Remember the section about the teachers' spending money in the summer and expecting to be reimbursed for their expenditures? Until the school board meets and approves the new year's budget, you do not have one. Once the budget is approved for the year, the money is yours. Well, not exactly.

Along with your many other duties as a principal, you are also the bank president, keeper of the records, and accounts manager for the money that has been given to you. Woe to the principal who forgets to either ask for a monthly account balance or forgets to read the one he or she received in the mail. I knew of a principal who was called to visit the superintendent's office to explain why she was $3,000 over in her budget. The principal sat dumbfounded and simply said that she had no idea how that could have happened. She had never received any kind of balance sheet on her budget. The superintendent calmly reminded her that it was her responsibility to check her budget balances, and that as of that point she had no more budget money. That meant that the copier maintenance agreement ceased, field trips were cancelled, and any supplies she had ordered to date would be returned to the company. Not good. Not good at all.

In my career I was very fortunate to have two of the best school secretaries imaginable. Mary Lou and Phyllis were wizards with budgets, and because I could trust them implicitly, I was smart enough to turn most of the budget matters over to them. These two wonderful women kept me from having to meet with the superintendent to explain any overages.

If one of the school's accounts started getting a little low, they would close that account off to me. They kept me updated on every account balance, helped teachers with the necessary purchase order forms, and informed me when teachers wanted something outlandish, like 100 pounds of glitter to make Mother's Day cards.

My usual practice when I received my yearly budget was to split the money in half, money for the first semester and money to get me through the second semester. When I reached that expenditure limit, the secretary at the time would simply tell me I could not spend any more money. Because there is no money in the summer months, I tried to save some money the second semester to meet some of the possible needs the teachers might have to start school the next year.

Here is a newsflash that you may not know: When the purchase orders are fully completed (that means they have the right budget code and the necessary signatures on them), they do not stay in your office. Let me say that again for emphasis. The completed purchase orders leave your office, go to the district's business manager or superintendent, and then go on to the school board for approval.

So if one of your grade levels asks for 100 pounds of glitter and you sign it and send it on its way without reading it, you may get a phone call from the superintendent wanting you to justify the purchase of 100 pounds of multicolored glitter before the superintendent presents it to the school board. This could and did happen to me.

Or take for instance, the purchase order that has been given to you by one of your teachers asking for a $59 stapler. Now, because you have already dealt with the justification of 100 pounds of glitter, you may be a little more wary of sending other unexplainable purchase orders to the superintendent's office. I suggest you meet with the teacher and ask her to explain the need for a stapler that costs $59. Because where I am from, many discount stores carry staplers for about $10. This magic $59 stapler had better be able to staple steel.

And let's say you find out that the students need this particular stapler when they make their biography books because it can staple multiple pages together. Here is your quandary: Do you let the stapler purchase order go through knowing the superintendent will ask questions, or do you request the super stapler for the school's use and let all teachers have the opportunity to use the stapler? Choose wisely.

Not only did I develop a plan for expenditures, I also learned about the hidden costs that will undermine your ability as a resource manager. When you begin to build your budget for the school year, be sure to include the copier maintenance cost. Do not do what I did once, and only once. I did not take into consideration that the rental cost for the school's copier came out of the campus budget, not the district's budget. If you do this, it will force you to use other dedicated money to pay for that cost, and the cost is accrued every month.

Along with the maintenance agreement is the cost of each copy that exceeds the agreed-upon number. For me, this meant that every copy made that exceeded 60,000 copies a month cost the school .008 cents a sheet. After awhile that seemingly little amount adds up. It even resulted in my having to limit the number of copies allotted to each teacher. This does not make a teacher happy.

Always investigate the cost of consumable textbooks that teachers will need for the upcoming school year. A consumable textbook means that the cost incurred to purchase those books will be a cost you have to plan for every year. These are usually textbooks that younger children use more frequently than older ones. However, many science and language classes at the secondary level require workbooks that carry an additional cost. Forgetting these hidden costs results in teachers finding very creative ways to provide the needed materials for their classes. I suggest you read the copyright laws for your state very carefully. Hint, hint . . .

AND ALL OTHER ASSIGNED DUTIES

A term contract is an integral part of any employee-employer relationship, especially within an organization as large and expansive as a school district. These contracts assure an employee of his or her right to a position. They are usually standard in their wording and expectations. For administrators, a catch phrase exists that usually states, "The principal shall perform any other duties assigned by the Superintendent pursuant to Board Policy" (Texas Association of School Boards 2006). I urge you to find this line in your contract and study it thoroughly.

Does this mean that the superintendent can ask you to pick up his laundry or wash her car every third Thursday of the month? Of course not. However, there are times when all other assigned duties mean just that, all and any other assigned duties.

Ms. Eunice, our beloved head custodian, was deathly afraid of mice, snakes, and small animals of any kind. Because our school was located near a wooded area, we usually had a host of woodland creatures come to visit. One morning, I heard a blood-curdling scream come from the direction of the long hall that happened to house Ms. Eunice's office. Knowing it was she, I immediately headed in her direction. Once I reached her office area, I found Ms. Eunice in the hallway still screaming, "Get it out of there, Ms. T!"

When I entered her office, I heard the tiniest little squealing coming from under her desk. I looked under her chair and found a tiny baby mouse stuck to the sticky paper we used to catch our woodland creatures when they entered our building.

Knowing Ms. Eunice would rather die than go back into her office, I picked up the sticky paper with the baby mouse still struggling and squealing, took it out to the dumpsters and disposed of the woodland creature. I have never seen any job description for the principalship relate the responsibility to take care of woodland creatures on sticky paper when they are squirming and squealing. Maybe I read the wrong job description.

Another incident of assigned duties came in September of 2006 when two little storms named Katrina and Rita decided to visit our area of East Texas. Because the Red Cross had designated our city and schools as shelter sites, evacuees from both Louisiana and south Texas headed our way. One Wednesday afternoon before the influx of people was due, the superintendent called all the principals, directors, and other administrative staff together and informed us of the severity of the impending situation and what would be expected of us.

During the meeting, he told all of us to go buy any groceries we might need, fill our cars with gas, and spend a little time with our families. He informed us that more than ten thousand people were expected, and because our schools would be used to house the evacuees, he expected his administrative staff to help cover the schools and assist in any way they could.

During the meeting, our superintendent informed us that he would be in contact with us about our assigned duties. By assigned duties he meant opening the schools for the evacuees; staying on the site to render aid, give directions, and keep a watchful eye on our schools; and readying ourselves to be on call for the duration of the evacuees' stay. Because our schools were being used to house the evacuees, our children were on a sabbatical from school, with no indication of when we might return to our regular school operations.

At the time, I could not fathom that ten thousand extra people would be coming to our little town. Why did I need to buy extra groceries? We had a Walmart and five additional grocery stores. Why did I need to fill my car with gas? We had a Walmart and a slew of additional independent gas stations.

Heeding the superintendent's advice, I did fill my cars with gas and I did buy extra groceries. And I am still grateful for his suggestions—because the next morning, despite my disbelief that ten thousand extra people would descend on us, they did, and they stayed for almost two weeks.

As the displaced families began to arrive, the administrative staff members were placed at various school sites. Some families came with only a blanket and the clothes they were wearing when they left their homes, while other families brought enough personal items to make their stay as comfortable as possible. The disparity was surprising and appalling at the same time.

Many of our schools were only equipped to house a limited number of evacuees because of their size, bathroom facilities, and space conducive to adults. In order to feed our visitors, the district's cafeteria manager cleared out all the freezers from the unused schools that she could and sent the food to the schools being used as evacuation sites.

City and county law enforcement officers were assigned to each school for the safety and welfare of not only school employees but for the sake of the evacuees also. Our schools and our city became a haven for these displaced families and we, as school administrators, were on nonstop duty.

I remember that first night very well because that was my first fourteen-hour shift. My school was not designated as a Red Cross site, so I was assigned to help other administrators on their campuses. The first day included registering the families, assigning them a place to sleep and keep their belongings, and establishing some kind of schedule for meal delivery and meeting personal needs. We truly tried to make the families feel as comfortable as possible.

During my second fourteen-hour shift, I happened to be lying on the floor of the principal's office of one school trying to get a few hours' sleep. The principal and I were sharing duties on her campus. As I lay on the floor of that office with the howling storm raging around us, I shared with the principal that I did not remember signing on for this kind of duty. She promptly reminded me that this was one of those "and all other assigned duties" that gives you an opportunity to become a seasoned leader. After a good laugh, we did get about an hour of sleep before the day's responsibilities hit us again.

This is only one example of when you might be called upon to per-form a duty that lies beyond the boundaries of standard operational procedures. In these cases, learn to accept the duty as an opportunity for growth and a willingness to help your school district when they need you. During our time with the Katrina and Rita evacuees, I experienced signs of selfless leadership that might not have been afforded to me on a daily basis.

I witnessed moments of kindness and generosity for others that still live in my memory to this day. I watched our superintendent as he wearily moved from school to school in stormy weather, on constant alert for his schools and his employees. I stood beside my friends and colleagues as they worked tirelessly and endlessly to provide what they could to the displaced families. We all learned a great deal from our experiences.

True leadership does not announce itself with a tickertape parade or with a loudspeaker at a sporting event. Sometimes it is a superintendent in a yellow raincoat visiting a school at 3:00 in the morning or a fellow principal who is visibly exhausted signing up to work an extra shift at a school in need. It is witnessing families who have very little themselves share with those who have next to nothing.

During all my other assigned-duties days while Katrina and Rita moved through our community, I met some wonderful and amazing people. I learned of the inner strength that true leaders need to accomplish even the smallest of tasks when their energy level is spent. This duty was an opportunity for a lesson in strength and perseverance. While I was glad to see our little community return to normal, I took away memories and experiences that I will never forget.

DEVELOPING YOUR OWN PERSONAL LEADERSHIP CAPACITY

You know by now that becoming a school leader makes you ultimately responsible for everything that takes place on that campus, from instruction to school safety and anything in between. In previous chapters, this responsibility has been discussed in a variety of ways and with reflective stories. But now I want you to consider all that you will really be responsible for and the possibility of any other assigned duties that may arise.

Bear Bryant said, "If anything goes bad, I did it. If anything goes semi-good, we did it. If anything goes real good, then you did it" (Holden Leadership Center 2008). This is the momentum and voice I want you to remember when your own experiences for leadership surface. In building your capacity for leadership, you in essence are helping others build theirs. Taking the responsibility for everything, good or bad, may not always seem equitable, but it is the way of a true leader.

There are also a few other suggestions I would like to offer as you learn about your capabilities as a school leader.

1. Leaders don't whine. I cannot imagine Sir Winston Churchill lazily lounging around Number 10 Downing Street complaining about the lack of gasoline to fuel the British tanks, or when finding out that the Germans had invaded another country taking out a hanky and crying, "Oh, woe is me." He took some action. He looked at his data. He made some crucial decisions. But I am fairly certain he did not whine.

2. Leaders look for opportunities for continued growth. This is not a new aspect of leadership. How can a true leader be expected to face new and challenging situations if he or she remains stagnant? If maintenance cannot come and fix the hinges on a door, pull out your tool box and fix it yourself. If you mess up the door and the maintenance department has to pull double-duty to fix the door correctly, then they might come a little faster next time you call. If you do not know where the gas and water mains are, learn where they are. If the cafeteria staff is short and an extra pair of hands is needed, grab a mesh hair net, get a scooper, and find yourself a place on the serving line so that the lunch schedule flows as smoothly as possible.

3. Leaders do not let their pride get in the way of doing a job. If the bathroom toilet is stopped up and the custodian is not available to help, put on a pair of work gloves and unstop the toilet. If you see a piece of trash in the hallway, pick it up and put it in the trash can. Hopefully, you will remember that the position you hold as a campus principal does not make you the leader of that campus. You are the leader of that campus because of what you are willing to do for that school.

4. Leaders accept responsibilities from their superintendents not because they are supposed to but because a job needs to be done. When you assume a new duty, be sure to gather as much information as you can to make you successful, to get the job done, and to allow the superintendent to recognize your leadership potential.

5. Leaders recognize the efforts of others. Humility is a forgotten grace for some, but not for a genuine leader. The quote from Bear Bryant

exemplifies this belief. If something does not go as well as planned, step up to the plate and take the responsibility for it. If something does go well, stand back and let others take the credit. This is such a small thing that leaders do that allows them to become great.

WHAT WILL MY PRINCIPALSHIP SAY ABOUT ME?

When I talk about my principalship and the many stories and experiences that I have lived through, I wonder myself why anyone would want to accept a position that is fraught with responsibilities, requires constant attention to details, and has very few tangible rewards. And then I think of Robert and Ben, of Callie and Hannah, and of all the other children I had the privilege of knowing. I think of the many talented teachers that I have dealt with in my career as an administrator and watched as they turned the art of teaching into a magical experience for children.

When you make the decision to be a school leader, I hope that you will never watch from the sidelines. I want you to actively participate in the learning on your campus, in the adventures that transpire, and in the relationships that you build with your staff and your students. Therefore, I hope that your principalship says the following about you:

- That in the face of any situation, you remained calm and readied
- That when additional duties came along, you offered your time and energy to help
- That when you dealt with people from any and every walk of life, you treated each person with respect and dignity
- That when others contributed to your principalship, you recognized their efforts
- That through every event, obstacle, or situation, you kept a smile on your face and gave back more than you received

USING YOUR 20/20 VISION

Even with all of this advice and helpful hints, no one person can prepare you for the variety and range of responsibilities that will come your way. My desire is to at least touch on those duties that I am certain you will face and provide some suggestions that will assist you in becoming a successful school leader. Once again, developing the gift of proactive thinking will provide you with a 20/20 vision regarding problem solving and decision making that requires you to

- ☐ Learn to ask questions of veterans in the field who have been a principal and may have advice they are willing to share.
- ☐ Adopt an understanding of the level of responsibility you hold as the principal.
- ☐ Introduce yourself to members of the custodial and maintenance staff as early as possible. Once these people learn you are sincere in your efforts to make their lives easier, you will have comrades for life.
- ☐ When you receive your very first school budget, visit with the district's financial manager and let him or her personally guide you through the many processes attached to the budget.
- ☐ Develop a systematic process for opening and closing a school year. This will save you countless hours every year.
- ☐ When asked to assist on a task not found on the district's job description for a campus principal, accept the task with a giving and willing nature.

MY WISH FOR YOU

At first you will be overwhelmed with all there is to do,
The things you must have ready—doesn't matter that you are new.
You'll need a pair of comfy shoes as you walk from room to room.
Everyone is coming back and they are coming back real soon.

Oh, you'll get tired and weary in the days before school starts.
Just ask for help from others; they'll always do their part.
With budgets, schedules, and so much more, you may sometimes feel alone,
Just view each task as a little chore and refuse to gripe or moan.

My wish for you when July creeps in is that you've had time to rest,
And with all your renewed energy, you'll get through every test.
Tests that challenge you to learn more about all the hows and whys,
To make you a true leader on whom teachers can rely.

ADDITIONAL RESOURCES

Reading Material

Belker, Loren B., and Gary S. Topchik. *The First-Time Manager*. 5th ed. New York: AMACOM, 2005.

Davidson, Jeff. *The Complete Idiot's Guide to Getting Things Done*. New York: Alpha Books, 2005.

Maxwell, John C. *The Twenty-One Irrefutable Laws of Leadership: Follow Them and People Will Follow You*. Nashville, TN: Thomas Nelson, 2007.

Stettner, Morey. *The New Manager's Handbook: Twenty-Four Lessons for Mastering Your New Role*. New York: McGraw-Hill, 2006.

Underwood, Jim. *More Than a Pink Cadillac: Mary Kay, Inc.'s Nine Leadership Keys to Success*. New York: McGraw-Hill, 2003.

Internet Sources

www.see.ed.ac.uk/~gerard/Management/art9.html
This article by Gerard M. Blais, titled "What Makes a Great Manager," explores the attributes needed by strong leaders as they become efficient managers.

changingminds.org/disciplines/leadership/articles/manager_leader.htm
This site examines the world of managers and leaders.

cnx.org/content/m14255/latest/
This research endeavor, "The Practitioner: How Successful Principals Lead and Influence," explores the connection between leadership and school success.

SOMEBODY HAS TO BE IN CHARGE, AND THEY CHOSE YOU

When my daughters were growing up, I always told them that if they ever found themselves in a place where they did not want to be or with a group of people they did not want to be around, to use my name in any situation that might arise.

For example, if they were at a party and wanted to leave early, they could always say, "My mama told me I had to be home early tonight." If a precarious situation occurred, they could say, "My mama told me I was supposed to call her and find out when I had to be home." Whatever the situation, my girls knew they could always fall back on that one statement, "My mama said," and make me the bad guy, if necessary.

I developed this same protection system for the teachers on my campus. If a situation arose and they needed my invisible backing, they could always use my name or my position to help them through it. For instance, if a parent became angry and the teacher was not prepared to handle the situation, I gave the teachers permission to say, "Mrs. Tareilo, our principal, said we were to contact her immediately if anything like this came up" or "Mrs. Tareilo advised us to involve her in all parent complaints." There is nothing unusual about this. I was the principal of the school—the boss.

Through the good times and bad, regardless of the reason for the situation, someone has to be in charge of the school and all that happens. The minute you accepted the principal's position, you became that person. Every one of us, when presented with questionable situations, likes to know that someone has the power and the authority to make decisions, solve problems, and be the support system we need. So get your "My mama said" slogan ready. You're in charge.

BEING THE BELL COW

According to Thornton (2007), a bell cow was the dominant cow of the herd who because of the bell she wore made it possible for farmers to locate the herd. Thornton also writes that the bell cow was chosen for her ability to lead the herd home after a long day of grazing in the fields.

Farmers chose cows instead of steers because steers were sometimes castrated and often used for laborious tasks on the farm. Thornton (2007) also describes the bell cow as "the queen cow, the leader, the boss cow." So what does this mean for you? It means: Whether you are male or female, find you an old bell, put that clanky bell around your neck, be ready to bring the herd home, and start learning to moo.

Let's take a moment and think about what it means to be the bell cow. Much as the farmers identified the cow with the most leadership potential, the superintendent and the school board of your district gave you the same distinction. You are the principal (or will be the principal) because someone believed you possessed the necessary leadership skills to lead a school toward success.

Farmers greatly trusted their bell cows to take the herd to a pasture and then return them safely home. For an entire school year, you have that same kind of trust given to you. This trust, which means respect and safety for all, and the instructional direction of the school, will be the two cornerstones of your principalship.

The bell cow does not stand in a field alone. She has a following of other cows and calves that tag along with her no matter what; they instinctively know that she is their leader. The men and women in the school that you serve also look at you the same way. Whether in a field, corporate office, or school campus, the bell cow is the one that not only has the authority to lead but also accepts the responsibility to lead.

Since reading about the bell cow, I have paid much more attention to cows as they move about their pastures. When the hay truck comes into the pasture to drop off new bales of hay, who leads them to the feast? The bell cow leads them. When it's time to settle in for the evening, who leads them to their evening resting place? The bell cow leads them. Are you getting the picture?

It's easy to lead a bunch of cows to newly mown hay. It's fairly simple for the bell cow to take the same path they take every night that leads to the herd home for the evening. Leading people in the direction you think they should go is a little more difficult. Some heifers don't like to be told what to do.

For the most part, the teachers on your campus will follow your lead, especially if you are trying to do something to help their children, improve their work climate, or make their jobs easier and more rewarding. But just like the stray cow who doesn't want to follow the predetermined path to the final resting place for the night, there will be a handful of teachers, maybe just one or two, who will resist anything you suggest or implement that might make their lives a little easier.

BECAUSE YOU SIT IN THE CHAIR

In one of the earlier chapters of the book, I mentioned having a pink desk chair when I was a principal. The pink chair became a symbol of my authority. When someone questioned an action of mine or wanted to know why I made a certain decision, I would simply say, "As long as I sit in the pink chair, I'll make the decisions for this campus. When you sit in the chair, you can make the decisions."

Usually I tried to be a democratic leader and gather information and input from others. On some occasions, however, this statement seemed to be the one people understood.

Think of the bell cow. She knows she wears the bell, and until the farmer takes the bell from around her neck, the herd knows she is the one in control of getting them to the fields for grazing and back home again. So far, I have called you a heifer and had you sitting in a pink chair. What a way to start a chapter.

Whether you wear a nice, new, shiny bell or sit in a leather-covered chair, the responsibility for running the school and taking care of everyone inside that school is yours. The staff, faculty, and students of the school look to you for leadership, direction, and even protection. The pink-chair-sitting bell cow in me usually emerged in emergency situations, such as the time a parent threatened to come to the school and steal his children.

The parents of these particular children were in the midst of a bitter divorce and custody battle. Both parents had called me with a warning that there was a possibility that the children would be taken from the school as a retaliatory action by the other parent. I have always thought that situations like this should stay within the home setting and not come to my school; therefore, I informed each parent individually that I would take all the necessary precautions to protect their children but that I did not want to make the school a battleground for their situation.

One day the father came to school wanting to visit with his children and then eat lunch with them. The children were residing with the mother at that time, and the father had not been able to see them as much as he would have liked. Because he still had legal custody as a biological parent, he was allowed to visit their classrooms and eat lunch with them.

I met with him in my office and informed him of the guidelines of his visit to the school. He agreed, and I directed him to his children's classrooms. I informed the teachers of his visit and asked them to keep an eye on him and the children.

In the infancy of my principalship and because I had talked with this father on several occasions, I felt I had fulfilled my legal duties as the principal of the school and went about my business. After a while, I received a beep from the intercom system. When I answered the intercom call I heard loud shrieking and screaming from the teacher as she cried, "He's taken them. What do you want me to do?"

Through the frantic cries of the teacher, I learned that this particular father had done exactly what I told him to do until he walked his children from the lunchroom back to their classes—when he grabbed his son and daughter and ran out the back door of the school toward his parked car. I alerted the superintendent's office and started running toward the back parking lot—in two-inch heels, no less.

Because my office was in the front of the building and the two-inch heels I was wearing were not conducive to sprinting, it took me a few moments to finally reach the back doors. As I rounded the corner of the building, I saw him as he was running to his car. He had purposely parked his car in the back of the school to make a quick getaway.

By the time I made it to the parking lot, he had loaded the children and their backpacks into the car and was backing up ready to leave the parking lot. I ran screaming for him to stop. He did not. He just sped off, with the children I had assured the mother I would protect.

Legally, the only thing he actually did wrong was his failure to comply with the school's student sign-out policy. He was the biological father of the children; no custody decision had been made. By all rights, he could take his children. Now someone had the arduous task of calling the mother and telling her that her estranged husband had taken her children from the school.

Stephen Comisky said, "You can delegate authority, but not responsibility" (Quotation Collection n.d.). I asked all the teachers involved to document in writing what had occurred and then send it to my office. After once again contacting the superintendent and letting him know what had transpired, I knew my next step was calling the mother. I would have loved to hand that duty over to someone else, but I sat in the chair, I was the bell cow, and it was my responsibility to make the call.

How do you tell a woman, a mother, that the man she warned you about, the man she told you would do anything to hurt her, had come to the school, and you allowed him to visit the classrooms, have lunch with the children, and then steal them from the school? I can still hear the teachers, the counselor, and the office staff asking me, "What are you going to say? How are you going to tell her what happened?"

In all my years as an educator, in my undergraduate- and graduate-level courses, with all the teachings of my wise professors and the theoretical texts I read, no theory, book, or person had ever prepared me to tell a mother her children were gone, taken on my watch, from my school.

Once I gathered the verbal and written stories from the teachers, I pieced together what the father had done and prepared myself to make the phone call to the mother. When I reached the mother, I told her everything I knew and explained to her that the children seemed fine and unafraid when I last saw them (being stolen from my campus by their father).

In a true motherly fashion, she became hysterical, hurling blameful questions toward me: "How could this have happened? You gave me your word you would protect my children. I warned you he would do something like this."

When something goes right on a school campus, the pink chair is where you want to be. When something like this happens, no one, and I mean no one, wants to sit in the chair for you, much less wear a clanky bell around his or her neck.

In the end, the mother and father ended up in court seeking a divorce and battling over the custody of the children. Not only did the father steal his children from my campus on my watch, he had the audacity to call me as a witness on his behalf. When I received the subpoena, I promptly called his lawyer and informed him I would not make a credible witness for his client. In fact, I would be considered a hostile witness, and he would be better off not calling me to speak. Both the lawyer and the father chose not to listen to me and called me to testify in court. Testifying in court in a divorce case or a child abuse case is just another unseen perk when you are the one who sits in the chair.

The judge ruled on the mother's behalf, granting her primary conservatorship over the children. The father received visitation rights. Did my testimony on the stand regarding his behavior at my school, his taking the children from my campus, and my unsuccessful attempts to make him stop and bring the children back to the campus have anything to do with the court's decision? I certainly hope so. Word to the wise: Don't mess with a bell cow and her herd. Better yet, don't mess with the person who sits in the chair.

It's here that I want to tell you about Tracy. Tracy started on our campus as a paraprofessional working in our special education department. She was the epitome of a caring and loving teacher, so much so that she was working on her teaching degree while working full-time. It was her ultimate wish to have a classroom of her own one day. Soon after she graduated from college and received her teaching certificate, she became one of our third-grade teachers. At the same time, she was diagnosed with breast cancer that had metastasized into her brain.

Tracy was able to start the school year and was determined to keep teaching while she was receiving chemotherapy treatments. One day she came into my office to discuss her future. Her main concern was being able to stay in the classroom with her children. I assured her that she could stay in the classroom until she told me she needed to take a break. That was my first mistake. I was to find out that Tracy's spirit was much stronger that her physical abilities.

Around October of that year, Tracy was beginning to show signs of fatigue. During lunch one day, Tracy's hand was shaking uncontrollably and her words were slurring when she spoke. As she walked down the hallways, she was seen leaning more and more into the wall for support.

Knowing she was scheduled for a checkup at her doctor's office, we as a faculty stood in the middle of our school, with hands held tightly together, and prayed for her healing. One of her family members assured us they would call the school as soon as they found out what the new tests revealed. True to their word, the family called us late that afternoon to tell us that Tracy's cancer had spread and she now had as many as ten more tumors in her brain.

Do you remember the lady in a previous chapter who wanted to conduct a petition on my campus and, when I told her no, wanted to file a grievance against me? She happened to be in my office asking for the grievance papers when I received the phone call from Tracy's sister. I interrupted our conversation, telling her that the phone call was one of great importance.

When I heard the news about Tracy's spreading cancer, I couldn't believe it. I slowly bowed my head and began to cry that heart-wrenching, shoulder-shaking kind of sobbing that causes others who witness it to feel the pain you are feeling.

I couldn't even speak. I could only cry. The mother who was in my office came around my desk and gently took me in her arms and held me as I cried. She patted my back and told me everything would work out and then quietly left my office.

Many of the staff members had already come by the office to ask if I had heard anything from Tracy's family. When the phone call came in, I knew I was going to have to be the one to tell the staff about Tracy's recent diagnosis. How was I going to tell the staff that the prognosis looked even grimmer than we could imagine? Why did I have to be the one to tell them that Tracy's place on our campus as a third-grade teacher was probably coming to an end? I didn't want to be the one in charge. I didn't want to sit in the pink chair anymore.

That afternoon, I called an impromptu faculty meeting. As I sat in the cafeteria about to tell our staff about Tracy's condition, I wondered how I was going to get through it. I started with the facts, moved into the doctor's findings, and then led the conversation into how we were going to support Tracy and her family through this diagnosis. I never knew it was possible to talk with a golf ball–size lump in your throat, but it is. I did have to stop talking when I feared my pain would overcome my ability to stay calm in front of the staff.

I know you are probably thinking that was the most difficult part of this story, but telling Tracy she could no longer be a teacher on our campus was the most difficult part. She sat in my office and asked if she could at least come and visit her children every once in a while. I told her no; they needed to remember her without her hands shaking or walking in a peculiar way. When she asked if she could just come and have Thanksgiving lunch with them, I told her no. She needed to rest if she was going to rejoin us in January.

Tracy sat in the chair across from my desk with tears rolling down her cheeks. I knew I had to remain calm as I broke this woman's heart. If not, I would never get through what I had to say. I explained that the most important thing to me was that she rested and healed. Having the rest of the semester off to do just that would mean that she could return to her classroom in the spring semester ready to finish out the year.

Tracy died in December of that same year. The cancer progressed at such a fast rate that in only a few short weeks after our meeting Tracy became homebound. At Tracy's visitation held at the funeral home, I was trying desperately to avoid her husband, thinking that he might blame me for not keeping my promise to let Tracy decide when she would quit teaching.

When he saw me, he embraced me, and we both stood there crying. When we parted, he thanked me for making Tracy take her sick leave when I did. By sending her home, I had given the family additional time with Tracy that they would have missed if she had still been teaching.

When I became a principal, I committed myself to taking care of the children at my school. I signed a contract in which I agreed to follow all the policies and practices and to ensure the education of each and every child. Nowhere in my contract did it ever say I was responsible for cleaning toilets, taking care of crazy witch ladies, or telling the staff that a beloved member of our faculty was going to die.

What do I want you to learn from this? The principal is in charge of everything and everyone at a school. The principal of a school accepts hidden responsibilities that aren't always written in the policy manuals or found in a contract.

Regardless of the type of news that has to be delivered, ultimately you, as the principal, have the responsibility of being the messenger. My only advice is that you always face every situation head-on, with knowledge of policies or practices, and use encouraging and sustaining words when talking with people.

Sitting in the chair does not mean that you constantly sit under a hanging sword of Damocles. Some days, sitting in the chair means you get to be a part of children's lives in a most rewarding way.

Most of our teachers built a recognition system into their classroom discipline plans. If a child had a perfect conduct grade, he or she might, for instance, get a homework pass or extra time on an assignment. Some of the teachers even built me into their reward plans.

For instance, if a teacher wanted to recognize a student for reading accomplishments, he or she might receive a coupon to read to the principal. If a child brought back all of his or her homework on time for a week, the teacher might send the child to my office so I could recognize the child's efforts and tattoo the child's arm. Yes, I said "tattoo."

I had a rolling stamp that had stars on it. A child would come to my office and show me his or her completed work, and I would ask the child if he or she had ever been tattooed and if his or her parents would mind if the child got one. (Now, I am not so sure I would do this with all the tattoos our children are actually getting.)

The child would beam as I pulled out the maroon ink pad, rolled the stamp over and over the ink, and then rolled the stamp down the child's arm. Not only were the children I "tattooed" proud of themselves for the work they had accomplished, but they knew I was also very proud of them.

The chair also allowed me to be the person who represented our school at various academic events. Every year, several of the area schools gathered for the University Interscholastic League (UIL) academic contest. This scholastic event allowed children to participate in a variety of academic contests that included music memory, art recognition, writing, and recitation.

At the end of the day's events, the schools with the most points would win a trophy for first, second, or third place. In fact, our campus hosted this event several times. Through the efforts of our teachers, students, and parents, we won a first- or second-place trophy almost every year.

Hearing the screams of happiness and delight when the judge announces that your school has earned the lovely, gold-toned, two-tiered trophy makes sitting in the chair a really nice place to be.

Any person who accepts a leadership position knows about the roller-coaster ride of responsibilities. Some days you will feel as if you are the warden of a prison and any minute the inmates will take over. On other days, you will feel as if you are Walt Disney giving tours through Disneyland, because things are so perfect.

It really does not matter about the color of the chair or the shininess of your bell, what happens at the school—*everything* that happens at the school—is your responsibility. Sitting in the chair brought me more joy and more involvement in the lives of children than I could ever imagine. While some days brought forth a slew of challenges, those challenges were also the trials that made me a better principal.

"LET'S ASK HER—SHE'LL KNOW WHAT TO DO"

Think for a minute about a person you would consider an expert. I think of Condoleezza Rice as an expert in foreign policy. I think of Tiger Woods as an expert athlete and golfer, and I know that Billy Graham is more than a door-to-door Bible salesman. Whether politician, golfer, or motivational speaker, they are simply good at what they do and they are considered the best at what they do.

They are so good at what they do they have a following. Members of the press clamor for just a few minutes of attention from Condoleezza Rice. Men and women from around the world fill galleries of golf courses in all kinds of weather for just one small glimpse of a putt, any length of a putt, from Tiger Woods. Thousands upon thousands of people pile into stadium seating to hear a passionate and charismatic message given by Billy Graham. People from all economic levels and in all parts of the world look to and listen to these experts for advice and wisdom when things happen beyond human understanding.

With just the same eyes, your teachers, students, and parents expect you to be the expert on the campus, even if you don't have many years of experience. Though you are only one person, people assume that because you are the principal you have a specialty in counseling, nursing, instruction, conflict resolution, and mechanical engineering, and the Houdini-like ability to be in all the right places at all the right times.

So in my office, to make people think I knew what I was doing, I kept a fully stocked tool box, a Bible, a box of tissues, and curriculum guidelines for every subject and grade level on the campus. I was just waiting for a call from Condi, Tig, and Billy Boy to offer them some valuable suggestions on how to handle problems or concerns they were facing.

Many times parents would come to my office, wringing their hands, with stories of how their child or children would not behave or listen to them. One such child was Jessica. Jessica was the youngest daughter of older parents. She had been coddled most of her life at home with a doting mother, a very attentive older sister, and a father who preferred that the mother handle school-related concerns because he realized the futility of trying to change Jessica's attitude.

Jessica was a very likable little girl who was always the picture of perfection. That is, until a teacher expected her to complete her homework assignments. Jessica did not think homework was that important. In fact, classwork was not that important to Jessica either. After several attempts to redirect this behavior and after several meetings with the mother, I thought it best to involve the father. Maybe he could persuade Jessica to complete her assignments.

A meeting with Jessica, her parents, and me was scheduled. Jessica and her parents arrived for the meeting, and I proceeded to give them an overview of Jessica's behaviors at school and what I hoped to accomplish with the meeting. Knowing that Jessica had a tendency to cry when she did not get her way, I informed Jessica and her parents that if she started crying she would be removed from my office and not allowed to return until she stopped crying. In addition, if Jessica interrupted the meeting between her parents and me, she would be asked to leave the room. I was establishing the parameters for Jessica's behavior. I was basically letting Jessica know I was not her mother and she was not going to run the show in my office.

Sensing that she might be losing a little control, Jessica proceeded to throw out inappropriate accusations regarding her teacher. When I told her that the comments were uncalled for, she started her crying fit. I merely got up from my desk and ushered her out the door.

The mother sat with her mouth open wide, and the father still sat passively without saying a word. I informed Jessica that when she thought she could return to the office without having another fit or saying inappropriate things, she could return to the meeting, but she would not interrupt our conversation again.

After a few minutes, Jessica knocked on the door and asked if she could return to the meeting. I said of course she could and continued describing Jessica's behaviors to her parents. When I reached the point of the discussion concerning her failure to complete assignments, Jessica once again interrupted the conversation with more tears and announced that everyone was "lying on her."

You guessed it. I rose from behind my desk, ushered Jessica out of the room, and told her she did not have permission to return to the office until the adults had finished their conversation. By this time, Jessica was wailing to her mother with outstretched arms, pleading for help. The father still sat there stone-faced, without saying a word. From this point on, the mother and I discussed the school's plan to help Jessica improve.

At the end of our conversation, Jessica returned to the office, and we proceeded to discuss the plan to help Jessica improve her attitude and her grades. Built into the plan were positive as well as realistic goals for Jessica. Throughout the entire meeting, the father had not said one single word.

I thanked them for coming and assured them we would do everything we could to help Jessica. As the father rose to leave, he looked at the mother and said, "I'm not coming back to this school. What she says [pointing to me] goes." And he left. I never had to meet with the parents again. It was on that day that I became an expert in the father's eyes on how to handle Jessica.

All of your expertise may not surface in your ability to handle children. Your expertise may come in the form of your mechanical abilities. In the third drawer of my third file cabinet lies the actual toolbox I kept in my office when I served as a principal. The red-and-black plastic tackle box holds a hammer, various kinds of screwdrivers, a pair of regular pliers, and my personal favorite, a pair of needle-nose pliers. I also have a wide selection of nails, screws, and picture-hanging equipment. Take my advice and gather some spare tools from your garage and keep them on hand.

In larger school districts, the maintenance department is highly specialized. One crew is assigned all the lighting responsibilities, and another crew is called when an electrical problem occurs. In some small school districts, the maintenance department may consist of only one or two people who serve the entire district.

Whether your school district is small or large, you will learn that the maintenance crews will only come when a work order has been filed in their office and the director of the maintenance department has seen it and assigned a person or persons to the job. If the request is not an emergency, the job may not be completed when you need or want it done. That's when I learned to become an expert with some of the campus maintenance requests we received in the office.

One afternoon as I was walking down the hallway to leave for the day, I heard a funny sound coming from the cafeteria. When I opened the door to the kitchen area, I learned that the sound was coming from the ice machine. It was making a horrible clanking sound. Knowing this was not good, I turned off the ice machine. Somehow, I also knew that the water had to be turned off to the ice machine as well.

I called the maintenance director and told him about the noisy ice machine. He said he would run by the school on his way home and check on it. He arrived before I left school for the day to look at the machine. He concurred with me that something was indeed wrong with the machine and he would send someone to look at it. He was not surprised that I had turned off the electricity, but he was surprised that I knew to also turn off the water. From then on when I called him about maintenance needs on the campus, he would ask me if I could handle it—and I usually could.

With my handy-dandy toolbox in tow, I replaced light bulbs, fixed door jams, moved desks up and down to fit the students' heights, opened doors without keys, repaired the copy machine, unclogged toilets, and hung various things on classroom walls with my trusty hammer. One might assume I had time in my hectic schedule to become an expert at small school repairs; I really did not.

However, I thought that if I could handle some of the small needs on my campus and save the maintenance department a trip to my school, they would be happy to help me with bigger needs if they arose. That is exactly what transpired. Not only did we keep our number of maintenance requests to a minimum, the maintenance department staff always came when I needed them without having to put in a work order. Another unseen reward of being an expert is that you gain the respect of other experts.

Handling a disrespectful child or being able to hammer a nail into a wall does not mean the school district will award you a plaque announcing your expertise in these areas. It simply confirms that the people on your campus look at you as the person in the know, the guru of all things, and the one person who can handle the crazy witch lady on Halloween. Yes, I said "crazy witch lady on Halloween."

Halloween for a school principal translates into stranger-than-usual behaviors from everyone, and on top of that, the expectation of a sugar fix for the children that could put the entire state of New York into a diabetic coma. One Halloween near the end of my principalship was no exception.

As a principal, you eagerly hope that your parents will want to take an active role in the school and the educational process their children experience. Schools actively encourage parent involvement through newsletters, calendars, and phone messages. And most of the time, the parents who want to be involved are truly caring and giving people. On this particular Halloween, however, one parent took her school involvement a little too far.

Many elementary schools, mine included, allowed Halloween parties where room mothers brought Halloween treats and goodies for the class. Younger children dress as storybook characters instead of wearing a Halloween costume. Even teachers chose to dress up in costumes such as M&Ms, chess pieces, or cereal boxes, to mention a few.

We did not allow any blood-soaked, skull-showing, or creature-like costumes. The name of the carnival held at that time of year was also changed from the Halloween Carnival to the Fall Festival. In lieu of ghosts and goblins, teachers focused more on the fall season in their room and in their hallway decorations. We really did try to move from the ghoulish side of Halloween. So when I was called from my office to check on a scary witch lady moving up and down the hallways, I leapt from behind my desk and immediately became an expert investigator.

One of my fourth-grade teachers buzzed in on the intercom to the school secretary asking if I knew there was a scary witch lady on campus. The school secretary promptly asked me the same question. When I heard the question, I flew from my office and headed toward the teacher's room.

She informed me that a lady dressed in a witch's costume was moving in and out of the classrooms saying scary things to the children. The teacher was pretty sure she had already been down the third-grade hallway doing the same thing. She really was not that alarmed because she recognized the scary witch lady as one of our parents she frequently saw while on car duty.

Sure enough, by the time I reached the scary witch lady, she was at the end of the fifth-grade hallway. I stopped her before she could enter another classroom. When I asked her what she was doing, she told me she just wanted to add a little extra to the Halloween parties that were taking place. I informed her that the teachers and I had decided to downplay the scary aspects of Halloween. I also told her how much I appreciated her thoughtfulness in thinking of us, but she would have to take off the scary witch's costume and return to her daughter's classroom party.

The woman was not happy with me or my request. She started spouting comments about how we were always asking parents to be involved in the school's activities, and when she did that we were prepared to "kick her out of the school." The mother refused to take off the costume, and I promptly informed her she would not be allowed to return to her daughter's classroom still wearing the scary witch attire. Upon hearing that, she stormed from the building, retreated to her parked car at the side of the school, and proceeded to announce to every parent who entered or left the school that I had kicked her out of the school for wearing black robes on campus. Thankfully, our parents paid little or no attention to her, and the rest of the afternoon parties went on without a hitch.

WHEN THE BAG IS EMPTY

Every self-respecting magician carries a bag of tricks. Once the magician says his magic words and dramatically circles the bag with his magic wand, endless multicolored handkerchiefs, beautiful floral arrangements, and hidden bunnies magically appear. The audience responds with thunderous applause because the wonders that come forth from the bag seem endless.

Because you sit in the chair, your staff, people in the district office, and your parents expect you to be like their favorite magician. Instead of hankies, pansies, and Mr. Floppy, the disappearing bunny, you are expected to make extra money appear for all the special things the teachers request, find the heavy-duty fairy dust that makes everyone happy and easygoing, and from somewhere in the magic bag pull out the super-duper pill that will turn every child on your campus into the next Einstein.

There should actually be a sign on your door or a midway barker announcing your abilities as the great Job, person of wonder and patience, or the spectacular Solomon, holder of knowledge and wisdom beyond that of mortal man. Your business cards should even have pictures of a magic wand and a magician's bag. You sit in the chair; you have all the answers—and that's what everyone expects.

However, I'll be the first one to tell you a little wizard-like secret: Some days when you are worn, spent, tired, and almost brain-dead, it really means that your bag of tricks is probably empty. In fact, I suggest you find some visual means to let your staff know that you have solved all the problems you are going to solve for one day, talked to all the crazy people you intend to talk to, and addressed all the district concerns that have crossed your desk that day. The next person who comes into your office with a problem, complaint, or grievance may actually end up sharing some bag space with Mr. Floppy.

Many days the hectic pace of the school found the assistant principal and me meeting in the hallway just pointing to the direction we were heading because of a classroom or teacher need. Those unspoken words and gestures were all we could muster at that particular time. We instinctively knew that when we reached our destination there would be a problem to solve, a child who needed redirection, or a teacher needing an extra pair of hands. Basically, we pulled out our bag of tricks and headed off.

One of my highest hopes for you is that your bag of tricks never runs dry or empty. The responsibility of running a successful school campus where children learn something every day and teachers and parents work as educational partners means your bag of tricks should look like Santa's gift bag on Christmas Eve.

After sixteen years as an elementary principal, I finally learned it was perfectly acceptable and permissible for me to go into my office and close the door. I realize this goes against what you have learned or are learning about creating a positive work environment by establishing an open-door policy with your staff and parents.

Almost every chapter of this book declares the importance of your accepting the many responsibilities that are yours as the principal, but I am giving you permission to once in a while, when your bag of tricks is empty, close your door. Tell your office staff that you do not want any phone calls, visitors, or problems for about thirty minutes. Would I make this a habit? No, but everyone needs to reenergize sometimes.

Consider this, if you will: Depending on the type of instructional schedule you have at your school, a teacher receives a conference period. You don't. Many teachers receive a duty-free lunch period. You don't. You will be walking the cafeteria with a tray in your hands or eating at your desk, if and when you actually remember to eat.

There will be days when you look at a clock and it's 2:00 in the afternoon and you cannot remember the last time you took a drink or had a bite to eat. So, once again, I give you verbal permission to treat yourself to thirty minutes behind a closed office door to take a breather and try to refill your bag of tricks. When your bag is empty, you do not always have the wherewithal to make the best decisions. Take for example, discipline issues.

Let's say you have a teacher on your campus named Ms. America, and Ms. America always sends little Billy to the office for rolling his pencil up and down his desk during reading time. And, let's say that on this particular day, Ms. America did not see the sign outside your door that said, "Sorry no magical answers today; the bag is empty." So, Ms. America leaves her classroom, asks another teacher to watch the remaining children, and heads to the office with evil little Billy and his maniacal rolling pencil.

Not seeing your head down, working diligently on a report that is due to the superintendent that afternoon, and completely bypassing the warning sign on the door, Ms. America barges into your office and demands you do something about little Billy and his pencil rolling. She has had her fill. Billy is always disturbing her lessons with his interruptions. By this time, a look crosses your face that translates into "I know exactly how you feel."

Forgetting all the positive ways you usually try to handle situations and trying to forget the fact that Ms. America is standing in your office with Billy while her other students are missing instructional time, you look up from the much-needed report and without hesitation calmly think, "Maybe if you weren't such a boring teacher, Billy would not constantly resort to rolling his pencil" or "Isn't this the seventh or eighth time you have been here with Billy and his rolling pencil? Did you ever consider just taking away the pencil?" or even "I wish you were as concerned with the academic success of your children as you are with Billy and his rolling pencil."

Now you and I both know that none of these comments are appropriate for a campus leader, a responsible principal, a professional educator to make out loud, but these comebacks are perfect to consider when your bag of tricks is empty. On the other hand, someone always has to be the adult in the room, and you are the one sitting in the chair. So help Ms. America with the pencil-rolling problem, do what you can to help Billy, and call the superintendent's office and let them know the report will be there that day but maybe not at 2:00 p.m.

One of the ways I dealt with the demands of the position was to find a quiet place on my campus where I could retreat for a few minutes of solitude. On one campus where I served as the principal (as I mentioned in an earlier chapter), this place happened to be in the special education center.

The rooms in this building were large and filled with the most caring and gentle teachers I have ever worked with. There I found beanbag chairs, a peaceful atmosphere, and the most loving children imaginable. Sinking into a beanbag chair listening to the children read calmed and quieted my anxieties and gave me a short reprieve from what awaited me in the office.

Just when I thought my bag of tricks was filling up again, my radio would crackle and interrupt with, "Unit 9, unit 9, what's your 20?" I guess you realize I was unit 9 and my 20 was the special education center.

Shortly after the call, I would press the send button and announce, "Unit 9 here," which would be followed by the all-too-familiar call, "You are needed in the office." In turn, I would take a deep breath and reply, "10-4, I'm on my way."

With some of my stories and memories, you may be wondering why I lasted in the principalship as long as I did. For one simple reason: I loved the job. Oh, there were days with empty trick bags, crazy witch ladies, and rolling pencils that certainly had me contemplating filling out a job application for Walmart. However, there were also days that filled my heart with so much love and reward that I wanted to burst with happiness. When a child from a broken home placed his little fingers in my hand and held on tightly because I was his safety net or when the mother of a special needs child hugged me because no school had ever treated her child with such compassion, I knew I was the principal of that school for a higher reason than a monthly paycheck.

DEVELOPING YOUR OWN PERSONAL LEADERSHIP CAPACITY

Having the responsibility for a school, being the boss cow, or sitting in a pink chair demands that you exhibit the leadership skills of Mother Teresa, Abraham Lincoln, and Lee Iacocca all rolled into one friendly, patient, and positive person. Even while you are reading this book, the situations I faced are minimal compared to the ones that you may one day face.

From the moment you drive your car into the school parking lot and until you leave that same parking lot at the end of the day, the situations you face will run from easy to unbelievable, all in one day's time. Here are a few thoughts that I hope you take with you when you begin your journey into the principalship.

1. First and foremost, school leaders accept all the responsibilities that come with taking care of teachers, students, and parents.
2. School leaders learn to seek the advice and wisdom of others when their bag of tricks runs dry.
3. Competent school leaders learn to recognize when they are emotionally drained and seek a place on their campus for renewal and rest.
4. School leaders know the importance of gathering all the data on any and all situations to help them make the best and fairest decisions possible.
5. School leaders stand on the sidelines and give credit to others when their school receives recognition and praise.
6. Knowledgeable school leaders look for the wonder and awe that is just waiting inside every child.
7. And like Winston Churchill, school leaders never, never, never give up.

WHAT WILL MY PRINCIPALSHIP SAY ABOUT ME?

From the moment you accept the principal's position on a school campus, no matter the age or grade level of the children, you automatically also accept the responsibility for solving any problem and making logical and defendable decisions. Even geese that fly south for the winter stay focused on the lead goose. Cows in a field know to watch and pay attention to the actions and movements of the bell cow in order to get home safely.

From the custodian to the assistant principal, your staff expects you to take charge, safeguard the school, and speak the educational language with such knowledge that student success is a guaranteed outcome. So, if and when you decide to leave the role of the principal, I hope your staff will say,

"I knew I could always come to her with anything. She always knew just what to do."

"I always trusted him to take care of our school and our kids."

"Even if she did not have an answer immediately, she always found someone who did."

"There was never a time I couldn't just go into her office and talk to her. She always found time to listen."

"I may not have liked or agreed with every decision he made, but I always knew he would explain it to me."

USING 20/20 VISION

I have no doubt that you will know what to do when the fire alarm sounds or how to rearrange a lunch schedule when necessary. If you cannot solve these small bumps, you are in for a long and arduous principalship. Once again, developing the gift of proactive thinking will provide you with 20/20 vision regarding problem solving and decision making. This checklist may provide you with a place to start when you become the person in charge.

- ☐ Stay calm when others do not.
- ☐ Always act in a professional manner; you are the adult in the room.

- [ ] Be a collector of data, all data.
- [ ] Develop a "gauge of emergency" when you see or hear a campus problem. The safety of the children always ranks as number one on this gauge, and rolling pencils rank somewhere near the bottom.
- [ ] Locate a safe haven for yourself.
- [ ] Keep current with research, literature, and the experiences of other school leaders and how they faced challenging situations.
- [ ] Accept the fact that all situations are learning situations.
- [ ] Learn how to make the hard decisions.
- [ ] Being wrong sometimes is not a bad thing. Being wrong all the time is. Be wise, and gather good and caring people around you to help you as you make legal and ethical decisions for your school.
- [ ] Stay focused on what your job is; everything is your job.

MY WISH FOR YOU

I won't be there to hold your hand when problems come and go.
So, I send these words, as a heartfelt wish, hoping that you'll know.
Whether bell cow or chair of pink, you now have the chore,
Of making sure that every day brings more joy than the day before.
My wish for you when you start this path is that your problems all stay small,
And that through each trial or turmoil you'll still be standing tall.
My wish for you when you sit in the chair is that you'll be filled with knowledge,
And to realize that sometimes the answers aren't in a book from college.
My wish for you when the school is yours is that you'll know just what to do,
And each and every bump you feel, somehow you will get through.
My wish for you when your bag of tricks runs dangerously low,
My wish for you goes far beyond these written words and thoughts,
Just always know the strength you need lies deep within your heart.

ADDITIONAL RESOURCES

Reading Material

Albright, Mary, and Clay Carr. *101 Biggest Mistakes Managers Make and How to Avoid Them.* Paramus, NJ: Prentice-Hall, 1997.
Carr, Clay, and Mary Albright. *The Manager's Troubleshooter: Pinpointing the Causes and Cures of 125 Tough Day-to-Day Problems.* Paramus, NJ: Prentice-Hall, 1996.

Ramsey, Robert D. *The Principal's Book of Lists*. Paramus, NJ: Prentice-Hall, 1996.

Ricken, Robert, Richard A. Simon, and Michael Terc. *The High School Principal's Calendar: A Month-by-Month Planner for the School Year*. Thousand Oaks, CA: Corwin Press, 2000.

Ricken, Robert, Michael Terc, and Ida Ayres. *The Elementary School Principal's Calendar: A Month-by-Month Planner for the School Year*. Thousand Oaks, CA: Corwin Press, 2006.

Internet Sources

www.mespa.net/Careers.html
While the information provided in this website focuses primarily on elementary school leaders, five major responsibilities of the principalship are discussed. These are applicable to any area of school leadership.

www.accessnewage.com/beststeps/Beststep.cfm?bs=557
Leadership is a universal concept that pertains to several professions; the principalship is no exception. This site offers basic information on accepting responsibility. Several links are provided.

www.free-daily-motivational-self-improvement.com/daily-motivation self-improvement-Become-an-Effective-Leader.html
This site provides a daily motivational and uplifting message that might be helpful when the responsibilities of leadership become overwhelming.

quotations.about.com/cs/inspirationquotes/a/Leadership22.htm
The quotations found at this site are inspiring. The site also provides several links to other quotation topics.

www.youtube.com/watch?v=Gr82xQi43Mg
This short video adds pictures, music, and motivational quotes that would inspire and uplift any principal. It would also be a great source of encouragement to use at a faculty meeting.

12

AND THEN, THERE ARE SOME . . .

Throughout this book, hopefully humorous and thought-provoking stories have made you reflect on the type of principal and school leader you want to be or the one you already are. Yet there are still some stories that need to be told, some that still make me laugh and some that to this day bring me to tears.

Therefore, this final chapter presents those stories. They are small vignettes from the life of a former elementary principal. Through my words, I hope to retell these stories in such a way that you will come to appreciate and accept the daily workings and people who will come into your life when you serve as a school leader.

SECOND-GRADE PET DAY

Our second grade had a wonderful tradition that took place around March or April and coincided with the end of their science unit on animals. The culminating activity for this unit involved all of the second-grade classes taking part in a Pet Day. Students, teachers, and parents all gathered for the event. First-place, second-place, third-place, and participant ribbons were awarded to the children for pets ranging from goldfish to horses. The agriculture department of the high school cooked hot dogs on a grill and also served as judges for the event.

One year on Pet Day, a third-grade child named Jerry brought his pet to school. He was so excited that he wanted me to be one of the first at school to see his special friend. Sure enough, Jerry ran hurriedly from the buses to let me see his beloved pet. I should have known something was a little disturbing when I heard the secretary assure Jerry that I would most definitely want to see the pet he'd brought to school that day. With a large glass pickle jar in hand, Jerry entered my office.

There he stood, beaming with pride, as he presented me with a pickle jar holding the biggest white rat I had ever seen in my life. This was not a mouse. It wasn't even a large fluffy gerbil. This was a full-fledged, card-carrying member of Rats-R-Us. But, there Jerry stood. I had to think of something fast because I could tell this rat meant the world to Jerry. The "quick comeback" god above must have seen my predicament and came to my rescue.

I told Jerry that as much as I thought his white rat would be a sure winner, I had to remind him that Pet Day was designated for second-graders only. Because he was currently in the third grade, he could not participate in Pet Day. I thanked him for introducing me to his special friend, but we would have to call his mother and let her pick up Snow-flake. Reluctantly, he agreed, and his mother was called.

MY ROBERT

Even in my teaching career some children just stood out. They grabbed hold of my heart and never let go. My principalship was no different. Robert grabbed hold of my heart and I hope I keep his smile and honesty with me forever.

Robert's wisdom and perseverance were only two of his many qualities. When he was in the 5th grade, he decided he wanted to read every chapter book he could find. When he finished reading the ones in his teacher's room, he thought it was time for some new books.

On his way to class one day, he stopped by my office for a chat. This was something he liked to do when he was supposed to be going to his class. On one such visit, he proceeded to tell me that his teacher needed some more chapter books. He had already read the ones she had and if I wanted him to continue reading chapter books, I needed to buy more for his teacher.

Robert told me that his reading was improving and he knew how important that was to me. He also agreed to share the chapter books with other students in his room so that they could become better readers also. I wholeheartedly agreed with him and asked what he thought I should do.

Robert offered to talk with his teacher about the books she would like to order and prepare me a list with an estimated budget, and that is exactly what he did. Because of our relationship and our little chats, he felt comfortable asking me for more books. He was the single guiding force that helped his teacher and his fellow classmates acquire a new set of chapter books for his classroom. I just loved that child.

THE CUSTODIAN AND THE UNDIES

I have already mentioned Ms. Eunice, our school's head custodian, several times. Usually in the morning, she was the first to arrive and open the school's doors. Soon after Ms. Eunice arrived, the cafeteria manager and her crew would come on duty. Most of the time, I was the next one to arrive. Early one morning, Ms. Eunice asked to speak with me about a very sensitive matter.

It appeared that when the cafeteria manager, Ms. Ruth, was about to wash a load of dirty hand towels, she found a pair of little black undies in the school's clothes washer. Ms. Ruth asked Ms. Eunice if she knew whose they were. Ms. Eunice had no idea, but she would certainly find out. Once Ms. Eunice had gathered her information, she wanted to talk to me.

There sat Ms. Eunice in my office holding the pair of little black undies. She told me she planned on talking with the evening staff to see if they knew who the owner of the little black undies was. Sure enough, about 2:00 that afternoon, Ms. Eunice had solved the mystery of the undies.

It appeared that one of the custodians had been doing her wash at school while she was on her shift and left her undies by mistake. I learned that her water had been turned off and she had no extra money to wash her clothes. Procedurally speaking, I should have called the custodial supervisor and let him handle the situation. If I had done that, she would have been immediately dismissed for using school equipment and resources for personal reasons. So I didn't call. But I did let the entire custodial crew know that if anything suspicious happened again, little black undies or whitey tighties, I would make the call to their director and someone would be dismissed.

THE LATE TEACHER

As a young, inexperienced principal, I knew I had a lot to learn about how to deal with teachers on an individual basis. Sometimes teachers needed only to be reminded one time about certain policies and once reminded, would never forget to abide by said policy.

Take for instance, the request to be on time and ready to meet their children for another exciting day of learning. This was so important to me that I mentioned being on time and not leaving children unattended in the morning during faculty meetings, on the intercom, and in weekly newsletters.

One of my teachers was continually late. For a few days, she would be on time, and then she would fall back into the same pattern of being late. Being a first-year principal and still striving and hoping people would like me, I let it go a little longer than I should have. When I told one of my fellow administrators what was happening, he gave me some sage advice.

He told me to wait in the hallway outside her room. If she was on time and in her room, all I had to do was just walk by and finish my morning rounds on the campus. If she was late, he suggested I go into her classroom, sit at her desk, and wait for her.

Because the back door of her room connected to another teacher's room, she was able to slip in the connecting door and I wouldn't be able to tell she hadn't been in her classroom. He said that when she came in late and started rattling off her excuses, not to say a word to her—just stand up, look her square in the eyes, and walk out of the room.

And that is exactly what I did. As I made my campus rounds one morning, I found her next-door teacher was standing in the middle of the doorway watching both her class and the late teacher's class. She knew how I felt about leaving students unattended and was carefully watching both classes.

I thanked her for her help and assured her I would watch the class and let her get back to her homeroom students. I began the morning routine with the kids, emptying backpacks, sharpening pencils, and preparing them to write in their daily journals. Then I sat down at the teacher's desk and waited.

About 8:15 a.m. the teacher appeared—not from the front door of her classroom, but through the connecting door of the other teacher's room. The look on her face was priceless. Just as the other principal had predicted, she started describing the trials and tribulations of her morning and emphatically apologizing for being late.

I never took my eyes off her as I rose from her desk. I never said a word as I walked out of the room. With that one silent act and a face of stone, I let her know that was the last time I would allow her to be late. It was the last time another teacher would leave her classroom duties to watch over her students. It was the last time it happened without a written reprimand. That old adage about actions speaking louder than words served me well.

MEETING WITH THE HUSBAND

One of my teachers decided she wanted to have a fundraiser for her grade level. After completing the necessary forms, we purchased several hundred pairs of curly shoelaces. The fundraiser began and was an immediate sensation. From the profits, the grade level was sure to be able to take an extra field trip or plan something very special for the children.

When the invoice came in for the shoelaces, I informed the teacher that she would need to collect the money and deposit it into the activity account, and then the office could follow through with a purchase order request to pay the bill for the shoelaces.

The first time I asked her for the money, she told me the sales were going strong and she wanted to wait a few days to deposit the money. I told her that wouldn't be a problem at all. I asked her a few days later how the sales were going and told her it was time to pay the invoice for the shoelaces.

Finally, I couldn't wait any longer to pay the bill and told the teacher the money had to be deposited that day. She once again assured me that everything would be alright and I would have the money that day.

Not long after that conversation, one of her fellow grade-level teachers came to the office to inform me that this particular teacher was acting kind of funny. Her co-worker was very worried about her. Suddenly, a lightbulb went off in my head and I realized what was happening. It was time to pay the bill and the teacher had taken the fundraiser money.

I headed straight for the teacher's room and found her in a state of panic. She appeared to be disoriented and nervous. I informed her that the instructional specialist would take her class so that we could go to my office and talk. Once in the office, she informed me that the fundraiser money was gone.

She had indeed used the money to take care of some personal bills. Her panic was not due to the fact she had taken the money; her panic was because her husband did not know what she had done. By the time the conversation was over, the teacher's mental and physical states had not improved. I became very worried about her condition.

I escorted her to our school counselor's office in order to give her a quiet place to calm down. I left school and went to her husband's office to meet with him. I proceeded to tell him about the situation with the fundraiser money and my concerns for her mental and physical health.

I also told him I believed she did not have the money and had used it for something personal. He had no idea what I was talking about. I asked him to come to the school and take her home with him. When we returned to school, he very calmly and gently spoke to his wife, assuring her that everything would work out well and there was nothing to worry about.

The next morning the teacher called in for a substitute and the husband came to see me. It appeared that I had been right. She had stolen the fundraiser money. By all rights, she should have been dismissed immediately; however, I felt such sorrow for this man and the situation.

Not only did I have to go to his place of work and tell him that I thought his wife was acting peculiar and that I was very worried about her, he had to face me and tell me his wife had indeed stolen money from the school. He told me it would take him a few days but he would repay the school the money that had been taken.

This was a judgment call. His wife had clearly broken a very serious school policy and faced possible termination, but she had been a dependable and caring teacher. A few days after the incident, the teacher asked to speak with me. She apologized over and over again, assuring me that nothing like this had ever happened before and would never happen again. She was simply going through a very difficult time and asked for my forgiveness.

Should I have given her the benefit of the doubt or dismissed her immediately? I let her stay. She had to deal with the embarrassment and shame of her husband, her immediate supervisor, and her fellow grade-level teachers discovering what she had done. That was enough penance for anyone to bear.

LITTLE CRITTERS

The nurse on our campus was a very capable and competent lady whose first concern was always the care of our children. So when she called me and said she needed me immediately, I quickly left my office and headed toward the nurse's station. When I opened the door, there was a small child sitting in a chair, holding a paper towel on her head.

Because I couldn't see any broken bones or blood, I just couldn't imagine why the nurse needed me so badly. The nurse called me over to her desk, out of the hearing range of the child, and told me she had just called CPS. The child sitting in the chair had an infestation of fleas imbedded in her scalp, and they had burrowed in so deeply that the child's head was bleeding. You can't make this stuff up.

Now, I have dealt with Mr. Crunchies, lice, and missing snakes, but I had never encountered fleas growing in a child's scalp. When CPS came, the caseworker was just as taken aback as I had been. We called the mother to let her know about the situation and said we had indeed called CPS. She informed us we did not have the right to do that and we had better not touch her daughter before she was able to get to the school.

Not one to be threatened by a parent, the CPS officer began asking the little girl questions about the flea infestation growing on her head. She told us her head had been itching for awhile and that she had indeed told her mother.

We didn't have to wait too long for the mother to arrive. Suddenly, the door to the nurse's station flew open and the mother came blowing in, yelling at the same time. The nurse, the CPS worker, and I just stood there as the mother proceeded to tell us that she knew exactly why her daughter had the fleas on her head.

The little girl suffered from asthma attacks and the mother had seen a story on television about how some childhood asthma had been cured when the child slept with Chihuahua puppies. So the mother, being a very caring and conscientious parent, had the child sleep with Chihuahua puppies to help cure her asthma.

Now, I do believe in some wives' tales. I believe that peppermint oil will help with toothaches. I also believe that "horse apples" from an Osage Orange tree, when placed around a house, will prevent roaches and spiders from coming in, but I had never heard the tale that curing childhood asthma could happen by having a child sleep with Chihuahua puppies. This was a new one to me.

The CPS officer stated that the mother had to remove the puppies from the child's room immediately and take the child to the doctor for medical attention, and that she would be visiting the home to ensure that all the requests had been followed in a timely manner.

Note to self: Always expect the unexpected.

THE TEACHER AND THE COMPUTER

One of our teachers liked using her computer. She liked to sit at her computer and chat with people so much that one of her fellow grade-level teachers felt I should know. The teacher gave me the heads-up, and I started walking the hallways a little more just to see what was happening in the classroom. Whenever I walked by, I saw her in front of the room teaching. I felt I had investigated the situation enough and thought nothing more about it.

Another teacher in the same grade level came to tell me that whenever she went into the teacher's room she was always on the computer. This being the second heads-up, I once again started walking the hallways. During my classroom visits, she was always teaching. That's when I got the brilliant idea to ask the technology department to provide me with an activity record for her computer for the last month.

The technology director called to tell me the report was ready and I could pick it up anytime. Off I went to the technology office to pick up the report. When I reached the office, the technology director handed me a forty-two-page report from this teacher's computer. The report gave a detailed listing of the times and the sites the teacher had visited in the last month.

As I began studying the report, I realized she had been on the computer more than she had been teaching my children. Not only was she on the computer during her lunch and conference times, she was on the computer continuously throughout the day. I was furious.

I called the instructional specialist into my office to read the report with me. I am quite sure that if my blood pressure had been taken at that exact moment, the little bead of mercury in the blood-pressure monitor would have shot through the cuff and knocked out one of my office windows.

I told the instructional specialist that I wanted her present when I met with the teacher, but it wasn't going to be that day. I knew that if I met with the teacher that day, as angry as I was, I would either say or do something stupid. The instructional specialist said she would let the teacher know I wanted to meet with her the next day during her conference time.

The next morning, during the teacher's conference time, the instructional specialist and I sat waiting for her. When she walked in, I was sitting in a chair at a small table I kept in my office. When she sat down, she asked why I needed to see her. I pulled out the forty-two-page report and flung it across the room (not at her, even though I had considered that). Forty-two pages of white computer paper flew across the floor.

The teacher, I am sure, thought I had gone absolutely crazy. The eyes of the instructional specialist flew open. I informed the teacher that the pages that were lying strewn across the floor actually held information regarding her computer activity for the last month.

Where she saw a yellow highlighted line, that was the documented time she was on her computer during instructional time—time that she should have been teaching my children. Each page had a number of yellow lines drawn on it. The teacher just sat there.

My questions were very simple. "What were the children doing when you were on the computer?" and "What were you supposed to be doing when you were on the computer this many times a day?" If this was just the computer activity for one month, what would I find if I looked back two months? Three months?

She started to cry and tried to explain to me that some of the computer activity was her attempt to locate additional information to help her with her classroom instruction. I must not have taken my forgiveness pill that morning because I didn't buy her feeble attempt to explain hours and hours of missed instruction.

I informed her that from that minute on she had forfeited her computer rights until further notice, that I would be in and out of her room on a regular basis and she had better be teaching her heart out, and that the instructional specialist would also be checking on the progress of her students. Even thinking about my children's missed opportunities for learning angers me to this day.

THE BAD NEWS

The principalship, like any other profession, is filled with many highs and lows. When you are responsible for an entire school and the people inside, you will face some responsibilities that challenge you to be strong when others cannot. This was the case when my friend and teacher, Markye, was told that her father had passed away.

Markye's husband, Richard, came to the school to see me and let me know that Markye's dad had passed away and he wanted me to be with her when he told her the news. I went to her classroom and asked her to meet me in my office. She later told me she saw Richard's car, but couldn't imagine why he would be at school.

When she entered my office and saw Richard sitting on my bench, she knew something was terribly wrong. I stood at my desk waiting to be the supportive friend Richard wanted me to be. But, when Markye heard the news, her support system and friend failed her.

Markye became very upset and on the verge of hysteria. She and her father had been very close because of his three children, she was his only daughter. As Markye reacted to the news, I slowly moved to the back wall of my office and as far away from her pain as I could. Richard held her close to him as he tried to soothe and bring her some kind of comfort. If I could have escaped out of the back door, I would have.

Not having a father when I was growing up, I have no real understanding of the father-daughter relationship. Markye was in pain and it was so intense, I could only stand in the corner and cry for her. I was not in any shape to help her at the time she needed me the most.

I know how to stand toe-to-toe with an angry parent and deal with almost any situation. I can grab a runaway kindergarten child while wearing a suit and heels if I need to and I can even break up a fight on a school bus.

But Markye's pain was something I couldn't deal with. Standing with my back against the wall of my office, I covered my mouth with my hands and silently sobbed for her loss. After a while, Markye calmed down and Richard was able to drive her home. When she was in the car and leaving, she held my hand and thanked me for being with her when she heard the news.

I was not prepared for real-world events to come into my school and affect those in my care. In my years as a principal, I have buried children who lost their lives to disease and accidents, I've held teachers' hands as they have gone through divorces and remarriages, and I have even helped CPS take children away from my school to ensure their safety. Real-world pains and hurts should be barred from entering schools and affecting the lives of those who live inside during the day. Schools should be safe for principals, too.

The stories in this chapter are just snippets of my twenty-four years in education. These are memories that did not particularly fit into any chapter but needed to be told. Many memories will be attached to your principalship, too. Keep them close to your heart and write them down so that you can remember and cherish the people and the events that made you grow and develop as a dependable, caring, and effective leader.

REFERENCES

Bennis, W., and B. Nanus. 2003. *Leaders: Strategies for taking charge*. New York: Harper.

Bond, K. 2001–2006. *Inspirational quotes for teachers and learners*. www3 .telus.net/linguisticsissues/quotes.htm (accessed November 20, 2007).

Brainy Quotes. n.d. brainyquotes.com/quotes/a/anthea_turner.html (accessed July 7, 2007).

Chicago Historical Society. n.d. *Build it with Lincoln Logs!* www.chicagohistory .org (accessed August 13, 2007).

Department of Workforce Services for Utah. n.d. *Sheepherder/Job* #8660798. jobs.utah.gov/jsp/utahjobs/seeker/search/viewReferralInfo.do?src=gsm&joid =2200662746 (accessed July 2, 2008).

Dynamite Entertainment. n.d. *A brief history of the Lone Ranger*. www .dynamiteentertainment.com/boards/showthread.php?t=530 (accessed August 19, 2008).

Foo, K. 2007. *Sixteen most inspiring famous failures*. November 5. bloggers journey.com/motivational-inspirational/16-most-inspiring-famous-failures/ (accessed December 16, 2007).

Gee, V., and J. Gee. 1999. *Super service: Seven keys to delivering great customer service*. New York: McGraw-Hill.

Holden Leadership Center. 2008. Leadership quotes. uoleadership.uoregon .edu/resources/quotes (accessed February 28, 2009).

Internet Movie Data Base. n.d. *The Lone Ranger.* www.imdb.com/title/
tt0041038/quotes (accessed August 21, 2008).

Layder, D. 2004. *Social and personal identity: Understanding yourself.* Thousand Oaks, CA: Sage.

Lewis, J. J. n.d. Power quotes. www.wisdomquotes.com/cat_power.html (accessed July 7, 2007).

———. 1995–2006. *Questions quotes.* www.wisdomquotes.com/cat_questions
.html (accessed December 16, 2007).

Lincoln Logs. 2007. www/the5and10.com/lincolnlogs.html (accessed August
13, 2007).

Lone Ranger. n.d. www.internationalhero.co.UK//lonerang.htm (accessed August 21, 2008).

Matthews, L. J., and G. M. Crow. 2003. *Being and becoming a principal: Role
conceptions for contemporary principals and assistant principals.* Boston:
Pearson.

Pedler, M., J. Burgoyne, and T. Boydell. 2004. *A manager's guide to leadership.*
New York: McGraw-Hill.

Servais, K., and K. Sanders. 2006. *The courage to lead: Choosing the road less
traveled.* Lanham, MD: Rowman & Littlefield.

Snowden, P. E., and R. A. Gorton. 2002. *School leadership and administration:
Important concepts, case studies, and simulations.* 6th ed. Boston: McGraw-
Hill.

Teachers Quotes. n.d. www.indianchild.com/teachers_quotes.htm (accessed
November 20, 2007).

Texas Association of School Boards. 2006. *Personnel positions.* www.tasb
.org/policy/pol/private/003903/pol_highlight.cfm?policy=DP(LEGA)
.html&QueryText (accessed April 20, 2006).

Thinkexist. n.d. thinkexist.com/quotations/he_who_asks_a_question_is_a_fool_
for_five minutes/164844.htm (accessed July 7, 2007).

Thornton, T. 2007. *The bell cow: A natural leader in the Hill Country.*
hillcountryofmonroecounty.blogspot.com/2007/09/bell-cow-natural-leader
in-hill-county.html (accessed December 7, 2008).

Tirozzi, G. N., and V. L. Ferrandino. 2000. The shortage of principals continues.
Education Week 1, no. 15. principals.org/publicaffairs/views/prin_short1000
.htm (accessed May 17, 2002).

U.S. Department of Education. 2004. *No Child Left Behind: A toolkit for
teachers.* Washington, DC: Author.

Walsh, J., F. Kemerer, and L. Maniotis (2005). *The educator's guide to Texas
school law.* Austin: University of Texas Press.

ADDITIONAL WEB REFERENCES

www.ncpublicschools.org/acronyms/
This site provides an extensive list of the many acronyms used in education.

omsd.omsd.k12.ca.us/departments/lss/hardy/admincoach/Documents/New%20
   Principal%20Responsibility%20Check%20List.doc
This site lists the primary duties of a principal in a month-by-month chronological format.

ABOUT THE AUTHOR

Janet Tareilo is an assistant professor in the department of secondary education and education leadership at Stephen F. Austin State University.

Made in the USA
Coppell, TX
14 March 2022

74947153R00163